SUSTAINABILITY AND PRIVILEGE

SUSTAINABILITY AND PRIVILEGE

A Critique of Social Design Practice

GABRIEL ARBOLEDA

University of Virginia Press

CHARLOTTESVILLE AND LONDON

University of Virginia Press
© 2022 by the Rector and Visitors of the University of Virginia
All rights reserved
Printed in the United States of America on acid-free paper

First published 2022

9 8 7 6 5 4 3 2 1

ISBN 978-0-8139-4748-8 (cloth)
ISBN 978-0-8139-4749-5 (paper)
ISBN 978-0-8139-4800-3 (ebook)

Library of Congress Cataloging-in-Publication Data is available for this title.

Illustrations not otherwise credited are by the author.

Cover photographs: The Makoko Floating School in Lagos, Nigeria, before and after its collapse (*left*, photograph © Aga Khan Trust for Culture–Image ID: IAA120895; *right*, photograph © Allyn Gaestel, 2016).

CONTENTS

ACKNOWLEDGMENTS

I would like to express my appreciation to the many people who contributed to the realization of this book. First of all, I am thankful to the residents of the communities where I carried out the field research, who openly shared their experiences with me. I hope that this book honors their struggle and that it is a fair representation of the lessons I learned from them.

I am also thankful to the designers who opened a window into their thinking through both direct interviews and their writings and buildings. This book is a critique, and as such it aims to honor their work as something significant enough to be critiqued.

Aside from what I learned from residents and designers, in forming the early ideas that led to this book I greatly benefited from working with my advisors at MIT, Reinhard Goethert and John Oschendorf, and at Berkeley, Nezar AlSayyad, Greig Crysler, Laura Nader, and Ananya Roy. Reinhard's long-standing mentorship on participatory practice as well as his professional advice have been transformative for my work. I also thank Laura for introducing me to the complexities, and the beauty, of ethnography's theory and practice.

As I finish this project, I also acknowledge with appreciation the influence of Harold Martínez, my advisor at the Universidad del Valle in Cali, Colombia. By revealing architecture's cultural and social complexities, Harold made this field make sense to me.

For their contributions, intellectual curiosity, and enthusiasm for this project, I am indebted to my research assistants Francis Goyes, Rebecca Jordan, Bahia Marks, Olive Murage, and Isabel Ontaneda, as well as my advisees Erika Linenfelser and Hester Tittmann. I also appreciated the sustained conversations about the book's topic with my advisees Cole Cataneo-Ryan, Emilie Flamme, Joshua Levitt, and Anna-Julia Plichta.

The comments received from reviewers at different stages of the writing process were essential to how the book shaped up in the end. Special thanks to

Felipe Correa, Arturo Escobar, and five anonymous reviewers. Thanks also to Jeff Dean, whose early interest in this project convinced me of its potential.

I also extend my appreciation to the people at the University of Virginia Press, including Suzanne Morse Moomaw and the members of the Board of Directors for their enthusiastic reception to this project. I thank Mark Mones for his patience, generosity, and undeterred commitment to having the book published. I also thank Boyd Zenner for having believed in the project from the very beginning and for sharing her wisdom with me. Lastly, I thank Maura High of High Editorial for her great attention to detail and for making sure that the manuscript had a consistent style, and Ina Gravitz for her excellent indexing work. The fact that most of the preparation for production happened during the worst of the COVID 19 pandemic makes everybody's efforts most meaningful to me.

At Amherst College, Nicola Courtright, Catherine Epstein, Heidi Gilpin, Justin Kimball, Biddy Martin, Samuel Morse, and Ronald Rosbottom offered unconditional support that made it possible for me to complete this project. Thank you, Ron for your welcome to Amherst and your ever-so-decisive mentorship. Thank you, Nicola, Justin, and Sam for championing my work at Amherst.

I am indebted to Karen Koehler for her decisive efforts to bring me to the Pioneer Valley and the Five College Architectural Studies Program. For their warm welcoming to the program, I express my appreciation to Thom Long at Hampshire College, Naomi Darling and Michael Davis at Mount Holyoke College, as well as Carey Clouse and Stephen Schreiber at the University of Massachusetts Amherst.

During the process of writing, my family helped me to not lose sight of the things that are most important in life. Noé and Isaac provided both the motivation to continue writing and the urgency to finish. Jennifer Rulf, *mi compañera de andanzas,* offered support in every sense—intellectual, emotional, and practical. Simply, this project would not have existed if it were not for you, J.

The big family in Colombia constantly reminded me that it doesn't matter what happens today: everything will make sense tomorrow. This book is dedicated to my mother and my late father, who taught me the two lessons that made it possible to complete this project: the importance of a work ethic and the power of persistence.

SUSTAINABILITY AND PRIVILEGE

Social Design

Since the late 1990s, the subject of poverty has reemerged as central to architectural design practice, as shown by the work of the now-defunct Architecture for Humanity and a number of other design nonprofits, as well as academic institutions and design firms that followed their lead. The activity of designing for social improvement is known by various names: design activism, pro bono design, architecture of social engagement, and others. One of the most frequently used terms for this field is *social design,* a term that can be limited, as some authors have noted (e.g., Jones and Card 2011; Antonelli 2012; Watson 2012). However, this is the term I adopt in this book because it is descriptive of the field's main subject of interest. It accurately reflects the field's essential premise that design can be a valuable tool to help solve critical social problems such as poverty.

Social design is an extensive area of architectural practice. As such, it appears in a myriad of projects, courses, conferences, publications, exhibits, and awards. In fact, along with LEED (Leadership in Energy and Environmental Design, the green building standard that consolidated the sustainable design approach to architecture), social design is arguably one of the most important developments in the last two decades of architectural practice. The architectural writer Christopher Hawthorne has gone even further, calling it "the single most visible architectural concern of the moment" (2011). Social design, in Hawthorne's view, eclipses the avant-garde movements of neomodernist, biomimetic, and parametric design.

The practice of social design is not new. In modern times, it dates back as far as the late 1800s, when socially minded housing developers began to produce better-designed housing as a solution for slums in cities such as New York (see Riis 1890, 1902). However, something quite unique happened in social design practice starting in the late 1990s. First and foremost, the practice became so widespread that for the first time in the history of architecture it became possible to talk about the social design *field,* rather than simply talking about social design projects, as those used to be relatively scattered; nowadays, social design projects number in the hundreds at any given time.

The second aspect, and one that has greatly contributed to the field's growth, is the "cool factor." In the old days of social design, architects doing this type of work were often chastised as too unsophisticated, too political, or too grassroots-oriented. Today, instead, social design practice is perceived as fashionable. It is no longer seen as a professional sacrifice that could marginalize the architect in the profession at large. Social design is now so integrated into the profession that it has in fact become a stepping-stone to mainstream practice in architecture. Many among the most celebrated rising stars in architecture today, including a few African and Latin American designers, started as social designers.

This has been possible because of a third factor that has made this new wave of social design radically different, which is the role of *high design.* By that I mean artistic, imaginative, and innovative designs that result in highly iconic pieces of architectural art (fig. 1). Different from previous historical movements (including modernism, where social building designs tended to be formulaic and thus repetitive) (fig. 2), social design practice today has a strong high design component. The notions of formal beauty and iconicity have become inherent to the practice today, shifting its focus from simply performing a social service to doing this with the regular tools of architectural design.

Fig. 1. The Soe Ker Tie houses in Noh Bo, Thailand (2009). A project by the Norwegian social design firm TYIN Tegnestue. (Photograph by Pasi Aalto, PasiAalto.com)

Fig. 2. The Pruitt-Igoe housing complex in St. Louis, Missouri. By the time this complex opened (1954), it was one of the most celebrated modernist social design projects in the United States. The complex was demolished in 1972. (Photograph by US Geological Survey, ca. 1963)

In essence, then, social design is regarded as "cool," it is visually appealing, and it fits well in the architectural establishment. This is the mainstream approach to social design today, and the one I am exploring in this book.

BOOK RELEVANCE AND CONTRIBUTIONS

This volume is a critique of social design, as its title makes clear. It places a question mark on today's mainstream way of carrying out social design practice by following the paradigms of regular architectural design practice, those based on high design and the architect's individual genius. Considering how widespread the practice of social design is today, it is surprising how, comparatively speaking, the criticism of this movement has not been nearly as profuse as its praise. In fact, social design tends to be celebrated across the whole spectrum of academia, from politically mainstream designers who see it as a laudable act of do-goodism (e.g., Bell 2004; Gould 2008; Cary 2010) to post-Marxist critics who regard it as the one possibility left for architecture and urbanism to reengage with the project of emancipation (e.g., Harvey 2014; Sassen 2014; Cunningham 2016).

Although there is a growing body of social design critique, this critique has mostly circulated through short-form works such as academic papers and popular press articles. To have an idea of the comparative rarity of book-form critiques to social design in the architectural field, it is worth looking at the decade 2006–16, when social design became a significant publishing area. The decade began with the publication of Architecture for Humanity's influential book *Design Like You Give a Damn* (AFH 2006) and ended with the publication of *By the People* by the Cooper Hewitt, Smithsonian Design Museum (Smith 2016). *By the People* accompanied an exhibit of the same name, and was the third of a series of influential exhibits and books by the museum, the other two being *Design for the Other 90%* (Smith 2007) and *Design with the Other 90%* (Smith 2011). During this decade, a host of other architecture-related social design books were published. By my own count, and considering only books published in English in the United States and Europe, the most significant books numbered about eighty in total. The overwhelming majority of these books were highly celebratory of social design practice. An edited volume published at the very end of that period (Lahiji 2016) was an exception, insofar as it proposed a conversation between critics and supporters of social design, and it thus included competing voices. However, the dominant tone of that book was still celebratory.

There is nothing wrong with celebration, and there are many reasons to applaud the massive movement of bona fide architects joining the global project of fighting poverty. However, not everything is to be celebrated, since serious issues exist in this practice as well, as I expect to demonstrate in this book. These issues are most evident in the field, when one observes what gets built and how people experience the construction projects. By strongly focusing on the field, this book fills a gap in social design literature. A major limitation of the laudatory literature is how often it relies upon self-reporting, that is, relying on project descriptions provided by their project designers. Unsurprisingly, those descriptions tend to paint a very positive picture of the projects. On the whole, much of the literature focuses largely on the viewpoints of designers, ignoring the people's experience of the projects. To overcome this limitation, this book focuses instead on that experience. In chapters 2 and 3, I describe how humble slum residents and rural villagers dared to challenge very ambitious and celebrated social design projects using simple yet powerful arguments from which we all can learn.

I rely upon extensive field evidence, studying six high-profile and/or large-scale social design interventions across three continents. One of the cases studied consists of thirty construction projects, so in total I examine thirty-five projects. This large volume of evidence allows for making safe generalizations about the practice of social design as a whole.

One of the reasons why it is also important to rely upon extensive field evidence is that the critique so far raised against social design has itself proven to be limited. One of its most noticeable limitations is that, just like the celebratory literature, the critique also seldom engages with the subjects of social design interventions. It often reads those interventions from a metatheoretical perspective, and therefore sometimes it becomes mostly an exercise in discourse analysis. Another reason is that critics of social design themselves have been accused of being simplistic. A prominent instance is the best-known critical piece on social design to date, Bruce Nussbaum's "Is Humanitarian Design the New Imperialism?" (2010), which I examine in chapter 1. A valid countercritique to the black-and-white nature of Nussbaum's argument was raised by the designer Emily Pilloton, who was the main target of this critique and who summarized it incisively: "If you're here, and you work there, you're an imperialist" (2010). Indeed, a no-nonsense yet passionate critique that overlooks the complexities of what Pilloton called the "serendipitous chaos" of the work in the field can come across as simplistic or superficial. It is therefore crucial to look carefully at the field in order to engage in a critique that is both strongly supported and nuanced.

By focusing on the field the book also seeks to address a crucial question often raised in architectural practice: What sense does the current critique of social design make for the purposes of practice? As with the Nussbaum controversy, in the eyes of design practitioners, this critique might sometimes sound as too theoretical or lacking in applicability. When it comes to the high academic critique of social design, indeed, it does tend to be more about "social" than about "design." That is, it is a powerful social science–based critique that proposes alternatives which, however, designers might find altogether unfeasible or at least hard to apply in practice.

Considering this factor, a central goal of my study is precisely to bridge theory and practice. Although focusing on the field, I make use of a theoretical framework to fully understand the critique of social design to date. I revisit the argument of imperialism, which is the main one raised in that critique, as will be explained in chapter 1. I examine that argument not only by parsing it through field-based evidence but also by placing it in its appropriate theoretical context. I carry out a close reading of the literature, including literature on sustainability and sustainable design, social design, and social science literature, the latter including development studies and postcolonial theory. With that, I strive to provide a deep and ample context to the imperialism critique by describing what the critique is about, its core concepts and rationale, and its main points of contention.

The connection between theory and practice is a central concern throughout. The book starts with a theory of practice in chapter 1. In that chapter, I introduce the practice of social design from a broad perspective, studying its history, main practitioners, and goals. Also, the book's source of analysis is practice, since I present a field-based study of social design projects in chapters 2 and 3. Then, on the basis of that study, I analyze the main challenge currently affecting social design practice. I close with a practice-based proposal to address this challenge in chapter 4. With this proposal, I intend to go beyond simply diagnosing the problem, by offering a feasible approach to social design that addresses it. Thus, the way in which this book bridges social design theory and practice is, first, by studying the problems of this practice as identified by critical theory; then, by explaining how these problems unfold in the field; and last, by proposing how they can be solved through an alternative approach to social design practice.

In sum, positioned midway between innocuous celebration and radical critique, *Sustainability and Privilege: A Critique of Social Design Practice* critically explores the role of social design in poverty alleviation; however, rather than quickly dismissing this practice, it highlights the lessons that can be learned, and on that basis it proposes a feasible approach to improve it.

ARGUMENT OF THE BOOK

The notion of sustainability is essential to social design's goal of poverty alleviation. I explore the paradigm of bringing sustainability to rural impoverished populations living in regions such as Africa or Latin America, and look at that paradigm in light of the main criticism that has been raised about social design practice—namely, that it is fundamentally imperialist. The basis for this argument is that social design projects often recall the purportedly do-good interventions of colonial times in so-called Third World settings. European and American designers often arrive with a comparatively high degree of power in places with which they are unfamiliar and, indifferent to this unfamiliarity, they make decisions that deeply affect local communities, which are often vulnerable communities in conditions of dire poverty. The designers set out to impose their own ideas, ignoring the expertise of local designers and the input from community stakeholders.

As a way to overcome the challenge of imperialism, both critics and supporters of social design agree on proposing *localism* as the solution. First, they propose that the practice of social design should be left to local designers. For example, Nigerian or Colombian designers should be in charge of the social design needs of their own countries. Second, they propose that designers should involve community participation in their work in order to include perspectives from local stakeholders.

Although in agreement with the imperialism critique, in this book I make instead a case for regarding class privilege as the most important factor for social designers to keep in mind. As a whole, social designers, regardless of where we practice or where we come from, must be aware of our own privilege when carrying out work with subaltern populations. The issue of the designers' inherent power over vulnerable populations equally affects the work of both so-called imperialist foreign designers and presumably more sensitive local designers.

In order to support this argument, I explore representative cases of high-profile and/or large-scale social design projects where local designers in a condition of privilege engaged in practices that ended up being very detrimental to the well-being of local subaltern populations. This happened even despite (or, as I will explain, actually because of) the fact that these designers invoked sustainability as the reason to tackle the projects in the way they did. It also happened even in cases in which these designers involved community participation in their work.

What exactly is the problem with sustainability advocacy in social design? I argue that the root of the problem lies in this field's use of sustainability as its standard for poverty alleviation. The problem starts with social designers' advocacy of sustainability initiatives such as greening urban spaces or, in rural settlements, using traditional construction materials such as bamboo and palm thatch. At first sight, these initiatives make sense; however, as was the case with the projects studied here, they made sense mostly from the standpoint of designers, who tended to ignore the negative impact of their sustainable design proposals on the particular conditions of people. The consequences of implementing those designs included displacement of people and expropriation of their property for green infrastructure projects, as well as the economic impact of having to build with traditional materials, which tend to be demanding and expensive. Consequently, the designers' advocacy of quite popular sustainability measures ended up reflecting their own privileged view of poverty, thus revealing a social class disconnection with the subjects of their advocacy. However, rather than aiming to bridge that disconnection, the designers decided to press on behalf of their own ideas, to the extreme of imposing them. For example, they pressed for the creation of parks while ignoring the destruction of homes and the displacement of homeless people, and for structures to be built with bamboo and thatch despite people having voiced their preference for materials such as concrete and metal roofing in order to allow for more practical and affordable construction.

Notably, the designers' imposition of their own viewpoints often took on the guise of community participation. Participatory processes were manipulated in a way in which people ultimately appeared as having accepted design proposals with which they had actually disagreed. In chapter 4, I identify six different strategies that were used to manipulate participation in these projects. The fact that similar strategies were used by different, unrelated practitioners in projects located far from one another attests to the widespread use of these biased participatory strategies in social design practice. It also attests to how limited the notion of participation is in and of itself, given that it lends itself too easily to be manipulated in these ways. The limitations of this notion are present from the very beginning of a participatory process, since the demographics of who participates can be easily restricted to only those community members who agree with the designers' ideas. As was the case in some of the studied projects, those community members tended to be the ones in positions of relative privilege in their own communities. Because of their higher social standing, they generally had a more influential voice in their community matters, and thus their opinions became prevalent in community-wide decisions, overpowering those of the community members in greatest poverty, despite the latter having been supposed to be the actual beneficiaries of the projects. Thus, the limitations with the notion of community participation involve both the notion of community (who is "the community," if only certain voices are taken into account?) and that of participation (in general, this approach is very easy to manipulate).

The social class disconnection between designers and project beneficiaries also becomes evident in the high cost of the projects. A common pattern in the studied projects was that these ended up being far more expensive than regular, simple alternatives that people themselves had unsuccessfully counterproposed. Importantly, these alternatives were quite simple from a formal standpoint, and as such they greatly contrasted with the intricately designed and/or artistic structures proposed by the designers. Still, despite the high cost of their structures, some of the designers presented them as affordable on the basis of excluding from the budget the beneficiaries' own contributions to the project, most notably their labor, which was designated as "free." Such a designation starkly contrasted with the perspective from beneficiaries themselves, as became evident during my field research. People usually had a clear recollection of what their labor investment had been in the projects, especially because it was a difficult investment for them to make, since they needed to procure for their daily subsistence but were mandated to contribute their labor at no charge. Another cost-related issue was that in many cases, the people's economic investment did not stop when the project was concluded, since they were left in charge of performing maintenance and repairs; these are essential tasks in order to ensure the durability of structures built, for instance, with bamboo and thatch, materials that deteriorate easily.

The economic burden on people was even higher when the structures were built defectively. This happened because often the designers were experimenting with daring, innovative structural framings or material combinations for which they had not carried out any previous testing. In fact, the projects themselves were regarded by the designers as their opportunity to carry out those tests. As I will explain, the practice of using social design as a field to carry out formal and technological experimentation is in fact quite widespread, and it is tremendously problematic because, as happened in the studied cases, this was experimentation undertaken without the informed consent of the subjects. That is, people had not been told that those projects were experiments, and had not been asked whether they agreed to be experimented upon. Those experiments put people at risk, especially children, as some of the projects were schools—some of them in fact collapsed. Finally, there was denial on the part of designers after the negative outcomes of the projects became apparent. Despite all these serious issues, including imposition, economic burdens, faulty experimentation, expropriation, and displacement of people, the project reports from designers and their supporters often described an unqualified success. To the contrary, there is considerable evidence that some of these projects actually made their supposed beneficiaries even poorer.

Thus, the problem of sustainability advocacy in social design concerns the imposition of an ideal of sustainability that might end up materializing as a quite dystopian reality. To summarize, then, although sustainability advocacy might reflect the problem of imperialism as described by postcolonial critics, it also very strongly reflects the problem of *privilege*. All of the projects studied in this book are projects by so-called local designers, "locals" as in nationals or residents of the locations where the projects took place, which is how localism proponents generally understand this notion. The problematic outcomes of these projects then suggest that in the end there is no significant difference between how local and foreign designers might carry out their work; when it comes to negative outcomes, the former's work can be just as detrimental as the latter's. This is the case even when designers invite community participation, which is a limited approach. In conclusion, the broadest challenge to social design work is privilege, rather than imperialism, because the challenge of privilege implicates both local and foreign designers. Furthermore, localism as the solution proposed to deal with the challenge of social design is limited with regard to both local designers (they could engage in questionable practices just as much as foreign designers) and community participation (in the way in which it is normally carried out, it does not really make a difference).

Now, why is it that sensible professionals like the designers of the studied projects, who honestly wanted to help fight poverty, ended up engaging in practices that actually caused more poverty? I argue that the reason is *design* rather than *designers*. That is, in the end it does not matter whether designers are local. The greatest challenge presently faced by social design practice is that its mainstream approach is too heavily based on high design. That is, the challenge lies in the fact that we are largely tackling social design by using the model of regular architectural design practice, which remains so highly based on creative strokes and individual genius. If the highest achievement in the architectural design world is largely considered to be that of becoming a star architect, a *starchitect*—an almost legendary status reserved for only a few—this system has been embraced to such an extent that it is now possible to talk also about *humanitarian starchitects*.

Social design's present focus on iconicity mirrors that of architectural design as a whole. There is today a fascination in the architectural design field with artistic, highly iconic forms, the result in part of technological developments in computer-aided design (CAD) software over the past few decades. These developments have allowed for the production of sophisticated architectural forms that had never before been possible in architectural history, such as the geometrically intricate and curvilinear architecture of Frank Gehry, Zaha Hadid, or Bjarke Ingels. Although this type of iconic architecture constitutes only one form of architectural practice, its visual impact has made it such a strong genre that it has in fact changed the discipline, which now confers a tremendous value upon such iconicity. I argue that this trend has deeply affected social design practice as well. In this field, too, the most famous projects tend to be those with more iconic shapes or more unique features. They include some of the projects described in chapter 2.

Granted, not every social designer is following this path. Many designers consciously resist the paradigm of iconicity, instead carrying out their work with more modest goals, formally speaking, and giving priority to the social goals of their projects. Despite that, however, iconicity remains the paradigm: the canon, the ideal to strive for. The opportunity to produce visually striking structures is what draws many young architects to get into the area of social design, as I will explain in chapter 4. Social design is often regarded as a stepping-stone for young designers to make a name for themselves in the high architectural world. They start as social designers; they become known for their iconic designs in say, rural Africa, and soon after they are designing museums and other high architectural design pieces for wealthy patrons in Europe and the United States. Although this is not bad per se, it explains the eagerness among some young designers to approach social design through the conventional architectural paradigm of high design. Doing this offers an advantage to them in terms of portfolio formation, and it could have a decisive impact on their careers. Consequently, the question of who benefits from social design, in the case of the mainstream, high design–focused social design practice, is a complicated one. The benefits can be sometimes quite asymmetrical; while designers might benefit a great deal, beneficiaries might get comparatively little, and sometimes literally nothing. I will provide powerful examples of this in chapter 2.

However, it is still necessary to consider an argument that has been often made to justify the role of iconicity and in general of formal beauty in social design, which is that the "social" and "design" goals of social design are not necessarily in contradiction (see Brillembourg and Klumpner 2013; Lepik 2013; Miller 2014; Quintal 2014). In fact, this is the core argument of present-day social design practice: that designers can make a social impact with their work while still doing it beautifully. However, the cases analyzed in this book demonstrate that in reality, when it comes to so-called real world practice, the social and the beauty goals are often in stark contradiction. This is best exemplified by the aforementioned conflict between designers who advocate for beauty, while project beneficiaries might instead ask for practical yet "ugly" solutions. Thus, although in theory there is no contradiction, in reality the element of beauty tends to be highly prioritized.

Now, why is this focus on formal beauty accepted as the norm in social design? Given that social design's main concern is poverty, social designers must deal directly with people in poverty. However, as architectural designers, we are not being educated to deal with people as much as, for example, anthropologists. The focus of architectural design is generally on buildings. Since this is what we as designers know, a key goal in social design then has become that of dealing with people in poverty by bringing them buildings. In addition, social design's current, mainstream high design paradigm dictates that we should not settle for bringing ordinary buildings, but rather visually striking structures in order to make an artistic architectural statement. Thus, today's social design practice relies upon a notion that continues to be highly prevalent in architectural design, namely, that the most important contribution that architects can make to society is beautiful buildings. Consequently, in social design, the notion of "design" has ended up becoming synonymous with formal beauty.

However, it often happens, as some of the studied cases demonstrate, that once designers arrive in the field with beautiful building designs, they discover that people have already identified that the best solutions to their poverty conditions are actually quite simple ones, and they might not even be "beautiful" (a gabled tin house, for example). In fact, in many cases, of which I will show a few, these solutions might not even require any buildings at all. These crucial factors put into crisis the beauty paradigm of social design: *we* want to give beauty, but *they* might not need it. People might be better off with more modest propositions from a formal standpoint, or if other non-building-related markers of poverty are tackled first. This is where the conflict of perspectives emerges. In the cases I studied, this conflict became contentious when the argument invoked by the designers in order to justify their imposition of beautiful buildings, over any objections from people, was that those buildings were *sustainable.* Engaging with the project of materializing beautiful buildings at all costs under the invocation of their presumed sustainability generates a conflict that exposes the designers' social class disconnection, with very troubling results. Thus, by invoking sustainability, a powerful argument, the celebration of social designers' individual genius is often privileged over the impact that their projects might have on populations in poverty. Consequently, the focus on beauty and the creation of exhibition-worthy pieces to be celebrated in architectural circles often works to the detriment of social design's goal of social improvement, to the extreme of putting people at risk and often leaving their conditions of poverty unchanged or even worsened.

Thus, evidently, the main focus of social design, which is poverty, cannot be appropriately tackled by using the conventional architectural paradigm of high design. Because of that, exploring a new approach to social design is imperative. I argue that the answer to the challenge of social design is to move this practice out of the realm of high architectural design and its designer-centered values, and instead to explore alternative models of practice that are people-centered. The most necessary change in the way of rethinking social design is to reconsider its focus on objects and bring back its focus on people. Therefore, the most effective way to implement this change is through incorporating in this practice the values from a discipline that has people as its central interest, which is anthropology. I propose a hybrid approach to social design that adopts the ethos of anthropology's ethnographic method, which relies upon the vision from the counterpart—in this case, the project beneficiaries. I call this approach *ethnoarchitecture.* The prefix *ethno-* here is understood in the conventional anthropological sense of *the perspective from the other side.* I will summarize the main premises of this approach at the end of the next section and give a fuller explanation in chapter 4.

SUMMARY OF CHAPTERS

This introduction presents the book's topic and its significance. Chapter 1 locates this topic within a larger theoretical context. In it, I introduce first some of the main players in the social design field, both individual designers and organizations, and their understanding of the notion of sustainability. Then, establishing a parallel, I examine the grounds of the imperialism critique of social design by explaining the connection between sustainability and imperialism from a postcolonial theoretical perspective. From there, I trace the main threads in the critical literature on sustainability, showing how imperialism constitutes one of its main subjects. I explain how the imperialism objection has also been raised with regard to social design, where it is indeed the critique's main subject. I describe the peak moment of social design's critique of imperialism, Bruce Nussbaum's 2010 question of whether humanitarian design (the term used by Nussbaum to refer to social design) is a new form of imperialism. I end the chapter with an explanation of the most widely proposed solution, one that comes not only from critics but also from supporters of social design, to overcome the challenge of imperialism in this practice—namely, *localism*. That is, local designers, as opposed to foreign designers, should take local matters into their own hands, and social design projects should be carried out with community participation.

Chapters 2 and 3 undertake a field-based exploration of localism. I explore in detail the two localism premises of local designers and community participation. I ask: Does implementing these two measures actually resolve the issues ascribed to imperialism in social design? To answer this question, in these chapters I look at six cases of social design projects by local designers. In chapter 2, I focus on five high-profile projects from reputable figures in the social design field: the Al Borde Architects' Nueva Esperanza School in Cabuyal, Ecuador; Kunlé Adeyemi's Makoko Floating School in Lagos, Nigeria; Alfredo Brillembourg and Hubert Klumpner's Torre David research and design project in Caracas, Venezuela; Giancarlo Mazzanti's Biblioteca España ("Library of Spain") and its umbrella project, social urbanism, in Medellín, Colombia; and last, Architecture for Humanity's Burrows Street Pocket Park in San Francisco, California, in the United States. In chapter 3 I focus on *ethnoengineering*, a large-scale social infrastructure project in Ecuador consisting of forty-eight constructions, of which I study thirty. For my analysis of the ethnoengineering project I rely in part upon my Ph.D. dissertation research (see Arboleda 2012), although the majority of the studied cases were not part of the dissertation and thus constitute a new contribution in this book.

The cases in chapter 2 form the basis of my study of localism's first premise, namely, that local social design matters should be left to local designers. In order to strengthen my point, I focus in that chapter only on high-profile projects. The collapse of one of the studied projects, Makoko, is well known in architectural circles. However, many of the problems with the remaining projects are less known. By exploring the outcomes of those projects, I intend to provide sufficient evidence to demonstrate that the problems of social design's high design approach extend also to the local designers who use it. Thus, in response to the localism premise of local designers, my study of these cases aims to demonstrate that being a local designer ultimately does not make a major difference. That is, these designers are not exempt from the problems that are normally ascribed only to imperialism.

In chapter 3, I focus on the second premise of localism, that of community participation. I use the ethnoengineering project to study participation because this project was explicitly and intentionally formulated as a participation-focused project. The project used a method that was conceived to incorporate the broadest possible degree of community participation in social development work. Following that method, project beneficiaries were theoretically able to participate in a far more extensive way and having more decision-making power than was offered by the participatory approaches used in the projects analyzed in chapter 2. Although the ethnoengineering project consisted of several dozen constructions, these were executed independently as separate projects, most of them using different designs produced by different designers. Thus, for all practical purposes, the ethnoengineering project was actually many projects in one, and thus provided the opportunity to work with a large research sample. Since I also study how participation was implemented in the five projects discussed in chapter 2, the field exploration of participation that I make in this book aims to be quite detailed and comprehensive.

After presenting, in chapters 2 and 3, an exhaustive field-based exploration of the limited outcomes of the two premises of localism, I start chapter 4 by gathering the findings from that exploration. I observe that, although sustainability has been critiqued as a global imperialist project, this notion was actually invoked as the justification for local designers to engage in very problematic practices as well. Thus, the problems of abuse of vulnerable populations that are ascribed solely to imperialism also occur in local social design practice; that is, the problems posed by imperialism extend to the supposed solution, which includes leaving social design matters to local designers. At this point, I introduce the book's thesis on privilege, arguing that, even though there are valid grounds for drawing a connection between social design and imperialism, the more significant challenge of social design is privilege, even more so than imperialism. Regardless of the designers' origin, their lack of awareness of their own privilege is what allows the abuse of subaltern populations to continue.

From here, in that chapter, I analyze the second localism premise, namely, that of involving community participation. I analyze the limitations of the notion of participation by studying the six strategies referred to earlier of imposition-via-participation, naming them *participation as labor, participation as information provision, deceptive participation, manipulative participation, anodyne participation,* and *participation as everything.* Identifying and describing these strategies is one of the most important contributions this book intends to make, because they constitute the mainstream ways in which participation is generally tackled in social design. This is what I call "top-down" participation: a form of participation that is controlled from above. I then observe that participation is a tool that lends itself too easily to manipulation, to the extent that, as it is currently used in social design, it becomes almost meaningless. Naming these top-down participatory strategies is thus a decisive step toward rethinking participation in social design.

I close chapter 4, and with that the book, by proposing ethnoarchitecture as a form of "bottom-up" participation, one that places human agency at the core of social design practice. In this proposed approach to participation, the social design project is driven by people and their own vision of problems and potential solutions. As for the designers, rather than driving the design process, and rather than assuming to be cocreators, they become instead *supporters* of the people's own design ideas by offering their technical expertise to materialize those ideas. Thus, in this proposed approach there is a positional change in which beneficiaries become *agents,* the agents of their own future, while designers move to the very bottom of the hierarchy in the design process. Thus, ethnoarchitecture is a response to the predominant high design approach to social design, which is so heavily focused on the image of a benevolent star designer and, with that, the celebration of individual authorship and artistic genius. The practice of ethnoarchitecture instead endeavors to bring social design to what it should be in principle—a practice that is more about service and less about the designers.

TERMINOLOGY

The terminology I use in this book consists mostly of simple terms, although many of them are subject to contradiction and debate, and because of that it is necessary that I explain my use of them. With regard to the terms used in the title of this book, I have already explained "social design," and I shall now define *sustainability* and *privilege.*

The question of what sustainability is belongs to a contested conceptual territory, as there exist many different understandings of this notion (see Cook and Golton 1994; Jacobs 1999; Bourke and Meppem 2000; Guy and Farmer 2001; Farmer and Guy 2005; Connelly 2007; Guy 2012). Consequently, there exist many definitions. However, and as I will explain in chapter 1, in the practice of social design at large there seems to exist a consensus. The predominant definition of "sustainability" in this practice is that of the Brundtland Report: "meet[ing] the needs of the present without compromising the ability of future generations to meet their own needs" (WCED 1987,

43). As I will also explain, this definition is limited. It is, however, the one I must work with since it frames the practice I am critiquing. That said, this is by no means a marginal or minor definition. Not only do many of the existing definitions of sustainability still follow the essential premises of the Brundtland Report, but also the Brundtland definition remains the most predominant and influential definition when it comes to practice, including the practice of social design as well as many other areas. The Brundtland definition is still largely used as the framework for sustainability initiatives by governmental, nonprofit, and corporate organizations. It is then sustainability's "hegemonic" definition. As for the limitations of this definition, as I will also argue in chapter 1, the main one is its emphasis on economic growth, as opposed to the *limits to growth* premise of other environmental movements. Such a focus on economic growth has had a decisive impact on social design practice.

As for the second key term in the book's title, *privilege,* this book focuses on social class privilege. Following Pierre Bourdieu, I define "social class" as a principle of differentiation based on how people have amassed different assets, including economic, cultural, social, and symbolic assets or "forms of capital" (Bourdieu 1986). Cultural capital is one of the forms of capital that, according to Bourdieu, most powerfully determines social class differentiation. Cultural capital comprises assets such as education and other markers of high culture, including taste and manners (1984, 1987, 1993, 1996). In this book I invoke the notion of cultural capital because it allows us to understand some dynamics essential to social design practice, such as manifestations of relative privilege within communities in poverty, and how privilege can eventually be an asset in social design practice.

I also use the term *positionality* as an alternative way of saying privilege. My use of this term follows that of Gayatri Spivak in the context of class consciousness (as in awareness) and the need for critical researchers to be aware of their own class positionality (see Spivak 2010). I use the term "positionality" also in the sense of class awareness, referring to the need for self-awareness among social designers as well. I find the term "positionality" illustrative insofar as it helps forming a mental image of privilege in the sense of the designers' default higher position in relation to the subjects of their work, and how this position can be shifted downward in addressing the challenge of social design.

In order to identify the class position of the subjects of social design, I refer to them as *subalterns,* a term coined in the 1930s by the Marxist thinker Antonio Gramsci to refer to the people who do not belong to the dominant classes (1994). However, I frequently use a much simpler term, *beneficiaries.* "Beneficiaries" is by far the most widely used term to describe these populations in social development literature and practice. This is a problematic term because it sounds very patronizing. However, there is hardly a better term to convey its meaning in social design practice. An alternative term could be *users,* which I also employ. However, this term still connotes a sense of passivity on the receiving end of a social design project. Other commonly used terms also fail to overcome this limitation. See, for example, the term *subaltern* itself, and also the term *subjects.* I also refer to *people,* as this term is often used in social design, to mean the common folk. However, even this term can be confusing because designers and community elites are also people; thus, the use of "people" does not inherently reflect social class or inherently represent the subalternity condition of the beneficiaries of social design. On the other hand, resorting to other more theoretically appropriate terms, social design advocates often use words such as "partners," "co-designers," or "cocreators." In reality, though, the use of these terms tends to be mostly rhetorical, since they are tied to an understanding of community participation that, as explained, is quite constrained and where participants are still limited to acting as subjects, users, or beneficiaries.

In conclusion, the terms most commonly used to describe the designers' counterparts either put them in a position of passivity or inferiority, or are too broad, or do not accurately reflect the current reality of the practice. Thus, using any other term to substitute for the uncomfortable "beneficiaries" ends up being either ineffectual or obfuscating the significance of the dynamics that this term so accurately reflects. Ultimately, the term "beneficiaries" bluntly reflects what social design practice has historically been about. This practice has been deeply affected by issues of privilege, where those who initiate the process often place themselves above the intended recipients. The latter are then usually constructed as passive actors in need of help, the subjects of *targeting* and *interventions.* These terms are also widely used in this and other social development fields, and as such I must also invoke them. Thus, my inevitable use of some problematic terms ultimately serves as an irksome reminder of a prevalent issue in social design that must be definitely addressed: the issue of privilege.

To address this issue, in the approach to participation that I propose, the counterparts shift from being beneficiaries to being *agents.* I use this term in reference to *human agency,* which Anthony Giddens defines as the ability to change history—that is, the ability of people to make history, as opposed to history making them; as opposed to their fate being predetermined by historical forces of oppression (see Giddens 1987). Thus, agency is *the power to act otherwise* (Giddens 1979, 1987, 1993) in contrast to the extreme opposite of *having no choice.* An agent is then the "'motor of events'" (1987, 216).

I adopt a view of *poverty* within this agency framework by embracing

Amartya Sen's definition of poverty as *capabilities*, that is, "having minimally adequate capabilities" (1992, 111; see also 1993, 42). For Sen, the difference between poverty and affluence is marked by different capability levels. In order to illustrate this difference, Sen appeals to a powerfully illustrative comparison between fasting and starving. As Sen describes it, the difference between fasting and starving is the difference between capabilities. Fasting "is *not* just starving; it is *choosing to starve when one does have other options*" (1992, 52, emphasis in original). Thus, the person who fasts has the capability to end their condition of starvation whenever they decide to. The notion of poverty as capabilities then relates to people's different capacities to overcome situations of scarcity by themselves. Embracing this notion, I understand poverty not as a given condition, but instead as a condition that people can overcome if they have the opportunity to develop their own capabilities. This understanding of poverty then challenges the popular understanding, which is that of poverty as deprivation or lack, and particularly of poverty as being marked by the fact that people are lacking *things,* which should then be presumably given to them. Thus, the notion of capabilities is fundamental in order to rethink the current prevalent framework of social design, which advocates addressing poverty by giving people objects, particularly buildings. When poverty is understood within the human agency framework of capabilities, then a different role for social designers emerges: to contribute to the generation of spaces, physical or otherwise, for people to develop their own capabilities.

Often in social design, subjects are described with a blanket term, "*the* community." This description reflects social design's broad understanding of *community,* which is that of community as in *commonality.* Community as so defined is a group of people who share common goals, ways of living, expectations, beliefs, visions, and in some cases even physical features. Thus, social design's prevalent notion of community relies on a presumed idea of homogeneity, that is, common factors among community members that in theory make them different from those who are not from the community. Therefore, community in this sense is defined by exclusion, by contrasting the community members with those who do not belong. These two characteristics in social design's understanding of this notion, namely, homogeneity and exclusivity, are what lead to one of the most problematic issues this practice currently faces, which is the hijacking of processes of community participation, as I have explained earlier and will elaborate on in chapter 4. In reality, communities are much less homogeneous than this understanding of the notion presupposes (see Hoggett 1997). Therefore, social design's purist understanding of community can be invoked to oppress subgroups within the larger group. For example, on the basis of the argument that they are not actually part of the community, people from these subgroups can be excluded from social improvement projects or from spaces that they should also have the right to inhabit. I examine a case of community being used in this exclusionary sense in a social design project in chapter 2. I will examine another case, this time of understanding community as homogeneous, in chapter 3. In chapter 4, I make a general critique of social design's predominant understanding of community. In general, when I use the term "community" in an unmarked sense, I use it simply to mean a group of people. In chapter 3, I refer to a territorial division in Ecuador that translates into English as "community." In order to avoid confusion between that and the sociological use of the term, for that territorial division I use its Spanish original, *comunidad.*

When it comes to the urban beneficiaries of social design, I use *slum* in order to refer to the areas with the greatest poverty in Third World cities. Specifically, I use "slum" to mean land takeovers by people in poverty, built in an informal and progressive manner. Like other terms I use, the term "slum" is limited but still more descriptive than any other. The term has been used since the 1800s in a derogatory manner to stigmatize urban poverty and, on that basis, to support problematic projects of "slum clearance." On the other hand, there is no other term that better describes the situations of inequality, marginality, injustice, stigma, and abuse that the residents of these settlements often endure on a daily basis. Its descriptive power is such that the term has been adopted by slum residents themselves for their own advocacy. This is manifest in the naming of Slum Dwellers International, the largest global network of slum residents' rights organizations. The term "slum" is also widely used in the sense I use it here in the technical literature; for example, the United Nations uses it (see, e.g., UNHSP 2003). For these settlements, sometimes I also use the term *barrio.* Although in some Latin American countries this term is used to simply mean neighborhood, in others it is synonymous with slum. I also use *favela,* which is a particular name given to slums in Brazil.

The other main target group of social design is rural indigenous populations, which, worldwide, tend to be the ones living in the greatest poverty (Hall and Patrinos 2006, 2012). However, defining the term *indigenous* is complicated, even for indigenous people themselves. A number of working definitions have been produced by international organizations in collaboration with indigenous people's representatives (see ILO 1989; UNPFII Secretariat 2004; World Bank 2005; UNPFII 2006). These definitions emphasize eight identifying characteristics of indigenous people: ancestry, difference, institutions, language, nonhegemony, self-identification, territory, and traditions. However, these organizations agree that it is difficult to produce an unified definition of indigenous people that goes beyond listing these characteristics. In fact, one of these organizations, the World Bank, explicitly refrains from defining the term (see 2005, paragraph 3). Another, the United Nation's Permanent Forum on Indigenous Issues, states that "no formal universal definition of the term is necessary" (see UNPFII Secretariat 2004, 4). On the other hand, there are other rural beneficiaries of social design for whom these characteristics might also apply and yet they are not legally recognized as indigenous people. For instance, this is the case with rural Afro-descendant populations in some countries in the Americas. Because of that, I often speak in terms such as "indigenous and other traditional people."

I use *traditional* in the sense of "the memory of a people" (Viollet-Le-Duc 1876, vi). There are many contemporary and far more sophisticated definitions of "traditional." However, I prefer how Viollet-Le-Duc links tradition to memory because memory defies time, and memory is selective. Thus, understanding tradition in terms of memory allows including within the category of traditional those indigenous and other people who are modernizing, and who therefore might no longer be considered traditional by outsiders. Despite their change, people in these communities might still see themselves as traditional, and embracing the notion of tradition as memory acknowledges this. First, traditional does not necessarily mean "old," since the adoption of recent technologies might also give rise to new traditions. Second, despite their adoption of modernism, people might still privilege their memories of forsaken traditions as still being prevalent. For example, in the past, a group of people might have built a particular type of traditional house, but they no longer build it. However, when these people speak about their traditions, they might still select their memory of that house and not the one of their modernist housing as being the house of their tradition. This way of including modernizing indigenous and other traditional people in the full category of "traditional" is crucial to this book's argument. As mentioned, a contentious issue in social design's sustainability activism is that designers often invalidate the decision by some traditional people to embrace modernism, and thus they set out to reimpose traditional construction approaches on these people. This becomes a source of conflict between designers and project beneficiaries, as I will explain in detail in chapter 3.

In connection to that conflict, I also refer to a classical understanding of traditional as the modern's other. As has been amply discussed in the critical literature, one limitation of the notions of traditional and modern is that they are normally defined by their opposite: We are modern because we are not traditional, and vice versa (see, e.g., Abu-Lughod 1992; Latour 1993; Roy 2001). However, despite that limitation, the modern/traditional dichotomy remains very popular in social design practice. In fact, this dichotomy constituted the very foundation of the ethnoengineering project, as I will explain in chapter 3. In this book I will use *modern* to mean modernism. Out of the many different manifestations of the modernist aesthetic, the one I focus on is the industrial, functionalist, and minimalist aesthetic of the early twentieth-century *International Style* advocated by architects such as Le Corbusier, Philip Johnson, and Ludwig Mies van der Rohe. When I say "modernizing" I mean *becoming modern,* as in embracing the modernist ethos, or *making something modern,* as in transforming traditional architecture with the addition of materials and languages associated to the modernist aesthetic. When I say "modern materials" I mean the iconic materials of modernist architecture, industrially processed materials such as cement, concrete, and corrugated metal sheets ("zinc"). Likewise, I also use "traditional materials" to refer to materials that are common to traditional housing in the most classical sense of this term, that of "old," for example, mud, bamboo, palm thatch, and raw wood. In the book I also use *traditional architecture,* meaning the architecture of traditional people, specifically referring to the architecture of subaltern traditional people in the Third World.

The term that I use for modernism's other is *traditionalism,* which I understand as a form of advocacy, particularly antimodernism advocacy. This is a type of advocacy in which social designers often engage in behalf of traditional subaltern populations, as I will show in chapters 2 and 3. Generally speaking, in social design, modernism is seen as a feature of the designers' world that is unacceptable for the case of traditional people because it is supposedly detrimental to them. The grounds for this argument are often those of sustainability: if traditional people embrace modernism, this would prevent them from being able to live a sustainable life. Indeed, a popular position in social design advocacy is that the modern is bad in general, but is particularly bad when embraced by traditional people. This view is so widespread and so deeply embedded in the practice that we have a name for modernism, but not for its opposite; that is, we do not have a name for our own advocacy of the opposite. *Traditionalism,* which is the term I am proposing, then refers to the opposite set of values, all of them positive, that designers normally associate with traditional life and which, as I will show in chapter 3, some traditional people might indeed defy with their wholesale embrace of modernism.

There is considerable exoticism in descriptions of traditional people, and this has serious political ramifications. In order to refer to those exoticist descriptions while keeping in mind their political context, I use the term *orientalism.* My understanding of this term follows that of Edward Said (1978). Broadly speaking, orientalism is a form of narrative, a way of describing other people that relies upon an essential dichotomy of "them" and "us." In orientalist narratives, people are spoken for. Thus, orientalism is a representation based on the representing actors' claimed authoritative knowledge of others. Orientalist narratives are positional, their main premise being that "Occidentals are superior to Orientals" (Said 1978, 15, capitalization in original), the former being the representing actors and the latter the represented subjects. However, and this is what makes orientalism an interesting notion, so-called orientals are not bluntly represented as inferior. Their material culture, including their traditional architecture, is often described with great admiration. Indeed, a fundamental discursive logic of orientalism is the paradox that, although the oriental creations are seen as worthy of admiration, the orientals themselves, the authors of those works, are customarily regarded as lacking something fundamental in terms of morals. In fact, the moralizing aspect is a staple of orientalist narratives. While orientalists normally represent the orientals' work as worthy of being preserved, they instead represent the oriental subjects as being in need of intervention. This notion of intervention is essential to orientalism's logic: the orientalism discourse is advocacy discourse. Furthermore, it proposes a very peculiar form of advocacy insofar as orientalist narratives often make an urgent invitation to occidentals to embrace the high moral mission to save the orientals. That mission is, for orientalists, an inevitable duty. As they claim, an intervention by the occident in the orient is necessary for the orient's own good, or for the well-being of humanity as a whole.

Consequently, there is a strong connection between orientalism and colonialism. As Said argued, historically speaking, orientalism has been the supporting discourse of colonialism, offering the narrative basis for that project. By narrative basis, I mean that colonialism, a problematic project that has had the plundering of resources as its ultimate goal, needs to be justified by the invocation of a grander goal, namely a moral goal, and the point on behalf of that goal—the "pitch" so to speak—has been the narrative of orientalism, that is, depicting the subjects of the colonial project as oriental others. For instance, the orientalist discourse was used to justify nineteenth-century colonialist interventions such as those of France in Algeria and the British Empire in Egypt. In chapter 1, I expand on the idea of orientalism in the context of social design's advocacy of sustainability by studying traditionalism as a contemporary form of orientalism. Specifically, I refer to the traditionalist narrative that indigenous and other traditional people should remain attached to traditional building practices, thus resisting modernization under the premise that those traditions are presumably essential for the global project of sustainability. As I will explain, some authors have argued that this is a narrative of *green orientalism,* which has in turn offered a basis for the project of *green imperialism.*

The next concept to define is then *imperialism.* This is a central concept to this book given that, as mentioned, imperialism constitutes the main critique leveled at social design. The issue, however, is that in this critique, the term "imperialism" is often used too informally. This use gives countercritics a strong reason to see the critique as superficial. I understand imperialism as it is defined in postcolonial theory, where imperialism is also the central concern. In fact, the subject of imperialism is what ultimately inspires the name of that field of studies, given that the "postcolonial" in postcolonial theory refers to what happened historically after the global colonial era ended with World War II—that is, after formerly colonialist powers from Europe started to let go of their colonies in regions such as Africa, the Caribbean, and South and Southeast Asia, and these colonies gradually became independent nation states. The central argument of postcolonial theory is that essentially nothing happened, since both the formerly colonial powers and now a new postcolonial power, the United States, managed to keep these nations in a condition of subjugation even without a sustained military presence in those territories. So, the argument of postcolonial theory follows that from colonialism, the Third World entered a period of postcolonialism, or imperialism. Consequently, for postcolonial theory the notions of colonialism and imperialism are related but different. The former refers to a territorial occupation, while the latter refers to other mechanisms of control and domination (see Said 1993). Those might include control by the economy (see Cardoso and Faletto 1979), or by cultural hegemony (see Gramsci 1971). Thus, under an imperialist regime, subjects theoretically govern themselves freely, but in reality they self-govern in a way that continues to serve the interests of the imperialist power. Therefore, both colonialism and imperialism are strategies of *governmentality* or the "art of government," as Michel Foucault understood this term (1991). However, their means are different; they are those of *power* versus *hegemony*. That is, if the colonialist governs by coercion, the imperialist governs by consent. For the purposes of this book, it is necessary to clearly state this distinction because, as it will become apparent from the literature review in chapter 1, in social design critique the terms colonialism and imperialism are often used interchangeably, although both are used in the sense of imperialism as defined here, that of hegemony.

In connection to the notion of imperialism, in this book I use the simple dichotomy *Third World/First World* to describe the two main regions in the imperialism debate. Third World/First World is a limited dichotomy that has been amply critiqued as outdated or inaccurate. However, I still find it more practical than any other existing alternatives. In fact, there does not seem to be a right way to describe that global division, although the division does undeniably exist. One popular alternative has been *developing countries/developed countries*. Yet, one issue with this alternative is that it is no longer (if it ever was) possible to talk in terms of such a neat distinction between stages of economic development. For instance, some suburbs and other pockets of wealth in developing countries, say in Latin America, are arguably in terms of income, infrastructure, and service provision more "developed" than some rural and even some inner-city areas of the United States, a developed country. There are other popular terms to express that division, including *East/West, West/Rest, and Global North/Global South.* The issue with those terms is also that global political and economic difference is not as geographically confined as these terms imply. It has lately become fashionable in social literature to use the latter terms, "Global North/Global South." This might sound like a more sophisticated way to refer to the dichotomy, but it is just as confusing as the others. Is Australia, for example, part of the Global North or the Global South? Besides, and going back to the issue of developed versus developing, what parts of Australia would be considered to belong to each of these realms, since generally speaking, there is a considerable gap between the living conditions of urban Anglo-Australian and rural indigenous Australians? Thus, this way of referring to the dichotomy does not really offer much advantage either. Consequently, I prefer to keep the old Third World/First World designation, which, although still limited, is very illustrative of the gap between both "worlds" (from Third to First), while being less confusing geographically.

Also in connection to imperialism, I refer to yet another simple dichotomy, that of *local/foreign* (I will use also "international" in the second case). This is a very simplistic dichotomy that I do not espouse, but that nonetheless I must invoke. The reason, as will be apparent from my description of the debate on imperialism in chapter 1, is that "local/foreign" is widely used in both social design critique and promotion, with both agreeing that *localism* is the solution to the problem of imperialism. The question, of course, is what does "local" mean? In an increasingly mobile world, anyone can call themselves a "local" at any given time. In fact, as I will also explain, it is a claim that some designers have actually made in order to exempt themselves from accusations of imperialism: *I lived there during the project, so I was also a local.* Despite the evident limitations of the notion, both the critique and promotion of social design still use "local" as a solid, stable category. Given that I am interrogating this category, I must use it as well. Specifically, and as I will explain in chapter 2, the way in which "local" is largely understood in social design is that of a *national* or a *resident* of the place where the social design intervention takes place.

There are other problematic dichotomies widely popular in social design that in my analysis I must refer to as well. In chapter 1, I refer to the simple dichotomy of good/bad, which is in turn connected to the also popular dichotomy of sustainable/unsustainable. Although I myself do not take ownership of these dichotomies, I must refer to them since they are essential in social design's sustainability advocacy, where the attribute of "sustainable" is commonly understood as *all that is good,* and "unsustainable" as its opposite. In turn, this dichotomy is connected to the already discussed dichotomy of modern/traditional, where, as I will also discuss in that chapter, modernism is largely assumed to be unsustainable, while traditionalism is assumed to be sustainable.

RESEARCH FOCUS, METHOD, AND MOTIVATION

I have written this book with architectural designers in mind, particularly designers interested in social design practice. Since the focus of the book is architecture, I use "designers" and "social designers" mostly in the sense of architectural designers. However, the book's argument applies also to other areas of design such as industrial design, which has been a major focus of social design practice. It also applies to other disciplines that have become concerned with this field of practice, including landscape studies, engineering, and anthropology.

From a methodological standpoint, this book asks a different question to those commonly asked in social design advocacy and critical literature. There is a major difference in how do advocacy and critique each relate to social design's subject of interest, that is, populations in poverty. Advocacy is normally concerned with questions of *how* and *what:* how the subjects of the advocacy live (i.e., the conditions of poverty in a given place), and what should be done about that (i.e., the design project). The critique, especially the postcolonial critique, instead focuses on the question of *why:* Why is the advocate concerned about this? Following the postcolonial critique of orientalism, the first of those questions, "how," is the question of representation common to orientalist narratives. In those narratives, the "how" question leads to the "what" question, which leads to the imperialist intervention: What to do? The answer is: *intervene.* Edward Said, however, argued that the problem of representation—which, in the case of social design, translates as representing subaltern populations as being in need of help—goes beyond representation itself because language inevitably represents (see Said 1978; Spivak 1990). The problem, he argued, is intent. *Why* do certain people decide to represent others in a given way at a specific moment in history?

Thus, the question of "why" relates to intention or purpose. The postcolonial answer to this question raises the issue of *humanitarian imperialism,* a type of benevolent advocacy on behalf of the oppressed subject that might actually do little to liberate this subject from oppression. I will explain this argument in detail in chapter 1. Although it is an argument that makes great sense, my intention is to expand upon it. By using a subaltern studies perspective, I focus on yet another question, *who,* as in: *Who is the advocate?* Postcolonial wisdom would discard this question as obvious: it is a foreigner. However, by formulating this question, I propose to shift the focus from the global sphere to the social sphere of the advocate. The question of "who" is the question of positionality—it is the question that deals with issues of privilege.

As I address the question of "who," I study both the position of the advocate, that is, the designer and the designer's patrons and supporters, and the position of the subject of advocacy, that is, the project beneficiary. I do this by exploring the materialization of social design's good deeds in the field. My description of the cases of the Nueva Esperanza School, the Biblioteca España Library, and the ethnoengineering project is based upon my own field research. As for the remaining cases, I describe Burrows Street Pocket Park on the basis of my own fieldwork and also field evidence from undergraduate research work for which I served as an advisor. For the Makoko Floating School case, I rely on the experiences of those participating in the project, as documented by Nigerian and international authors. For the case of Torre David, I study the designers' own literature.

The main criterion to select these projects has been notability. The projects in chapter 2 are among the most celebrated, published, and awarded projects in the social design field. The ethnoengineering project was a paradigmatic endeavor of implementing a comprehensive community participation approach in about two hundred communities throughout an entire country, Ecuador (as I will explain, it would end up materializing in only thirty-one of them). Notability was the most relevant criterion to use because, the practice of architecture being so reliant on the study of precedents, the most notable projects tend to be the ones that most heavily influence new design production. Designers who try to reproduce the notable projects' presumed success readily adopt their premises, which then become the practice's ruling premises by the means of their constant reproduction. This will be evident when I study the projects in chapter 2. Although they were carried out by different architects in different parts of the world, they all followed similar premises.

I study the ethnoengineering project through a representative sample of the constructions. For this sample I took into account geographical, ethnocultural, typological, and technological considerations, as well as the completeness of the construction works and each of the individual projects' relative significance in the context of the larger project. On the basis of those criteria, I selected thirty different construction projects in twenty villages, out of the forty-eight projects in thirty-one villages that constituted the total of the intervention. My sample then constitutes over two-thirds of the projects and villages involved in this project, which provides a very accurate picture of how the overall project played out.

In the cases in which I carried out field research, I did so through inspecting the built work and carrying out unstructured interviews. In the book I quote from beneficiaries, especially in my study of ethnoengineering, since the research focus of that case is community participation, and obviously the best way to explore participation is to ask the actual participants. All of the interviews for this research were carried out in Spanish and have been translated. To avoid repetition, I abstain from restating that these are all "my translation." (This is also the case for the literature and other material translated from Spanish.) In my translations I try to stay faithful to each interviewee's style of speaking Spanish. This will be particularly evident in the case of Ecuadorian indigenous villagers, most of whom are bilingual; their mother tongue is Kichwa, which they use to communicate with each other, switching to Spanish when they communicate with outsiders. Their Spanish is then very special, grammatically speaking; it is a mix of archaic Spanish once taught by missionaries, present-day Spanish slang, and Kichwa syntax. Given this peculiar way of speaking Spanish, the English translation might in some cases sound peculiar as well.

As mentioned earlier, by paying careful attention to what the subjects of social design have to say, my goal is to propose an alternative to social design's laudatory literature, which largely reflects the perspective of designers. However, I still pay careful attention to what designers say, vis-à-vis what they do. In this book I name the designers behind failed or problematic projects. This is unavoidable because those projects are deeply attached to the names of their creators. As I have also mentioned, this is a result of the high design paradigm of social design practice, which places so much importance on individual authorship. In fact, most of the iconic projects that I study in chapter 2 are so linked to the names of their designers that it is not possible to simply talk about a school in the Makoko slum to describe one of these projects. Instead, in social design literature, this school is often described as *Kunlé Adeyemi's Makoko Floating School*. This description strongly indicates that the school is of Adeyemi's authorship, as Adeyemi himself has also made it clear in his publications, interviews, and presentations. Thus, due to those strong claims to authorship from the designers, it is inevitable that when I discuss the problems with these projects, I also use their names.

However, I believe that those problems are the result of honest mistakes rather than ill intention. I believe the designers of these projects were acting in good faith, but they were blindsided by the strong high design paradigm currently ruling the practice of social design, which pushed them to engage on practices that, had they been aware of the framework they were acting within, they probably would never have done it. This is one of the reasons why I have decided to write this book, namely, to bring to light the issues with this paradigm. In that sense, an unintended contribution from these designers' work, and one to be greatly appreciated, is that it allows us all to learn from their mistakes.

That said, I am less interested in individual figures than in the *pattern;* that is, when a number of designers with little to no relationship to each other engage in the same type of problematic practices. Thus, the focus of this book, rather than the assessment of individual social designers, is the aspects of those designers' work that constitute a pattern across social design as a whole. This pattern includes a narrow understanding of environmentalism, a particular way to relate to beneficiaries, the tendency to impose the designer's vision at all costs, and other commonalities I identify in this book. One of the most important contributions this book attempts to make is to bring to light the existence of this pattern. Very importantly, I have selected only a sample of cases that demonstrate this pattern's existence. The studied projects are far from being the only ones I have identified as following this pattern, which is in fact deeply ingrained in social design practice.

As mentioned earlier, one of the aspects that make this book different as a critique of social design is its strong focus on the field. My emphasis on the field comes from the fact that I am a social design practitioner myself, working with a wide spectrum of partners from small local nonprofits to international organizations. The latter include the IDB (Inter-American Development Bank), the institution that funded the ethnoengineering project, in an unrelated project in Guyana. It was my own experience as a practitioner that prompted the general direction of this research. As a research project, this book started from reflecting upon lessons learned in my career as a practitioner, including the limitations of my own early work in the Ecuadorian Pacific Coast. One of these limitations had to do with cost issues associated to traditionalism, particularly the use of a traditional construction material, bamboo. The purpose of my bamboo work was demonstrative; that is, to show the people I was working with the many environmental and constructive advantages of building with this material. Despite these advantages, and the fact that bamboo was available, people still preferred concrete block construction. From this type of paradox I learned that our viewpoints as designers, in this case the advantages of bamboo that I intended to promote, can be valid. However, people's opinions should be honored as authoritative because they are the experts on their own poverty. When people experience poverty, they think a great deal about their conditions and as a result often conceive very good yet simple and doable ideas as to how to overcome those conditions. These ideas are often lost when we as designers press our own good ideas.

As I will explain in chapter 4, one of the reasons why we as designers press our own ideas comes from our training in architecture school. I began the process of unlearning what I had learned in school after I became involved in other projects, particularly one in which I worked for a Canadian environmentalist who intended to build community infrastructure using thatch palm and bamboo in indigenous Amazonian settlements. However, villagers in these settlements actually preferred metal roofing and other industrial materials for their construction. This was the moment when I began to see that there might be a pattern in villagers' opposition to traditionalist ideas on sustainability, that it was not simply an isolated issue of the Pacific Coast area where I had been working. In both locations, people wanted practical solutions to their situations of poverty, declining sophisticated traditionalist alternatives. Later on I found the same pattern of opposition among other people I carried out building and research work with, not only in Ecuador but also in Colombia, El Salvador, Guyana, and Suriname. As for the villagers' objections to traditionalism, one of the most common was affordability: working with traditional materials had become too onerous for them. Although to an outside observer this argument might not make much sense at first, given that these are locally available materials, I had indeed experienced that situation in my own bamboo work. Although the raw material itself was low-cost, the process of construction demanded a great deal of care (I will refer to this issue in chapter 3 as I explain the ethnoengineering project, which used this material as well). Thus, the high cost of working with a traditional material did not pertain to the cost of the material itself, but to the amount of labor involved; it took too long to prepare the material and to build with it.

Given the time investment, the bamboo projects I was working on took too long to build, and thus the labor costs made this work far more expensive than construction with the premanufactured concrete blocks that people favored, and which explained their preference for this material. On the upside, the fact that the projects took much longer also meant that they generated a salary for local workers for much longer than usual as well. Rejecting the customary practice in social design of relying on "free" community contributions, from the very beginning of my career I have observed the practice of paying for community labor. Although the projects I worked on included some of those contributions, I kept them to a very minimal level and with the only goals to train users in bamboo construction techniques and to encourage a process of appropriation of the projects, which were my organization's cost-free contribution to their community groups.

The fact that the paid workers were able to generate an income for much longer was significant because these were some of the areas in greatest poverty in Ecuador, and as such they had a dramatically low employment rate. However, the projects' comparatively high costs still defeated the common premise in social design that a traditional material is a low-cost solution.

When I began to carry out research on other designers' work, I realized that the issue of high costs and the villagers' subsequent rejection of traditionalism was also a pattern in their case as well. Thus, I realized that this was far from being my own isolated experience. In fact, the issue of unaffordability of traditional construction is now so generalized that it has clearly become part of the very own nature of this type of construction, as I explain in chapters 2 and 3. This explains why is it so problematic to press for traditionalism in traditional communities in poverty. The objections from villagers, the experts in their own poverty, are generally based on affordability: if there is funding available for construction projects in their villages, it better be used efficiently, because money in those places is scarce. Thus, if architects go to those villages to help people address poverty, they should not be advocating high-cost solutions.

The fact that this book project began as a reflection on the mistakes that I made in my own practice means that, beyond its being a critique, this book is also a self-critique. I have myself made some of the mistakes that I am critiquing here. However, the book also bears witness to my having become aware of those mistakes.

I will close this chapter by coming back to the question of imperialism, with which I will be in conversation throughout the following chapters. I was born in Colombia and was trained as an architect there, and have done most of my work in Latin America and the Caribbean. Thus, I am one of those so-called local designers that both the critique and the promotion of social design idealize as the solution to the challenge of imperialism in this practice. However, being fully aware of the complexities of working locally, I am well positioned to question the argument of localism as the solution to imperialism. I intend to turn the mirror back on us as local designers as being a part of the problem. However, I do not intend to absolve foreign designers from their role in the problem as well. I could write yet another book on similarly troubling social design projects carried out by European and North American (and, in fact, also Asian) designers in the Third World. In reality, and this is my main argument, it does not matter where designers are from. We are all implicated in a practice that very easily lends itself to abuse of vulnerable populations, and hence, the challenge of social design goes beyond imperialism.

CHAPTER 1

Social Design, Sustainability, and Imperialism

SUSTAINABILITY IN SOCIAL DESIGN

Social design's central goal is social improvement, and this practice generally envisions that goal as one of sustained improvement. Thus, the notion of sustainability is fundamental to social design, to such an extent that social design and sustainable design are in fact closely connected fields. This connection is evident in a host of books devoted to the topic of social design published since the mid-2000s (e.g., Kennedy 2004; Feireiss and Feireiss 2008; Feireiss, Feireiss, and Sloterdijk 2009; Fuad-Luke 2009; Aquilino 2011; AFH 2012a; Lepik 2013; Meinhold 2013; Charlesworth and Ahmed 2015; Krückeberg, Putz, and Willemeit 2016; Lucente and Trasi 2019). Indeed, the connection made in the literature between social design and sustainable design is so direct that some authors have described social design as being a form of sustainable design (see Bergdoll 2015), while conversely, others have described sustainable design as a form of social design (see Falkeis and Feireiss 2015).

Such a direct connection has existed since the early days of social design. This is evident from the work of three of the main figures in the history of this practice: Hassan Fathy, Victor Papanek, and Samuel Mockbee. Fathy, who carried out the bulk of his work between the 1930s and the 1980s, was the designer of New Gourna in Egypt (fig. 3). This pioneering social design project remains the most classical example of social design practice. Papanek, who carried out his work between the 1950s and the 1990s, was arguably social design's first theorist, as he authored a series of influential books that offered an early roadmap for what the practice of social design should strive for. Mockbee, who was active between the 1970s and the 1990s, was the foundational figure of the current social design movement through his Rural Studio, the most celebrated service learning program in US architectural education.

Throughout his New Gourna project and his career in general, Fathy was highly interested in the climate and overall energy performance, as well as the

Fig. 3. The mosque at New Gourna, Hassan Fathy's pioneering social design project. (Photograph by Marc Ryckaert, Creative Commons)

economic and structural feasibility of the mud-based structures traditionally used by the Egyptian rural poor, structures that provided the model for his designs. Indeed, Fathy's approach has been described as "solar building for the poor" (Behling and Behling 1996). Papanek's last book, illustratively named *The Green Imperative* (1995), outlined the argument for embracing sustainability in social design practice. In this book, Papanek argued that the dismal environmental condition of the planet is real and present, and that global poverty is a direct consequence of those environmental issues (10–11). Arguing that conventional design practice is part of the problem, Papanek called for designers to radically change their practices, adopting what he called an ethical design perspective that would embrace ecological and social responsibility. He concluded: "Sustainability can be helped or hindered by design" (235). Mockbee described sustainable architecture as "a combination of values: aesthetic, environmental, social, political, and moral" (Mockbee in Fox 2000, 208). Following that premise, his Rural Studio projects used materials such as hay bales and rammed earth, as well as reused elements such as car tires and windows. This was, in Mockbee's view, a way to extend the benefits of sustainability to communities in poverty.

Besides these three pioneers of the practice, sustainability remains a central concern in social design today. Indeed, it is so central that the vast majority of the world's most influential social design organizations either explicitly or implicitly declare sustainability as being their goal or the means towards that goal. This has been the case since the late 1990s, when Architecture for Humanity, the organization that made social design mainstream, was established. Architecture for Humanity was founded by Cameron Sinclair and

Kate Stohr, and at the time of its closure it was headquartered in San Francisco, California. In addition to establishing the organization, Sinclair and Stohr also published *Design Like You Give a Damn* (AFH 2006, 2012a). This is a two-book series promoting Architecture for Humanity's activities and is one of the most influential pieces in social design literature to date. Sustainability was so important for Architecture for Humanity's activities that the notion was not only often invoked in these two books, but was actually part of the organization's own mission: "Building a more sustainable future using the power of design" (2013a, 3). It was also part of its vision, which was to "plan, design, and build beautiful, sustainable spaces" (10), as well as one of its goals: "To build communities based on sustainable prosperity" (Sinclair 2007).

Sustainability is also explicitly stated as the goal and/or the means toward the goal by the world's most prominent social design practitioners and organizations today, in the so-called First World and the Third World alike. I will study examples of the centrality of sustainability for the latter in the next chapter. As for the former, one example is Article 25, an organization based in the United Kingdom and self-described as the world's largest architectural nonprofit: "We design, manage and deliver sustainable building solutions in areas affected by disaster, poverty and need" (Article 25 n.d.a). A second example is Orkidstudio, another prominent social design organization established in the United Kingdom and later relocated to Kenya: "Our aim is to explore the potential of architecture as a tool for relieving poverty, transforming lives, and promoting sustainable urban and social development" (Orkidstudio n.d.a). A third example is Architecture Sans Frontières (ASF), a global network of social design nonprofits with a presence across six continents: "[ASF members] cooperate for fair and sustainable development initiatives in active collaboration with disadvantaged people or communities" (ASF 2017b).

WHAT DOES "SUSTAINABILITY" MEAN FOR SOCIAL DESIGN?

Considering both past and present social design practitioners and organizations, the degree to which sustainability is essential to social design is evident. However, what does the notion of sustainability exactly mean for social design? The answer is clear from the mission, methods, goals, and other position statements from the organizations cited above, as well as other leading social design practices, both international and local. The international practices are based in the United States and Europe and carry out their work mostly in the Third World. They include those mentioned in the previous section, and others such as Architectes de l'Urgence, MASS Design Group, and TYIN Tegnestue. As for the local practices, some of the most prominent are either based in or have originated in the Third World itself, carrying out most of their work in that region. They include Al Borde Architects (Ecuador), Kunlé Adeyemi's NLÉ Works (Nigeria), Alfredo Brillembourg and Hubert Klumpner's Urban-Think Tank (Venezuela), Alejandro Echeverri (Colombia), and Giancarlo Mazzanti (Colombia). In the next chapter, I will be discussing these local practices' understanding of sustainability in the context of a few illustrative projects. Below I will focus on the international practices.

First and foremost, it is worth looking at the meaning of sustainability for social design through the lens of Architecture for Humanity, whose pioneering approach to social design was so highly influential that its echoes still reverberate in the work of many organizations large and small. Architecture for Humanity explained its understanding of the notion in the following terms:

For us sustainability is about more than building green. We think about how a building will affect the environment, how it will improve the lives and livelihoods of its occupants, and its impact on future generations, including its vulnerability to disaster. (AFH 2014a)

In other words, Architecture for Humanity focused not only on the environmental impact of a given building but also on how that building would bring social improvement both in the present and in the future. This is similar to how Article 25 understands sustainability as a long-term concept: "Sustainable building and projects are vital, in every sense: working for the long term" (Article 25 n.d.b). Victoria Harris, a cofounder of this organization, explains the significance of this principle with respect to emergency reconstruction, arguing that many humanitarian organizations define their focus too narrowly as emergency work, and consequently "they have no truck with the long-term, complex matter of building sustainable, resilient systems" (Harris 2011, 16). Instead, she argues, Article 25 aims to go beyond the emergency focus on "plastic sheets and lean-to structures—temporary fixes" (16). Rather, the organization considers that the first phase of an emergency must be part of a long-term recovery process: "Disaster relief and long-term development must be inextricably linked, and development opportunities assessed and insisted upon in every aspect of the reconstruction process" (17).

Orkidstudio expands this understanding of sustainability by focusing on the use of local human and material resources:

Our approach is founded on a celebration of local people and resources. We select local materials and source from nearby suppliers, supporting the economies around our sites and promoting sustainable and responsible procurement. (Orkidstudio n.d.b)

Orkidstudio also emphasizes its view of sustainability in economic terms, particularly with respect to growth and self-sufficiency:

Alongside our buildings, we are engaged in a diverse range of small and medium sized enterprises, working with individuals and communities to develop sustained resources and enter new markets. We create scalable models to enable self-sufficient access to key infrastructure and shelter. (2015)

Expanding the notion of sustainability further, Architecture Sans Frontières understands it as going beyond resource efficiency to consider also local needs and traditions:

ASF-International members promote an architecture that is environmentally sustainable and respects local needs and traditions, using low-impact materials, appropriate technologies, and renewable sources of energy to create more resilient cities and places. (ASF 2017a)

With regard to other global leading organizations, it is worth looking at what sustainability means for *Architectes de l'Urgence*. This is a French emergency reconstruction organization with a membership of over 1,600 architects and other professionals, conducting reconstruction programs in thirty-three countries (FAU n.d.). In the view of Patrick Coulombel, one of the founders of the organization, and in agreement with Victoria Harris, sustainability should be an essential component of emergency reconstruction, in the sense of making sure that emergency solutions proposed by designers will last over time and will be friendly to the natural environment (Coulombel 2011; see also 2019). Architectes de l'Urgence also states on its website that it is "always involved in a real logic of sustainable development and risk mitigation," since its programs aim to be not only "adapted to the technical and architectural context but also the social, environmental, and cultural [contexts]" (FAU n.d.).

Another illustrative conception of sustainability in social design is that of the MASS[1] Design Group, currently the highest-profile US social design organization. In describing its method of work, MASS asks: "Are our projects sustainable?" The answer is:

Our projects go beyond a checklist of metrics. . . . Working with locally sourced materials and labor when possible, we assess the entire supply chain for environmental impact, and assure that the majority of capital invested in construction flows to the community we are serving. (MASS n.d.)

Thus, according to this statement, MASS's projects are sustainable because of their use of local resources, the buildings' reduced environmental impact, and their positive economic impact. Also, in a series of toolkits and reports providing examples of successful architectural and urban design interventions, MASS emphasizes instilling a sense of ownership among project beneficiaries to ensure they will take charge of the sustained maintenance of the project, and with that, to ensure not only that the project lasts over time, but also that its operational cost is reduced (see MASS 2017a, 2017b).

Finally, it is worth looking at what sustainability means for TYIN Tegnestue, a Norwegian firm that started as a social design practice and remains one of the most highly awarded practices in this field. These awards have been conferred to TYIN for a number of projects built in Southeast Asia, projects that are among the most iconic in the field of social design (fig. 4; see also fig. 1). Explaining one of these projects, TYIN makes clear its view of sustainability as simplicity, durability, and adaptability—the three notions coming together in order to ensure the sustained usability of the project, even when needs change:

The main construction's simplicity, repetitive logic and durability enables the local inhabitants to make adaptations that fit with their changing needs without endangering the projects structural strength or the general usability of the playground.

Fig. 4. TYIN's Cassia Coop Training Centre in Sungai Penuh, Indonesia. (Photograph by Pasi Aalto, PasiAalto .com)

This way the project runs in parallel with the ever changing surroundings and fits with the idea that the project could be part of a larger call for a more sustainable development in the Klong Toey area. (TYIN n.d.a)

In its description of another project, TYIN extends its understanding of sustainability to resource efficiency: "Important principles like bracing, material economisation and moisture prevention, may possibly lead to a more sustainable building tradition for the Karen people in the future" (TYIN n.d.b).

SUSTAINABILITY

The organizations mentioned above are widely acknowledged as the leaders in the social design field. As such, they have ultimately modeled by their example the social design agenda. Their vision, approaches, objectives, and consequently their view of sustainability have been followed by a myriad of smaller social design initiatives, becoming paradigmatic for this discipline. For example, in chapter 3 I will study the work of a group of very respected but lower-profile designers from Ecuador. As will be evident, their idea of sustainability is very similar to that of these high-profile organizations, which attests to a broad understanding of sustainability in social design practice as a whole.

What is this broad understanding of sustainability? What do all those diverse definitions of sustainability ultimately mean? The definitions share a few common themes, as well as some specific themes in the case of practitioners that connect sustainability to their particular area of interest. Both commonalities and specificities constitute the predominant meaning of sustainability in social design. Characteristics of sustainability in this field are then first and foremost the idea of social improvement as the general goal, with a focus on *localism*. That is, designers strive to make sure that their projects cater to local needs, using local labor so that income from construction expenses goes to local builders and thus supporting the local economy. There is also emphasis on the notion that involving local beneficiaries in the process of construction, as well as building with local materials, significantly reduces construction costs. Additionally, the economic impact of the project goes beyond delivering a building project, involving other initiatives that stimulate the capacity of beneficiaries to engage in business, thus keeping a general eye on self-sufficiency. Consequently, economic resources are a great focus in social design's overall understanding of sustainability.

Another focus is the idea of *culture*, as in traditional culture. This is something to which social designers usually assign great importance. Along with the interest in traditional culture goes the concern for the natural surroundings. Social designers mind the environmental impact of their buildings, making sure that the materials they use are locally sourced, have a low environmental footprint, and are appropriately and efficiently used. Social designers also consider renewability, both in terms of materials and the energy sources of their buildings. Thus, there exists a strong consideration of resource efficiency, which is partly motivated by the interest in protecting the natural environment.

One important goal of resource efficiency is to consider the project's impact in the long term. Social designers aim for their buildings to be durable. One of the ways to ensure this is that, during the process of work, designers endeavor to instill in beneficiaries a sense of ownership of the donated building, so they feel compelled to perform maintenance, which brings the extra economic benefit of lowering the buildings' operational costs. Another strategy for the long term is to design structures that are intentionally simple, or lend themselves to easy adaptions with which the structure might remain useful, even when the beneficiaries' needs change. This is the culmination of social design's general idea of sustainability—the future. There is a great emphasis in social design on the idea that buildings should serve both present and future needs; that the project should be carried out in a way that makes it a resilient project; one that lasts, is maintained, and is adaptable, thus remaining useful over time.

This is social design's broad concept of sustainability. Social design sees sustainability as the combination of two general categories: on the one hand, resources, understood both as economic resources and resource efficiency in the construction, and on the other the emphasis on the long term, the future. Thus, by and large, social design's notion of sustainability relates to implementing a number of efficiency measures in order to ensure that there are resources available (including economic resources) in order to satisfy present needs and ensure that those resources will still be available in the future.

Such an emphasis on resources and the future means that the predominant understanding of sustainability in social design actually mirrors the classical definition of sustainability given in the Report of the World Commission on Environment and Development, a United Nations report also known as the *Brundtland Report* (WCED 1987).[2] The Brundtland Report's definition of sustainability is "meet[ing] the needs of the present without compromising the ability of future generations to meet their own needs" (43). This is the best-known and by far the most predominant and influential definition of sustainability.

It is then critical to study the Brundtland Report's notion of sustainability because this report in the end has provided the template for sustainability practice that social design at large follows. What does the wide adoption of the Brundtland Report's notion of sustainability mean for the field of social design? The fact that social design has so widely embraced the report's classical definition as its preferred way to carry out environmental advocacy makes this a very particular form of practice. This definition has been amply critiqued in the literature, resulting in many other definitions, including the very popular arithmetic and alphanumeric definitions of sustainability. They are the *three pillars* (environmental, social, and economic), the *three Es* (environmental, ethical, and economic), the *three Ps* (people, planet, and profits), the *six Rs* (reduce, reuse, refuse, rethink, repair, and recycle), and others.

Notably, the arithmetic and alphanumeric definitions generally aim to revise the Brundtland Report's idea of sustainability by expanding rather than contesting it. That is, they do not seek to challenge this idea as much as to improve it. As is clear from these and other definitions, essential to the report's view of sustainability is the proposition of *economic growth*—in particular, the fact that growth has to be integrated rather than challenged when it comes to the project of environmental preservation. Although this is not a bad thing per se, it makes sustainability a very particular form of environmentalism, as it is in a stark contrast to the notion of *limits to growth,* which was the essential premise of early 1970s environmentalism. In fact, the limits that the Brundtland Report stresses are technological. As the document states, when technology finally reaches a point at which it is possible to engage in sustained economic growth, while not affecting the present and future availability of resources, then the key environmental issues of the planet would have been addressed (1987, 8).

This vision actually began to materialize two decades after the publication of the Brundtland Report with the emergence of green building standards such as the *Living Building Challenge,* a net-positive approach to construction (see McLennan 2004; ILFI 2016; Thomas 2016). Living buildings give more to their surrounding environment than they take from it by procuring their own water from the rain and electricity from the sun, providing the surplus of this operation to neighboring buildings and their natural environment. The fact that it is now possible that the operation of buildings not only does not take resources away from the environment around but also actually helps to enrich that environment, is something very significant. Theoretically, it means that humanity might have reached, invoking Francis Fukuyama (1992), the end of history when it comes to environmentalism. However, what does such an achievement mean in the end?

DECONSTRUCTING THE NOTION OF SUSTAINABILITY

The main critique that has been made of social design practice is that it is imperialist. This critique has also been raised with regard to the sustainability paradigm that social design pursues. I will explain in detail the arguments of these interrelated critiques for the remainder of this chapter. The imperialism critique of social design has been prompted by the proliferation of organizations from Europe and the United States working in African, Latin American, and Southeast Asian countries, as is the case of the organizations mentioned earlier. However, as social design advocates have passionately counterargued, this might be an unfair critique because these organizations are doing mostly pro bono work targeting emergency situations and poverty in those countries. Considering that, and the fact that they are proposing to target poverty by the means of sustainability, how can advocating for sustainability in global poverty alleviation be considered part of an imperialist project?

The best way to understand the imperialism argument is by deconstructing the notion of sustainability through a postcolonial theoretical lens. Essential to postcolonial theory is the principle that ideas cannot be considered as separate from their history. The origin of sustainability has been placed by various authors roughly between the late 1960s and the late 1980s (see Dasmann 1985; Redclift 1987; Worster 1993; Marcuse 1998; Baeten 2000; Borowy 2014). It was by that time that the notion of sustainability was widely invoked in connection to environmental preservation. This is a fundamental factor in deconstructing sustainability for critical purposes. Sustainability is historical, that is, it is a notion that can be traced back historically; it is not simply an unqualified notion. By the time that the sustainability movement took shape, other environmental movements were actually proposing forms of environmentalism that were fundamentally different than sustainability. These included movements such as deep ecology, animal rights, and ecosocialism. This difference was later extended also to movements that emerged after sustainability and partly in response to sustainability, most notably the environmental justice movement. Indeed, the key environmental premise in most of these movements was and continues to be to challenge the notion of capital accumulation. Sustainability instead proposed the groundbreaking notion that environmental preservation and capital are not at odds—that, indeed, they can coexist. The Brundtland Report put this idea in well-finished form: There is no contradiction between environmental preservation and economic development (WCED 1987, 40). That is, one can act in an environmentally friendly way and still make a profit.

The issue with this premise is that the Brundtland Report's vision of sustainability went beyond seeing economic growth as a regular economic process. Instead, the report made its appeal for sustainability in terms that were quite welcoming to growth as a supercapitalist, uncontrolled growth. The report catered directly to the largest global market players, whom it saw as essential to have the notion of sustainability widely adopted. Indeed, the report made an explicit and insistent appeal to global financial institutions such as the World Bank, as well as global corporations, proposing that "the World Bank can support environmentally sound projects and policies" (18), and that "transnationals [corporations] can have a substantial impact on the environment and resources of other countries and on the global commons" (86). Thus, central to the Brundtland Report's appeal on behalf of sustainability was the promise that sustainability as a new form of environmentalism would not disrupt the economic status quo.

Due to both its embrace of economic growth and the promise that no radical change was necessary, sustainability ended up being enthusiastically adopted by the financial and corporate world. A number of authors have studied the World Bank's "green turn" in the 1990s (see Escobar 1995; Goldman 2001a, 2001b, 2005; Li 2007, 2011; Mosse 2011). Other authors have argued that sustainability was "hijacked" by the corporate world (Welford 1997; Parr 2009; Dauvergne and Lister 2013). I argue, instead, that sustainability was *designed* to be hijacked. From reading the Brundtland Report, it is clear that this notion was formulated in the exact terms that would allow for its easy adoption by banks and corporations.

Besides those institutions, sustainability was embraced by virtually everyone. I argue that it became so popular because of the style of environmental activism that it proposed, one that, besides not posing any threat to the status quo, was also *optimistic*. That is, it was based upon motivation and excitement about acting upon environmental issues rather than emphasizing the urgency of those issues, which was largely the model of ecologism, as in the presustainability and later alternative environmental activism movements. In fact, out of the many readings that have been made of the Brundtland Report, one aspect that has received less attention is its writing style, which was key to how the report made its point on behalf of sustainability.[3] The Brundtland Report is indeed a peculiar piece of writing. It was intended to be first and foremost a policy document, one of those thick, dense stacks of paper that nobody seems to fully read (it ran to nearly four hundred pages). However, this policy piece was written with great prose in mind. For example, it is common for policy reports to have an executive summary plainly named as such, but the executive summary of the Brundtland Report instead has an elegant proper title, *From One Earth to One World*. The report's narrative starts by invoking a visual reference, the moment at which humanity first saw the planet from outer space. Throughout its many pages, the report continues in this vein, powerfully and passionately inviting readers to become enthusiastic and excited about the harbingers of a new era.

The Brundtland Report's style is indeed peculiar because this document was supposed to address the toughest issues at stake in the international arena: famine, disease, pollution, natural disasters, and the like. However, it describes these issues in such a way that ensures that its readers will continue to read with great optimism. It does so by employing a narrative method consisting of first talking about how much humanity has achieved, then describing these critical issues as improvements that need to be made, and finally concluding that no major structural changes to the world order (not only economically but also socially and politically) are necessary; rather, the solution is simple and commonsensical: sustainability. This narrative style thus suggests that we have done well so far, there are a few things to be improved, and it will be easy to do so. This is how the Brundtland Report made a promising offer of environmentalism within the institutional order and the status quo. But also for individuals in general, the report extended an inspiring invitation for everyone to change the world. With that, it set the tone for a new model of environmental advocacy, that is, that of optimistic action, as opposed to the earlier alerts about socioenvironmental catastrophe. The report speaks of change, harmony, mutual understanding, and the world as a big family. Thus, I argue, it was partly by adopting this style that the Brundtland Report avoided being yet another policy piece to be only glossed over, to become instead one of the most quoted books in the second half of the twentieth century.

With that, the Brundtland Report was instrumental in making sustainability a mainstream phenomenon. As a form of environmental activism, sustainability ended up dwarfing every other environmental movement, in fact becoming in the popular imagination *the* environmental movement. For many today, sustainability *is* environmentalism; this is the scale at which it obliterated in the collective imagination all competing forms of environmentalism. Thus, in a process analogous to the one that Don Mitchell observed with the shifting understanding of the concept of culture (1995), sustainability went from being an *ideological* notion—that of the globalizing framework of the Brundtland Report—to becoming an *ontological* notion, one that is used to explain everything with regard to the environment and it is now the standard for most discussions of environmentalism.

It is then understandable that social design at large adopted sustainability as well. In fact, arguably, it was thanks to the adoption of sustainability that social design went from having been for decades a marginal form of architectural practice to becoming one of architecture's most important fields.

I argue that social design ended up adopting sustainability on the basis of this concept's popularity. However, by doing so, the discipline unintentionally ended up siding with an agenda of uncontrolled economic growth with serious social ramifications—it has been called *green neoliberalism* (Goldman 2001a, 2001b, 2005).

Hence, the imperialism critique of social design can be understood in terms of the limitations of its preferred form of environmental advocacy, that being sustainability. Granted, this reading of sustainability might be disappointing for social design advocates. It might also sound extreme, since it might be misread as "sustainability is all about profits, and all social designers are wrong." In sum, it might be misread as a rather extreme depiction of sustainability in connection to wild profit-seeking and a disapproval of an entire discipline by characterizing its main paradigm in such narrow terms. However, this is far from my point. By shedding a critical light on the problematic origins of sustainability, my goal is to simply call for a halt, even if brief, for self-reflection. If we as designers consider the historical origins of the type of environmental activism that social design favors, we might be able to reflect upon the limits that social design practice has met.

The reason behind this call is that something is clearly wrong with current social design practice. This should become evident from the troubling projects I examine in the next two chapters. A large number of social designers, including those from many of the organizations mentioned earlier, do very commendable work with excellent results while still using sustainability as their paradigm. However, at the same time, other designers engage in seriously questionable practices, and this situation in fact includes, as the next chapter will show, some of the most admired social designers today, our "humanitarian starchitects," so to speak. I argue that one of the main reasons why, despite these designers' projects being so obviously problematic, the projects get to be built is precisely social design's high reliance upon the notion of sustainability as its preferred form of environmental activism. That is, these problematic projects get built because their designers are able to argue that the projects are sustainable.

Thus, I believe that it is imperative to shake the very foundations of social design practice, and we will be able to do this only by interrogating our most deeply esteemed paradigm, that of sustainability. With this goal in mind, for the rest of this chapter I will focus on the consequences of the limitations of sustainability by studying those limitations from a theoretical standpoint. I will explain from a postcolonial theoretical perspective why it is so problematic for social design to blindly embrace sustainability as its preferred form of environmental advocacy. In subsequent chapters, I will focus on the consequences of sustainability's limitations from the standpoint of practice by showing what can happen in so-called real life as a consequence of the wholesale adoption of sustainability in social design.

SOCIAL DESIGN, SUSTAINABILITY, AND RURAL POVERTY

The limitations of the fact that social design's preferred approach to environmentalism is sustainability go beyond sustainability's socioeconomic premise. They also extend to this movement's environmental premise, which makes sense (as I explain in this section), but it runs into a fundamental challenge (as I will explain in the next section).

The environment-related limitations of sustainability are most evident when it comes to social design's main target populations. As mentioned, the practice of social design has coalesced around the paradigm of bringing sustainability to populations in poverty. Among those populations, rural populations in the Third World have long been among social design's main targets. This makes great sense, given that worldwide, the people in greatest poverty tend to be rural dwellers, particularly indigenous populations (see Hall and Patrinos 2006, 2012). When it comes to these populations, social design's environmental focus on sustainability is often justified on the grounds that sustainability contests the predominant social improvement approach that has historically been indiscriminately applied to them—namely, the notion of development based on the paradigm of modernization.

In fact, sustainable development was proposed in the Brundtland Report as a response to the unmarked modernist development proposed by the Bretton Woods 1943 conference. That type of development is, even to this day, the solution most commonly used by governments and international organizations for indigenous and other traditional populations living in poverty. It consists of "developing" them by imposing a social and economic paradigm meant to absorb these populations into the larger society. To meet this end, traditional rural communities are provided with physical infrastructure (houses, schools, health centers, etc.) that follow the premises of the International Style of modernism; that is, functionalism, formal minimalism, and reliance on industrial materials and technologies. This infrastructure is regularly implemented following a "top-down" centralized planning approach that relies on outside expertise and excludes community participation.

As social theorists have long argued, this development-via-modernization paradigm is very detrimental to traditional populations, making them essentially poorer. The reason, as these authors have discussed, is that it forces dependencies on transnational economic forces (Cardoso and Faletto 1979); consequently, it inflicts great damage on these people's natural habitats, affecting their occupations and causing displacement (Escobar 1995). In general, this approach espouses a unilinear, evolutionist view of growth that rejects local visions of a better life (Esteva [1992] 2007); thus, it ignores local technological solutions that, if properly improved, can be more effective in a local context (Schumacher 1973).[4]

In addition to these charges from social theory, in the architectural field another argument has been made for the notion that modernization is detrimental to traditional populations: simply, that modernist design is not sustainable, as in environmentally friendly (see Behling and Behling 1996; McDonough and Braungart 2002; Stang and Hawthorne 2005; Krier 2006). "Unsustainability is utterly endemic to modernity," asserts the architectural theorist Peter Buchanan (2012, 77). The key reasons he gives are, first, modernism's reliance on fossil fuels for the manufacture and transportation of construction materials and the operation of buildings; and second, its technological focus, which disregards more subjective aspects such as culture (77).

Thus, the possibly harmful effect of the modern on indigenous and other traditional people is invoked as yet another powerful argument behind sustainability advocacy. In fact, this very issue contributed to the United Nations' adoption in 1987 of the recommendations from the Brundtland Report on behalf of sustainability. The report explicitly argues that the modernization of traditional people poses a challenge for sustainable development in and of itself. It observes that these people tend to be connected to ancestral practices that are in harmony with natural environments. Thus, the report argues, their modernization entails a loss of knowledge of how to live sustainably that is necessary for the society at large. Consequently, the report recommends that any improvement initiative targeting indigenous and other traditional people should be carried out in a way that balances development with traditional lifestyles (WCED 1987, 116).

Following on this recommendation from the report, within the discipline of architecture the notion of *culturally appropriate building* matured with the work of traditional architectural theorists such as Paul Oliver (1997, 2006), Howard Davis (1999), and Amos Rapoport (2005). This notion later became a ruling principle in social design's sustainability advocacy. Culturally appropriate building follows a *traditionalist* (as opposed to modernist) approach, insofar as it embraces traditional building practices to counteract the perceived detrimental effects of modernization on traditional populations. This approach dwells upon early social design work such as Hassan Fathy's, mentioned earlier. An example of a traditionalist social design project is that of a day care center designed by architect Bolívar Romero as part of the ethnoengineering project in Ecuador, which I discuss in chapter 3.

Fig. 5. Traditionalist day care center in the village of Michacalá, Ecuador. This structure was designed and built as part of the ethnoengineering project, discussed in chapter 3. In the hill behind the building there is a great deal of modernist construction, which is now very common in this Kichwa indigenous village.

As it can be seen from figure 5, this architect-designed project essentially looks like a traditional house.

TRADITIONALISM AND ORIENTALISM

At first, social design's "culturally appropriate" paradigm makes great sense. Adopting traditionalism might be an effective way to counteract the detrimental effects of the modern, and with that to implement a sustainable alternative in poverty alleviation practice. However, what happens when traditional people themselves resist the premises of traditionalism, instead embracing the modern?

The fact that traditional building practices around the world are becoming "extinct" (Rudofsky 1979) has long been documented, and lamented, in architectural literature (e.g., Rudofsky 1964, 1979; Fathy 1973; Zevaco in Aga Khan Award 1980; Sinha 1994, 2012; Robledo 1996). The main reason for this so-called extinction is that traditional people are massively adopting modernization (fig. 6). Thus, the social design rationale to embrace traditionalism relies on sensible observations, but the problem is that it assumes that traditional people as a whole are in agreement with this idea—in particular, that they are in agreement with both the issue (i.e., the modern) and the measures to address it (i.e., traditionalism). In reality, though, traditional people might resist traditionalist design projects, as I will explain happened with Romero's day care center and many other traditionalist ethnoengi-

Fig. 6. The Kichwa village of Yanaturo in Ecuador, 2016. Most of the newer buildings in this village are of modernist construction, with concrete blocks and metal or fiber-cement roofs. A few remaining traditional structures, like the one visible in the foreground, are used only as corrals for household animals.

neering structures. The issue, as the traditional architectural researcher Paul Memmott has observed, is that there is a "dilemma often imposed on designers by their Aboriginal clients: although they wish to maintain certain customary aspects of their domiciliary lifestyle, they invariably aspire to a house that conforms to Western norms of appearance and status" (2007, xiv). That is, the modern is an aspiration among traditional people who, unlike traditionalist designers, generally do not see that preference as betraying their condition of traditionality.

Although traditional people worldwide are massively and rapidly modernizing and thus might decline the sensible traditionalist proposals offered to them by social designers, the designers themselves often dismiss this modernization trend as senseless. It is common among social designers to argue that modernization among traditional people results from external impositions, which is not always the case, as I will explain when I present the Ecuadorian ethnoengineering project. On the basis of this not-always-accurate observation, social designers often conclude that traditional people who pursue modernity should be persuaded to give up on that interest, or that designers should find a way to implement their traditionalist designs while ignoring people's rejection, under the assumption based on the arguments outlined above that doing so is ultimately more beneficial for them. Social designers usually speak with a sense of pride about having managed to build traditionalist designs despite people's objections, and they display these buildings in online and printed publications, celebrating how they accomplished that feat. An illustrative example is how TYIN Tegnestue describes one of its projects in Sumatra, Indonesia:

The project is mainly constructed from the use of two materials; locally crafted brick and the trunk of the cinnamon tree. The trunks are a by-product from the cinnamon production and it has [*sic*] a low status among the locals. This low status, however, seem [*sic*] quite undeserved, and so we chose to utilize the trunks in everything from the main construction to the interior of the centre. (Cifuentes 2012)

The TYIN project indeed looks beautiful (see fig. 4), and the rationale from the standpoint of natural resource use does make sense. However, this seemingly sensible decision raises some questions. The statement that the cinnamon trunk *"has a low status among the locals . . . so we chose to utilize the trunks in everything from the main construction to the interior of the centre,"* can also be read as *"You don't like it? Here, have more."* Thus, a project like TYIN's can be logically thought out and beautifully solved, but it leaves questions open with regard to *who* chooses to do *what,* and *how* that imposition might be perceived among the subjects of the imposition.

Little is known about what happens in traditional communities on a social level after such impositions take place. This is in fact what motivates my detailed field-based study of those types of projects in this book. As will be evident, the outcome of those impositions can be very problematic in many aspects, not least the political aspect. It is then imperative to look carefully at cases such as TYIN, in which European designers set out to tell people who have historically been subjugated by European colonialism how they should live (i.e., adopting construction materials they dislike). Given that this type of situation is actually very common in social design, it is imperative to reflect on it by considering the question of what it means in a larger sociopolitical context to force (or "persuade") traditional people to reembrace their own traditions, while seeking to justify this imposition by invoking the notion of sustainability. In turn, such reflection is essential for understanding the point of the critique when it equates social design, and sustainability in general, to imperialism.

The imperialism critique can be better approached by means of studying the narrative element, which, as I explained in the previous chapter when I discussed terminology, has historically been key to the project of imperialism. As a narrative, traditionalism is very explicit in the Brundtland Report. In fact, one of the most interesting aspects of the report is its portrayal of indigenous people. As prominent characters in its passionate account, indigenous people are given a central role in the report's project of sustainable development. From the very first pages, the report establishes itself as a positional narrative of two worlds, wherein indigenous people are conspicuously depicted as socially monolithic groups in a state of generalized poverty that they are unable to overcome by themselves—*we* have to do something for *them,* the report urges. The reason, besides the humanitarian concern, is that they are the primitive conservationists of sorts; that is, they are the people who have maintained humanity's connection "with its ancient origins" (WCED 1987, 114). This connection, the report argues, has been maintained as a consequence of some indigenous groups' geographic or sociopolitical isolation, which "has meant the preservation of a traditional way of life in close harmony with the natural environment" (114). However, the report warns, these groups are becoming less isolated, and consequently the areas in which they reside are now prone to natural resource exploitation. The report explains that "this exploitation disrupts the local environment so as to endanger traditional ways of life," to the point that "their traditional practices disappear. They become the victims of what could be described as *cultural extinction*" (114, emphasis added). The problem, the report concludes, is that, since "these communities are the repositories of vast accumulations of traditional knowledge," then "their disappearance is a loss for the larger society, which could learn a great deal from their traditional skills in sustainably managing very complex ecological systems" (114–15). Thus, the Brundtland Report's narrative emphasizes how indigenous people possess the key asset necessary for the sustainable development project, namely knowledge on the natural environment.[5] They are the example that we as nonindigenous people must follow, but *we* must help *them* to preserve those now-threatened exemplary practices because they are convenient for the larger society.

With this appeal, the report offers a postcard example of *green orientalism.* In this particular form of orientalism (which I defined as a general phenomenon in the previous chapter) the oriental other is the indigenous person, and the high moral mission behind the orientalist advocacy is natural preservation. In introducing the notion of green orientalism, Larry Lohmann (1993) invokes the feminist historian Donna Haraway on "the cannibalistic western logic that readily constructs other cultural possibilities as resources for western needs and actions" (Haraway 1989, 247). This observation fittingly describes the way the Brundtland Report sees the role of indigenous people in the sustainable development project—they are largely considered a resource for the global project of sustainability.

Arguably, if orientalism offers the narrative support for imperialism, green orientalism similarly offers the narrative support for green imperialism. In introducing the latter notion, Manuel Lizarralde (2003) notices tremendous asymmetry in terms of resource consumption between "Western" people in the First World vis-à-vis indigenous people in the Third World, the latter being those people idealized by the Brundtland Report. The former, which constitute only a small fraction of the planet's population, consume most of its resources. However, "Westerners, practicing hyperconsumption of resources, expect rainforest inhabitants to live a way of life that consumes relatively little" (2003, 43). The role that the Brundtland Report confers to indigenous people in the global project of sustainability is based on this expectation. A reading of the report under a green imperialism critical lens is that indigenous people are supposed to take a higher burden for the environmental problems of the world, as they are supposed to withhold themselves from accessing the advantages of modern technologies that people in the First World freely enjoy. They are not supposed to aspire also to the comforts of modern life, since it is presumably in their "nature" to remain attached to their old traditions.

Ultimately, according to this critique, green orientalist narratives like that of traditionalism perpetuate what has historically been an unequal relationship of power between the First and Third Worlds. When it comes to the historical transition from imperialism to green imperialism, the stated justification of imperialism was morality, and the intent was actually domination; but ultimately domination was only the means toward an economic end, namely the plundering of natural resources. For instance, missionaries who were part of the Spanish Empire in the Americas were fascinated by the religious beliefs of indigenous people, who, for instance, would drink concoctions to reach altered states of mind for ritual purposes. As the missionaries described those practices with fascination, they also pronounced them diabolic. That was a typically orientalist stance: admiration was followed by moral condemnation. On the basis of this orientalist characterization, Christianization of indigenous people became a central project of the Spanish Empire. However, what really motivated that project was the interest of the empire to gain control of the extraction of gold, silver, and other precious resources in indigenous lands.

Under a green imperialism lens, there exists a clear connection between this history and the present, with a special twist. A key resource today is knowledge, particularly traditional knowledge on natural resources, as the Brundtland Report states very clearly. Thus, the present-day orientalist stance is no longer about forcing indigenous people to abandon their traditional practices as the missionaries of old did, but instead the opposite, since now they are supposed to keep those practices. The green orientalist narrative of indigenous people as traditionalist by nature is based upon the argument that they should stay traditionalist in the name of sustainability. However, the natural resources from the forest are still today at stake, since the concern is that, if indigenous people lose their traditions, then a great wealth of knowledge might be lost, as the report states. This knowledge notably includes knowledge of medicinal plants, which, once they are revealed to scientists and entrepreneurs, often end up being patented by First World corporations.

That was the case of *yagé* (*Banisteriopsis caapi*), a tropical vine used for a brew essential to the most important shamanistic rituals among Amazonian indigenous people. Also known by the Kechwa name *aya waska* ("vine of the soul"), one of this plant's major active constituents is DMT (N,N-Dimethyltryptamine), a psychoactive drug said to trigger psychedelic experiences far deeper than those from LSD. Thus, the great potential of this plant for the medicine industry led to its being patented in 1986 by the California-based International Plant Medicine Corporation. Loren Miller, who ran this company, had traveled to the Ecuadorian Amazon and learned from indigenous villagers about the traditional use of the yagé. He then took a sample of the plant to the United States and filed for the patent as if he had invented the plant. The United States Patent and Trademark Office (USPTO) granted the patent. This caused outrage among indigenous rights organizations across the entire continent, given that Amazonian indigenous people regard this plant as highly sacred. These organizations included COICA,[6] one of the most important indigenous organizations in the hemisphere, which is formed by the national-level indigenous organizations of all nine South American countries that share the Amazon forest. As COICA's general coordinator, Antonia Jacanamijoy, commented, "We would like to believe that, as the millennium is ending, so is the time of paternalism, protection and colonial practices—but it seems that we have the sin of optimism" (Knight 1998, 24).

About a decade later, COICA and other organizations challenged Miller's patent on legal grounds, arguing that the plant had long been in use (in fact, for over one thousand years, according to archaeological evidence). They also argued that the plant was used by millions of indigenous people. It was their common knowledge, which they used for religious and cultural purposes, and therefore it could not be patented. In 1999 the USPTO nullified the patent, but fell short of acknowledging the organizations' argument that indigenous people were the owners of their traditional knowledge: the patent was canceled on the grounds of a technicality. Washington, DC–based public interest attorneys working in support of the indigenous organizations found that the plant had been previously described in a herbarium. This meant that there had been a previous disclosure of the supposed invention, and therefore it was no longer patentable. However, the USPTO later reversed its decision, and in 2001 it reinstated the patent in Miller's name. The patent followed its due course until expiry, as any regular patent does.

The fact that a US company was able to patent the most sacred plant of the indigenous people of an entire continent, and that the patent was awarded by the US government, ignoring any legal challenge by those people who had discovered and mastered the use of the plant, reflects how critical the issue of traditional knowledge is to the project of green imperialism. In particular, this case highlights how critical is the issue of indigenous people's agency with regard to what can be done with their knowledge. In fact, this issue also works in the opposite direction, that of the widespread trend toward modernization among indigenous and other traditional people. The fact that they might want to do away with traditional technologies and embrace modernism deeply defies the outsiders' economic interest on traditional knowledge. If traditional people abandon this knowledge, then it might be lost, and no outside corporation would be able to economically benefit from it. Thus, the embrace of modernism arguably puts the essence of the green imperialist project into crisis.

SUSTAINABILITY AS HEGEMONIC

So far, I have covered two postcolonial theoretical perspectives in the imperialism critique of sustainability, namely the history of the idea of sustainability and the notions of green orientalism and green imperialism. In this section, I will discuss hegemony, a third and final perspective that is closely related to the previous two.

I introduce the notion of hegemony with an anecdote from my own social design work. Early in my career, I worked in a slum outside San Lorenzo, a small port in Ecuador. The slum residents, who were families in great poverty, had been encroaching upon a protected forest area, part of the Chocó forest, one of the most biodiverse regions in the planet. Although by the time of my work this area still kept some of its natural wealth, including wild animals and some patches of rainforest, residents were progressively clearing it out. I worked in partnership with a number of community-based groups, offering them support with infrastructure building.

One morning, I was walking to the work site with a resident when he suddenly darted away from me and started chasing a small rodent that ran past us. As the man eventually caught up with the animal, he aimed for its head with his machete. However, rather than beheading the animal, he suddenly flipped the blade sideways, instead using it as a whip. He hit the animal on its head with such vigor that the stroke immediately left it stunned and paralyzed. Then, the man carefully lifted the tiny body and let it lie under the shadow of a tree. I came close and saw the little animal lying on its side, with its shiny dark eyes lost in the deep blue sky, its nose moist and leaking some blood. The animal was breathing intensely, clinging to life. Horrified, I inquired of the man why, out of mercy, he did not simply kill the animal rather than leave it there suffering. Indignant, he asked me if I was out of my mind. At that point it was only 9:00 in the morning. The animal would be his dinner, so if he killed it, by the evening it would have already gone bad. In a place where poverty was such that hunger was a daily occurrence, this sudden extra source of protein had appeared as a blessing to this man's family.

I invoke this experience to exemplify, first, the limits of traditionalism as an orientalist narrative, and second, the hegemonic character of the notion of sustainability. First, quite often we as outside observers in privilege engage in Brundtlandesque depictions of traditional populations as being so closely attached to their natural environment, ignoring the fact that the predicament of many among these people leads them to challenge those narratives, sometimes in a brutal fashion. On the other hand, though, there is another reading of this story, which is also about sustainability: Only semikilling the rodent could be argued to be *sustainable.* In fact, the man was actually using a quite sustainable technological alternative to refrigeration. It was a self-regulating, natural system to keep the meat fresh, even warm, for hours by inflicting a brain injury. However, few in the sustainability movement would advocate practices like this as being exemplary of sustainability. This story is significant because it highlights how in sustainability advocacy the notion of sustainability in and of itself is not sufficient. When we advocate for sustainability, we are not simply looking for technological efficiency; instead, we look beyond. It must be efficiency plus something else. The moral aspect of the outcome is tremendously important as well.

This factor is implicit in the very notion of sustainability and how it is often posed as an argument between good and bad. Such an argument is evident in William McDonough and Michael Braungart's *Cradle to Cradle* (2002), which remains one of the most influential manifestos on behalf of sustainability in architectural design theory. In fact, the key argument of McDonough and Braungart's classic book precisely invokes that dichotomy: "Being 'less bad' is no good" (2002, 45). This is the case for virtually any definition of sustainability—the notion of sustainability is related to only positive attributes, while the opposite is negative. *Webster's* dictionary, for example, relates the term "sustainable" to adjectives such as "rational, reasonable, sensible, well-grounded, acceptable, admissible, allowable," while listing its near antonyms in negative-connoting terms: "absurd, illogical, irrational, ridiculous, unsound; extreme, outrageous, unreasonable" (Merriam-Webster 2019).

The notion of sustainability is then largely understood as *all that is good.*

No one, for instance, would espouse the idea of sustainable dictatorships. Dictators tend to be very good at finding ways to make sure that the resources they plunder are still available for their future generations—there exist entire lineages of dictators, including grandfathers, fathers, and children, in quite a few countries. Given that this practice conforms to the Brundtland Report's definition, it can then be fairly argued that dictatorships are sustainable. However, when it comes to the Brundtland Report's focus on resources and the future, we draw a line; this is not sufficient. It must be resources, the future, and something else, and this is what explains our potential outrage when we are confronted with stories of animal cruelty such as that of the San Lorenzo man. Given then that there exist practices that we do not allow ourselves to consider as sustainable, despite how they might technically conform to the Brundtland Report's notion of sustainability, it is clear that the element of morality is also essential to sustainability advocacy.

There exists another emotional component in sustainability advocacy, which is *fear*. The essential fear here is that of death—this is ultimately what the fear of planetary extinction is about. This explains the anxiety triggered by the fact that the families of a San Lorenzo slum were destroying a protected forest, and that a starving man might have been contributing to the extinction of a wild rodent species. Indeed, as different as sustainability has been as a form of environmental activism, especially because of its optimistic tone, this form of advocacy has historically kept, from the earlier ecologism movement, the tone of urgency in the motivation to act on environmental issues at all cost. We are on the verge of environmental catastrophe, so we need to act now. This was the central plea of environmental advocacy in the early 1960s (see Carson 1962), and the plea continues today in sustainability advocacy, despite sustainability's being so different as a form of environmentalism.

What does the central role of fear in sustainability advocacy mean in a political sense? The *politics of fear* is an increasingly popular political strategy, which relies on instigating fear of some things, or some people, as a way to garner public consensus around controversial issues, thus rallying the public in support of indefensible political agendas. The politics of fear became a staple in the United States after September 11, 2001 (Hazen 2002; May 2004; Glassner 2018). The politics of fear is directly linked to the economics of fear—as a reaction to living with the persistent sensation that we are surrounded by threats, we buy our peace of mind through the purchase of products that offer the promise of protection, even if those products are more expensive than normal.

Why is the discussion about the politics and economics of fear relevant to the imperialism critique of sustainability? Since sustainability is ultimately the environmentalism of capitalism, its advocacy often relies upon consumption, and the consumption of green products often relies upon the latent notion of environmental catastrophe. Thus, it has been argued that the link between capitalism and environmental activism is indeed the politics of fear (see Žižek 2007). When we are confronted with the fear of all fears, that human existence in the planet might become impossible, then we are ready to do whatever it takes for sustainability. We are sold.

Morality and fear make sustainability a tremendously powerful form of environmental activism. After all, it is very difficult to overcome an argument of good and bad, and it is instinctive to act on fear. Morality is the driving force of sustainability's advocacy, the "pull factor," so to speak: Sustainability is good. However, the "push factor," which is what urges us to embrace this morality, is fear: We must act now or we are doomed.

The logic of morality and fear combined is so powerful that it has allowed sustainability to become a *hegemonic* notion. That is, sustainability has become a form of "soft power" that is all but impossible to resist—a powerful notion that is very difficult to argue with. This is in fact one of the most problematic issues with the notion of sustainability: how little room it allows for dissent. Questioning sustainability, especially in social design practice, is often equated with advocating for something akin to the destruction of the planet. This actually compels me to state my position here very clearly. Although I am a critic of sustainability, that does not mean that I am a climate change denier. In fact, I have seen climate change unfold through my years of practice in social design—and here another reference to my own work is necessary. I normally ask when the rainy season starts to figure out the best time to break ground in a given place. Over time, I have heard villagers' answers shift from something like June or September to "We don't know anymore." This is only one example of how I have witnessed the impact of climate change through my own work. Like many people, I am convinced that this is not a natural occurrence; it is instead anthropogenic.

However, I still argue that the paradigm of sustainability must be taken to task, because quite troubling practices are being carried out worldwide in the name of sustainability, and this includes not only social design practices. They are happening because the hegemonic character of sustainability allows for this notion to be invoked in order to support the deployment of strategies of domination. That is, given that it is such a hard-to-oppose notion, sustainability is being invoked to advance projects that are detrimental to vulnerable populations, including those indigenous populations that the Brundtland Report idealizes and that social design largely caters to. Common nowadays are situations of exploitation and abuse—or at the very least of perpetuation of inequality—in the name of sustainability. Many of these situations have been documented in literature and the press. They include, first, displacement by wealthy investors of impoverished settlers in the interest of natural restoration in Uganda, Botswana, and Mexico; second, high investment in natural preservation projects while those who live around the preserve endure abject poverty in Myanmar, Philippines, Zambia, Brazil, Costa Rica, and the Ecuadorian Galápagos; and third, burdensome experimentation of green technologies in marginalized communities in China, Nicaragua, and Suriname. This is happening precisely because sustainability is such a hegemonic notion; that is, these practices get justified because they are done in the name of sustainability. As a consequence, by using sustainability for the rampant abuse of people in the name of environmental preservation, we are instead creating "conservation refugees" (Dowie 2009).

In the next two chapters, I will show exactly how these situations of abuse in the name of sustainability have become quite common in social design. Invoking the logic of sustainability, some designers, including quite prominent designers, inadvertently carry out projects that end up subjecting populations in poverty to all forms of abuse, including impositions, economic burden, displacement, expropriation, technological experimentation, and even risk to people's lives since the buildings sometimes collapse. Before that, however, I will turn to the literature to explore how those and related problematic situations are being studied, and how they have been attributed to the geopolitical project that uses hegemony as its tool, that is, imperialism. After explaining in this chapter the logic of the green hegemony argument behind the critique of imperialism, I will be in conversation with this critique for the rest of the book. I will carry out a field test of this argument and its most commonly proposed solution, namely, localism, starting with the next chapter.

IMPERIALISM IN SUSTAINABILITY CRITIQUE

The charge that sustainability advocacy bears imperialist connotations has been often made in critical theory, to the extent that imperialism constitutes, along with social equity, the dominant theme in the critical literature on sustainability. Both strands of the critique are interrelated, since the imperialism critique tackles the question of social equity in the context of Third World affairs. The sources I examine here include both design and social science literature, the areas of critique I engage with most directly in this book.

Before introducing the social equity and imperialism critiques, it is worth looking at the keystone of the critique overall, namely the notion of

sustainability itself, which some authors see as a limited notion. One limitation that has been identified is that it proposes an instant gratification
approach that is too focused on economic outcomes (Worster 1993). Another
limitation is that it is too comprehensive, general, open-ended, and abstract,
and as such it is left open to every possible interpretation (Mitcham 1997;
Petrucci 2002; Crysler, Cairns, and Heynen 2012; Droege 2012). Thus, it is
argued, the Brundtland Report's notion of sustainability is insufficient, and
for this reason an approach that improves its fundamental premises must be
adopted (Norgaard 1994; Van der Ryn and Cowan 1996; Ben-Eli 2005; Ehrenfeld 2008; Fry 2009, 2011, 2017; Buchanan 2012; McDonough and Braungart
2013; Jackson 2017; Farley and Smith 2020). The real issue, however, could
be the opposite: that the problem is with the notion of sustainable design in
and of itself, because of the underlying assumption that it is possible to find
designed solutions to the environmental crisis (Hill 2008). Another area
of critique problematizes the notion of sustainable design from a different
political lens: since global warming is presumably a "hoax," then there is no
need for sustainable design (Pawley 2000; Guldberg and Sammonds 2001).
In fact, this argument continues, the sustainability paradigm hinders design
innovation and economic development; therefore, sustainability poses a
danger to progress (Williams 2001, 2008).

With regard to the themes of social equity and imperialism, critics argue
first that there exist limitations to the usual emphasis on the environmental
and technological aspects of sustainable building, since such an emphasis
neglects the social, economic, and cultural aspects (Gunder 2006; Moore
and Karvonen 2008; Henn and Hoffman 2013; Vellinga 2013, 2014; Moore
and Wilson 2014). In fact, the practice of sustainable design can replicate the
problems of the modernist approach when implemented in a top-down fashion that excludes community participation (May 2011). Regarding the cultural aspect, part of the literature focuses on the role of traditional people in
the sustainability narrative and how, as mentioned, they are often presented
as de facto conservationists or "ecologically noble" people (Redford 1990;
Schmink, Redford, and Padoch 1992; Krech 1999; Bruckner 2013). Thus, the
fact that they engage in small extractive agricultural practices might be seen
as contrary to their nature, and this can be cited as grounds to evict them
from their lands (Anaya 2010). Indeed, and as mentioned earlier, in the interest of conservation, many traditional people worldwide have been and
continue to be displaced from their ancestral lands to make space for natural
preservation sites (Dowie 2009). In another argument, the popularly upheld
notion that traditional building is inherently green might well be regarded
as a myth (Rapoport 1994; Røstivk 2011). Even if this notion was accurate
in the past, such building practices are no longer feasible due to issues such

as the forced displacement of traditional populations in the name of natural preservation (AlSayyad and Arboleda 2011). Paradoxically, environmentalism's devotion to nature as an entity removed from all human experience disregards the fact that nature is indeed a culturally constructed and deeply political notion (Oelschlaeger 1991; Evernden 1992; Cronon 1996; Latour 2004, 2008; Drenthen, Keulartz, and Proctor 2007; Swyngedouw 2007, 2010b).

An important body of the social critique focuses on issues of social justice vis-à-vis environmental sustainability in urban environments. Communities of color tend to benefit less from green infrastructure projects, despite being the ones most directly exposed to living and working in polluted environments (O'Connor 1988; Bullard 1990; Agyeman, Bullard, and Evans 2002, 2003; Agyeman 2005, 2013; Logan 2020), including environments polluted by presumably green industries, such as those engaged in biomass production (De Puy Kamp 2021). Such deep inequality in connection to who benefits from green initiatives amounts to a form of *environmental racism* (Chavis and Lee 1987; Bullard 1994, 2001; Bryant 1995; Melosi 1995; Cole and Foster 2000; Holifield 2001; Bullard et al. 2008; Saha 2010; Purdy 2015). Expanding on this argument, some authors observe that the notion of diversity in general (class, gender, race) is regularly obfuscated in sustainability celebratory literature (Allen and Sachs 1991; Scott, Park, and Cocklin 2000).

In addition, and echoing early critiques of environmentalism as a marker of social class privilege (e.g., Enzensberger 1974), another part of the critique specifically looks at social class positionality in the advocacy of sustainable living, in the sense of whose concern sustainability really is, and who gets to embrace and materialize those green ideals. The answer to this question, generally speaking, is affluent people (Allen and Sachs 1992; McGranahan, Songsore, and Kjellen 1996; Hope and Agyeman 2011; Greenberg 2013).

Thus, "sustainable," as it is commonly understood—namely, feasible and self-perpetuating—does not necessarily mean socially just (Marcuse 1998). This disconnection is particularly evident in the case of "starchitects" who have championed sustainability while ignoring the social and human rights consequences of their monumental, "green" work (Hadley 2020). Also, the sustainability logic of creating or improving green spaces in low-income neighborhoods is nowadays often invoked to actually propel the gentrification of those neighborhoods; this process has been called green, environmental, or ecological gentrification (Hagerman 2007; Dooling 2009; Checker 2011, 2019; Gould and Lewis 2012; Wolch, Byrne, and Newell 2014; Curran and Hamilton 2017; Anguelovski et al. 2019).

The fundamental argument of the postcolonial critique of sustainability has to do with the role of global capital in the sustainable development paradigm. I referred to the basic premises of this critique earlier, when I was examining the notion of sustainability. Several authors argue that the concept of sustainability was coopted and made to serve corporate interests (Greer and Bruno 1996; Parr 2009; Thyssen 2009; LeonVest 2011; Krupar and Al 2012; Dauvergne and Lister 2013; Klein 2014). This means that, in the midst of growing evidence of environmental deterioration, capitalism actually found a way to reinvent itself (Keil 2007); it is now the "green economy." However, the significant irony of the green economy is that people in privilege can simply maintain their overconsumption patterns, as they presumably consider themselves absolved by the fact that they are now consuming only so-called green products (Dauvergne 2016). In terms of architecture, if thermal cost-efficiency is being refashioned as sustainability, then sustainable design practices are just business as usual (Jarzombek 1999). Indeed, the sustainable development premise that the environmental impact in a given city can decrease while this city experiences an economic growth might be unfeasible, because there is an inherent contradiction between the notions of a "green city" and "growth," a contradiction that only embracing the idea of "degrowth" could solve (Krähmer 2021). As a whole, the discourse of sustainability became attractive in the first place because its ambiguity allowed for advocates of big business to engage in environmental discussions without challenging bourgeois politics, and this was particularly true in the case of mainstream architecture (Jarzombek 2006). Taking all of the above into consideration, sustainability advocacy is then one of the most representative examples of today's postpolitical condition—a politics of consensus based on accepting the now uncontested hegemony of the neoliberal political and economic model (Swyngedouw 2009, 2010a).

Ecological activism has also come under criticism in the postcolonial critique of sustainability. The radical passion within part of the ecologism movement, in addition to some ecologists' desire to reembrace preindustrial practices, have been compared to religious fundamentalism (Lal 1995). Along the same lines, and as mentioned in the previous section, the very notion of fear, namely a quasi-religious fear of a natural catastrophe that so strongly animates ecological activism, has been argued to ultimately embody the very logic of global capitalist domination—the politics of fear (Žižek 2007). Several other significant criticisms have been leveled at ecologism. The notion of natural preservation has been criticized as embodying yet another instance of the Western imperialist paradigm of global domination, in this case the domination of wilderness (Birch 1990). It has been argued, too, that the ecological rhetoric of equitability is "essentially imperialistic and patronizing" (Wigley 1999). As also mentioned earlier, there is, in green imperialism, a widely held expectation that, as the supposed stewards of the planet, indigenous people will make sacrifices such as abstaining from consuming even the most basic Western commodities, while the rest of the world rampantly continues its habits of overconsumption (Lizarralde 2003). This is a view that "both arises from and perpetuates power imbalances" (Lohmann 1993). A serious critique has been also leveled at the claim, popular in the ecologism movement, that overpopulation is the source of environmental problems; this claim, it is argued, is only a mask for xenophobia, neocolonialism, and ultimately ecofascism (Baeten 2000), as in the race-based discrimination and subjugation of people in the name of environmental preservation.

International financial institutions (IFIs) such as the World Bank, whose role in the Brundtland Report's sustainability project I described earlier, are a key target of the postcolonial critique of sustainability. It has been argued that, by making environmental problems "global," these institutions are extending their monopoly over the natural resources of poorer countries while forcing vulnerable populations in these countries to share the responsibility for environmental problems they did not cause (Shiva 1993). Indeed, although most global greenhouse gas emissions have originated in industrial and land use models developed in the United States and Europe, their environmental consequences are most deeply felt in the Third World (Young 2020). In connection to these arguments, it has been observed that the sustainable development project is no different from what it was intended to substitute for, given that it is also about development—a project of global economic and political domination (Esteva [1992] 2007; Esteva and Prakash 1992; Sachs 1993; Sachs, Loske, and Linz 1998; Esteva, Babones, and Babcicky 2013; Raco 2014). The limitations of such overfocus on development are still evident in the United Nations' 2015 Sustainable Development Goals (SDGs), which stress quantitative gains while not explicitly making respect for democracy and human rights part the goals (Smith and Gladstein 2018).

An important trend in the IFIs' critique adopts a Foucauldian perspective, connecting the notion of sustainable development to issues of hegemony, truth, and governmentality. These critiques characterize neoliberalism as a new technology of governance that relies upon the rejection of the planner state in favor of the rules of markets. On the basis of that characterization, a number of authors have focused on the hegemonic role of the World Bank with regard to the green knowledge it produces, and the fact that this knowledge becomes the truth that the bank uses for its own policy interventions. These authors also regard the bank's community participation approach as an ecogovernmentality technique, concluding that its sustainable development operations basically constitute imperialism in a green disguise (Escobar 1995; Goldman 2001a, 2001b, 2005; Li 2007, 2011; Mosse 2011).

A similar critique has been raised with regard to environmental advocacy by the United States and other First World countries to have Third World countries strengthen their environmental standards. Critics contend that this advocacy relies upon the premise that, by way of strengthening those standards, these countries will acquire green technology from the First World, thus ensuring the latter's economic hegemony (Pratt and Montgomery 1997). In architecture, the Foucauldian argument has been invoked to argue that the production of authoritative green knowledge has historically nurtured colonialism (Piers 2006; Chang 2012). On the other hand, also echoing the Foucauldian notion of hegemony, some authors have reflected upon how, given that it is now regarded as an absolute standard, the notion of sustainability has become the new normative and dominant discourse in architecture (Jarzombek 1999; Pyla 2008, 2012).

SOCIAL DESIGN AS IMPERIALIST

The imperialism argument has also been widely made in the literature with regard to the practice of social design. In fact, and as I referred to earlier in this chapter, imperialism constitutes the main critique of social design practice. The Foucauldian critique in this case also invokes the notion of governmentality. It has been argued that international NGO[7] humanitarianism constitutes a form of biopolitics without the state, as well as a reconfigured form of governance where NGOs fill the void of state presence in so-called failed states (Redfield 2012a). It has also been argued that by offering a *design fix* (i.e., objects) for problems entrenched in imperialism, humanitarian designers are failing to address structural dynamics such as underdevelopment, echoing in turn the principles of colonial-era humanitarianism, which regarded the global poor as the subjects of elite benevolence. Therefore, today's celebrated humanitarian design projects "constitute a form of soft cultural imperialism" (Johnson 2011). An often-ignored dimension of the design fix is how green technologies such as dry toilets and other ecological toilets can be perceived among subaltern populations as solutions that perpetuate colonial inequalities. Facing the lack of a proper sanitation infrastructure, these populations historically have had to resort to alternative and less dignified toilet systems such as buckets. Now, they are targeted by humanitarian organizations with yet more alternative toilets that ultimately reaffirm the notion that subaltern populations are not deserving of the regular technological solutions that upper classes enjoy, namely regular flush toilets (Redfield and Robins 2016). One of the main issues with the present trend of addressing humanitarian crises through the design fix is that groups of people who were in the past encouraged to self-manage are now instead regarded as "'users' who are permanently enrolled in the continuous prototyping of the technologies that govern them" (Duffield 2019). Even in the less common cases in which those humanitarian objects still allow for a user's modification, such as in the Red Cross shelter kits, they might still "fail to work as a tool for involving communities in their own relief and recovery" (Fredriksen 2014). As it evades the political question, this technocratic emphasis on objects—extending also to an IKEA-sponsored refugee shelter that was developed with support from the United Nations Refugee Agency—represents an official focus shift from refugees to refuges. With that, it represents "an evasion of the political or, more specifically, an institutionally sanctioned politics of evasion" by which the fact of cruel dispossession becomes subordinated to, and obliterated by, the architectural icon (Monk and Herscher 2021).

The Foucauldian notion of expert knowledge in connection to governmentality has also been raised in social design critiques. One such critique is that present-day social design activism has paradoxically adopted the ways of thinking it originally sought to challenge. From the 1960s paradigm of challenging expertise, social design practice has now turned into a realm of experts' technical rationality—a governmentality approach that is the preferred power device of the neoliberal state (Crysler 2015). Thus, present-day social design practice is a continuation of the premises of the Bretton Woods modernist development project, which privileges outsiders' over indigenous solutions (Schwittay 2014). In fact, the development project has recently found a new frontier of expertise application and a source of contracts for big design firms; development is now being reframed as a project of innovation and design, where people in poverty are targeted as "clients" (2014). However, the notion that only so-called Western design companies are able to generate innovation ignores non-Western design solutions developed by local designers in response to specific challenges in their communities; thus, the prevalent notion of design innovation ultimately perpetuates neocolonialism and imperialism (Tunstall 2013). When it comes to Sub-Saharan African countries, which are by far the favorite sites of Euro-American humanitarian design interventions, such a notion is also problematic as it relies upon the assumption that "in terms of design, Africa has little to offer, but much to receive" (Pereira and Gillett 2014). Instead, it is necessary to consider the question of who designs for whom, and with that the question of the role that design should play in the project of decolonization (2014; also Ambole 2020). Design can become a force of change and help to strengthen the autonomy of subaltern populations, if designers adopt a decolonial perspective by which they become more critical of the role of design in the context of inequality and a "modern/colonial world system" (Escobar 2018).

Consequently, critics suggest, humanitarianism as a whole is also a manifestation of the postpolitical condition, as it seeks to address issues of social justice through the market rather than engaging with political action (Swyngedouw 2016). That is, it targets these issues by, for instance, encouraging people in the First World to consume Starbucks or Whole Foods products, under the assumption that these acts of consumption will presumably benefit Third World workers or farmers. Such an assumption, however, immediately precludes any engagement with a politics of emancipation (Žižek 2010). Also, by favoring the global market approach to deal with issues such as lack of access to water, humanitarian products thwart the formation of local capabilities and the political project of postcolonial nation-building. In fact, there is a great contrast between the LifeStraw, a water filter designed in Europe to be used in African countries, and the Bush Pump, a water collection system designed in an African country for local use (Redfield 2016). The focus on innovative products as the solution to humanitarian situations, then, fails to address the structural factors that have led to these situations in the first place (2018). These products only provide short-term fixes, but their fetishization, which confers upon them an almost miraculous power to solve critical issues such as hunger, depoliticizes the causes of those issues (e.g., poverty and its roots); consequently, it hampers a debate on long-term solutions (Scott-Smith 2013). Instead of rushing to design "moralized goods" directed to "problem-solve" the issues faced by vulnerable populations such as refugees, designers in the so-called Global North should first and foremost become aware of the politics of borders that have created those populations in the first place. Subsequently, they should realign their practice in a way that actually supports refugees in their struggle with the politics of violence they normally face as they attempt to cross national borders (Keshavarz 2020).

In general, the present boom of humanitarian products reflects how people in poverty are now seen as a new frontier of markets, being directly catered to with innovative and attractively designed humanitarian objects for them to buy (Cross 2013). On the other hand, these products tend to be designed as context-agnostic, universal solutions. However, the fact that people in different places might react differently to them reveals their limited scope as elements of a "philanthro-capitalist utopia" (Scott-Smith 2018). As a whole, the pragmatic idea that the most serious socioeconomic and environmental problems of the world can be solved simply with design innovation funded by corporations ultimately assumes that the consequences of capitalist growth can be solved with more capitalism (Rule 2008). Indeed, the logic of the humanitarian design movement relies upon a false dichotomy of greedy economic capital versus benevolent aid capital. In reality, as long as it uses the means of capital to reach its goals, this movement cannot play a socially disruptive role, as it usually claims to do (Watson 2012).

As for critiques of specific areas of social design practice, one body of critique targets practice in slums, which is a very popular form of social design work. One critique focuses on the ever-popular romantic representation of life in favelas or Brazilian slums, and its aestheticization in the form of artistic and architectural pieces (Williams 2009). Another critique refers to the depiction of the strategies of survival by slum residents as "ecological virtues," given that these residents for instance recycle discarded materials for their housing. According to this critique, such representation serves only to perpetuate stereotypes that make slum residents into oriental exotic others—that is, new, urban versions of the noble savage myth (Varley 2013). One of the highest-profile social design organizations focused on slums is Urban-Think Tank (U-TT). This is an award-winning practice led by Alfredo Brillembourg and Hubert Klumpner (I will discuss their work in the next chapter). U-TT's work is based on studying slum dwellers' housing strategies and using these as a model for architectural and urban design practice. Their work has been criticized as a parasitic appropriation of the dwellers' work, equal only to the Spanish Empire's plundering of Venezuela's natural resources in colonial times (Hancox 2014).

The social design model of service learning has also been the subject of imperialism critiques. Critics argue that service learning studios held in the Third World, while aiming to train architectural students from the First World, might indeed embody a form of educational neocolonialism. These studios' strong focus on exotic, primitivist architectural imagery customarily ignores local social, political, cultural, and even environmental contexts. Those who benefit more from these studios are seemingly the foreign students, since the studios tend to reduce "local communities" to the role of recipients without involving them as active participants in the process (Berlanda 2015). As a way to overcome this issue, one service learning educator offers that both architecture students and faculty members must be exposed to basic resources on international aid (e.g., by reading relevant literature and participating in field trips) so that they can gauge the complexity of the task at hand and recognize in advance the perils of the new imperialism (Zaretsky 2011, 2016). On the other hand, when so-called Global South students in, say, Arab countries design for local people in poverty, they often do it by also using the intellectual framework of the so-called Westernized university model. Thus, while the effort to "decolonize" social design is important, decolonization must also involve an overturning of the Eurocentric mind frame with the goal to pursue "a knowledge produced with and from rather than about" (Abdulla in Schultz et al. 2018).

Another major line of commentary examines the nonprofit model of social design, studying it also through the lens of imperialism. One critique focuses on Architecture for Humanity, the organization that made social design mainstream as a form of architectural practice. This critique notes how Architecture for Humanity's motto "Design like you give a damn" actually reflected a bias of rampant privilege that is highly celebrated in this practice—designers presumably have "a birthright to do what we want and design where and for whom we want." Instead, designers should aim to emancipate the profession from this neocolonialist do-good paradigm (Linsell 2014). The same critic also targets Architecture for Humanity's policy of forbidding its members from places like Asia from taking any payments for design work they did under the organization's name. By instituting this policy, the author argues, Architecture for Humanity perpetuated the dominance of foreign designers because they can afford to work for free more easily than their local counterparts and, in doing that, they cripple the agency of local designers from the developing world. In this sense, the practice of humanitarian design could then be equivalent to "a 'revisionary form of imperialist nostalgia'" (2015).

The general argument on imperialism in practice-based critiques is that a social design intervention in a remote country might be perceived as intrusive to people who are still recovering from more than a century of colonialism (Stairs 2007). Frequently, the oft-repeated claim that design can change the world is made synonymous with controlling the world, thus "the road to neo-colonialism is paved with good intentions" (2009, comment 19). However, a countercritique argues that it would perhaps be more neocolonialist to assume that people in African countries do not want good design; humanitarian design is not neocolonialist when the foreign designer deeply and authentically engages with the "local community" (Shioiri-Clark 2013). Thus, a "truly humanitarian practice" will be possible only if, in their overseas work, designers engage in a conscientious way with their local partners (Golden 2014). One of the issues with humanitarian design practice in Third World informal settlements is that construction projects are usually addressed and described using the perspectives and reference points of the so-called Western world. Embracing the different perceptions of reality held by local residents is essential for practitioners to effectively carry out their work in places they are new to (Gaestel 2019). Additionally, humanitarian designers should become aware of the complex social, political, and even legal implications of their work in foreign settings. It is necessary also to develop an ethics of humanitarian design practice that considers learning and listening from project beneficiaries, even if this implies having to rethink one's original design ideas for a project (Harris-Brandts 2015).

However, it has been highlighted that the claim that foreign design interventions offer great socioeconomic benefits is generally anecdotal, since no quantitative evidence is usually provided to support it (Haar 2014). In addition, there is a blatant contradiction in the work by design offices that claim to work to "empower the poor" of the so-called non-Western world, and the fact that these offices are led and staffed by an overwhelmingly American majority (Stairs 2015). In fact, there exist salary and other inherent inequalities between the expatriate and local staff members of a humanitarian organization operating under the *sans frontières* or *without borders* label. Thus, the "without borders" discourse ultimately reflects a privilege of mobility that not all the staff members of such organizations enjoy. Local staff from Third World countries often have to remain within their own countries' borders, as they might hold passports that are not easily accepted internationally. If this situation were to be left unaddressed, then "the maps of aid organizations would uncomfortably resemble those of empires" (Redfield 2012b).

THE NUSSBAUM CONTROVERSY

As it can be seen, the critiques leveled at imperialism in social design have been numerous and have targeted many aspects of this practice. However, nowhere has the imperialism issue been raised more contentiously than during the controversy unleashed by Bruce Nussbaum, which remains the most impassioned public debate on the practice of social design to date. The debate started with a short piece written by Nussbaum, an author, designer, and educator, and published in Co.Design, a Fast Company magazine website, in July 2010. The piece was provocatively titled "Is Humanitarian Design the New Imperialism?" (Nussbaum 2010).

"Humanitarian design" was the broad term used by Nussbaum to refer to what I call in this book "social design." The focus of Nussbaum's critique was Project H, a nonprofit initiative led by the social designer Emily Pilloton. Project H became famous after the redesign of the *Hippo-Roller*, a water transportation device intended for rural African women (fig. 7). Nussbaum based his critique on criticism that he had in turn overheard from a few Asian designers, who seemed unhappy with "Western design intervention." In Nussbaum's words, these designers pondered what makes American designers like Pilloton think they have the solution for other people, considering that in countries like India there might exist better local solutions to local problems. Commenting specifically on the closing line of Project H's mission statement, "We believe design can change the world," Nussbaum pondered whether European and American humanitarian design initiatives might be perceived as colonialist in the countries to which these initiatives are directed. He asked whether Euro-American designers are perhaps being too presumptuous and whether they are establishing the right partnerships, learning from the best local people, and being perceptive of postcolonial

Fig. 7. The Hippo-Roller, one of the humanitarian design pieces at the center of the Nussbaum controversy in 2010. (Photograph by Hippo Roller, hipporoller.org, Creative Commons)

sensitivities in the countries where they work. In his conclusion, Nussbaum reflected upon the need for designers to consider the question of who, in the end, has the right answers; he pondered whether there might exist important design lessons that Euro-American designers could learn from designers from India, Brazil, or African nations. He closed by asking why it is that the former's focus is on Asia and Africa, and not for instance on Native American settlements in the United States, where poverty indicators match the worst in those continents.

Nussbaum's piece generated an impassioned reaction among influential figures in the social design circle. One of the first to respond was Cameron Sinclair, the cofounder of Architecture for Humanity. Sinclair accused Nussbaum of selecting the wrong target—aim higher than pro bono designers if you want to take on imperialism, he said (Sinclair 2010).[8] Sinclair argued that the type of humanitarian Western interventions that Nussbaum described was something of the past, since the humanitarian design movement had already transformed "into a complex global network of multi-disciplinary, multi-cultural and diverse teams working locally hand in hand with communities on the ground." Sinclair also argued that the majority of architects affiliated with Architecture for Humanity lived and worked "in the communities they are designing/building for." He also provided a few examples of

Architecture for Humanity's projects in order to demonstrate how this organization supported local professionals. He added that collaborating and partnering with local designers was in fact a requirement of his organization. Last, he highlighted the dozens of local Architecture for Humanity chapters in cities from Dhaka to New York, working for instance on issues of homelessness. "Local designers create real change," he stressed.

Another reaction was published in the weblog of the MIT IDEAS Global Challenge, authored by Lars Hasselblad Torres, a social entrepreneur. The *One Laptop per Child* project, also initiated at MIT, had been another target of Nussbaum's critique. In his post (Torres 2010), he also countered Nussbaum, arguing that the first step currently involved in humanitarian design is usually "to get to know the needs of the poor, by living, working, and conversing alongside," rather than simply getting their feedback on the designed product. Consequently, Torres argued, many of the best-designed humanitarian products available today have been developed in close partnership with beneficiaries (or "customers," as Torres referred to them). This happens through a process of cocreation that, in addition to resulting in a good design, increases the capacity of people in these communities by bolstering local productivity and skills. This, Torres argued, defeats the premise that what these designers do can be equated to colonialism.

Also, Emily Pilloton, the founder of Project H, objected strenuously to Nussbaum's article (Pilloton 2010). She accused her critic of being ill-informed and oversimplifying the practice of humanitarian design. She clarified that most of the work her organization did actually took place in the United States. As of the time of her response, Project H was in fact based in Bertie County, which Pilloton described as North Carolina's poorest county—the organization would later move back to Pilloton's home base in California. Pilloton added that her case was not unique, and she mentioned a number of US-based organizations doing similar work in impoverished communities throughout the country. Commenting on the fact that the Hippo-Roller had ultimately become one of social design's most visible "marketing and infrastructure failures" (Stairs 2010), Pilloton conceded that undertaking that project had been a mistake, partly "because of its lack of direct collaboration with end users." She highlighted how, after that experience, the organization had decided to undertake only local projects "run by local designers invested in their own communities, in places they understand, with people who are fellow citizens." Pilloton eloquently advocated for such type of local engagement as the ideal for humanitarian design practice, arguing that it allows people to become no longer beneficiaries but instead co-designers of a given project.

Many other reactions to Nussbaum's article appeared in design blogs and other publications. The majority of those pieces adopted a stance deeply critical of Nussbaum. There were some notable exceptions, however, including a reflection by the writer Maria Popova on Design Observer, a web-based publication that closely reported on the debate (Popova 2010). Popova highlighted how the voices of local designers had been generally lacking in this debate, and also how the language used throughout the whole debate reflected little awareness in the design field of the value of cultural diversity. A second favorable reflection came from Niti Bhan, a social designer and entrepreneur who introduced herself as a multicultural professional, unlike most of the other participants in the discussion (Bhan 2010). Bhan highlighted first the importance of mutual respect over the paradigm of patronizing the recipients of humanitarian design aid. Second, she underlined the importance of what she called a "give and take," as in the fact that First World designers should acknowledge that they do also have something to learn from their Third World counterparts. Third, Bhan highlighted the political filter with which the activities of First World designers can be perceived in the Third World, where a designer "doesn't see you simply as a designer but as an American designer (or British or white or whatever etc), with all the political ideology and history that your nationality entails."

A third supporting piece was an open letter to Nussbaum penned by David Stairs (Stairs 2010), a social design educator and practitioner who had been raising the issue of imperialism since 2007 (see Stairs 2007). He had been himself at the center of a previous controversy when he had questioned whether the seemingly endless number of existing social design initiatives was really doing much to help the world (2009). Stairs agreed with Nussbaum's point, in turn citing Arvind Lodaya, an Indian industrial designer who "once called design in the non-Western world a 'cultural WMD'" (weapon of mass destruction) (2010). With that, Stairs reemphasized that "designers from the developed world need to be very careful about how they 'intervene' elsewhere." Still, he predicted that as the economic playing field becomes more level, the next upsurge of design innovation might originate from studios in cities such as Delhi, Rio, or Cape Town.

LOCALISM AS THE SOLUTION

From this extensive literature review, a few key aspects of the social design imperialism critique can be identified. First, imperialism is currently considered to be the main challenge faced by social design practice. This challenge is extensive to social design's focus on sustainability. The general argument of the imperialism critique is that local communities are affected by decisions made by outside institutions and actors that are located in centers of power in Europe and the United States. Those outsiders' decisions seldom have a positive impact in these communities' life conditions, and they might even make those conditions worse. This then constitutes a form of imperialism, notwithstanding the discourse of sustainability that outsiders might invoke to justify their decisions.

The second key aspect pertains to the solution that the critique regularly proposes to tackle the challenge of imperialism. The critique focuses on two main questions. The first is *who designs.* According to critics, the protagonist role of First World designers in the Third World displaces local designers, despite the fact that the latter might be better equipped to deal with local design issues, and consequently overlooks the fact that local designers' practices might positively contribute to further emancipation of postcolonial states. The second question is *how designs are carried out.* As critics argue, First World designers are often unaware how the design solutions that they propose for Third World countries can be perceived locally. The reason for this is that designers often carry out their work in a top-down fashion, disregarding community input. Therefore, it is necessary to also involve community participation in the design process.

The third aspect became quite evident during the Nussbaum controversy, given that its "viral" online dynamic allowed for many voices to be heard, including those of critics and supporters. Very notably, this debate made it evident that, although there exists a clear disagreement between critics and supporters of social design with regard to the issue of imperialism, actually both sides tend to agree on the solution, that being *localism.* The main argument on localism during this controversy was that social designers as a whole should ideally focus on their own national context—for example, the focus of US designers should be the United States, addressing for instance issues of homelessness. More ideally, in fact, designers should work in their own communities or become part of the community where they work. This was presented by some in the debate as a gold standard to strive for in social design practice. However, it was also argued that when this is not the case, foreign designers should work in partnership with local designers. Indeed, it was generally agreed in the debate that local designers normally have the right answers, as they are better enabled to find solutions that work best in their local contexts. Consequently, Euro-American designers indeed have much to learn from designers in the Third World, so much so that the next great wave of innovation in design might actually emerge from those regions. Last, there was also strong agreement between critics and supporters that

designers as a whole should work in close collaboration with project beneficiaries. Solutions should be developed in direct conversation with them
through a process of community participation. This approach, it was argued,
offers great advantages both in terms of the resulting product, which works
more effectively, and also in terms of increasing local capacities.

Thus, as seen from the literature and especially from the Nussbaum controversy, there is consensus among critics and apologists in that localism
is the best way to carry out social design practice. Localism in this consensus refers to two main principles: First, socially speaking, local designers'
interventions are more beneficial than those of foreign designers. Second,
awareness of local conditions from resources to risks is imperative, and this
awareness is only possible through a profound and sincere engagement with
local communities through community participation. In simpler terms, the
two principles are that local designers should ideally lead local social design
projects, and that designers, local or otherwise, should involve community
participation in their projects.

In the next chapters I will explore these two premises. My goal is to establish whether deferring to local designers and involving community participation really makes a difference. Is localism the solution to the issues
normally pointed out to as exclusive of imperialism? And to what extent is
community participation a solution? These two questions will guide my exploration for the rest of this book.

CHAPTER 2

Is Localism the Solution?

On Local Social Designers

In the previous chapter, I explained how central sustainability is to social design practice—it is, indeed, the main focus of this practice. I also explained how social design practice generally understands the notion of sustainability, in the Brundtland Report's sense of the term—that is, to ensure the availability of resources over the long term. I then focused on the postcolonial critique to sustainability, explaining the idea of sustainability as a hegemonic notion, one that is very hard to oppose. I explained how the hegemonic character of sustainability is what ultimately makes it into a convenient tool to support strategies of imposition on vulnerable populations that critics have deemed imperialist. I examined those critiques and then focused on the critique of social design itself as imperialist. This is by far the most serious and recurrent charge that has been made in both popular and academic literature about social design practice. I closed by identifying the way out of imperialism, as it has been agreed upon by both critics and apologists of social design. The solution in their view is *localism*—namely, the double premise that local designers should take local matters in their own hands, and that social design practice should involve community participation.

In the next two chapters I will conduct a field-based exploration of these two premises. In this chapter I will explore the first premise, concerning local social designers, by asking the following question: If, as the imperialism critique regularly points out, the main challenge faced by social design relates to the abuse that so-called First World designers might inflict on Third World local populations, are these populations better protected from abuse when the project is in the hands of a local designer? The kernel of my exploration will be a simple question: Does it matter in the end? Does "being local" actually make any difference in terms of the outcome of a social design intervention?

To address this question, it is necessary first and foremost to define *local*. In this book, I understand "local" as social design literature generally understands this term. As the literature review in the previous chapter shows, in social design "local" is generally understood in the simplest and most self-explanatory sense of this term—that is, local as in not foreign. On the one hand, a local in this literature is commonly understood as being a resident of the place where the project takes place. Granted, the understanding of this term in connection to residence is problematic, partly because anybody at any given time could then call themselves a local. Take for example the case of Emily Pilloton, who was the focus of Bruce Nussbaum's imperialism critique. Pilloton moved back to California after ending her involvement with the North Carolina's Bertie County project that she had offered as a counter-example to Nussbaum's accusation of imperialism. However, during the controversy she was able to legitimately argue that she was a local in Bertie County, since she was living there at the time of the project: "I now call it home," she asserted (Pilloton 2010).

On the other hand, when it comes to a Third World context, in social design literature "local" often defaults to *national,* as in the designer being a national of the country where the project takes place, in this case regardless of whether or not they live in that place or even in the country. For example, in social design literature, a Nigerian designer who lives in Europe and designs from there a school for a slum in Nigeria where he has never lived is, regardless of that, still considered a ' local designer." This reflects the importance conferred on being a national in social design when it comes to the Third World and in connection to the discussion on imperialism. Yet, one of the main issues with such understanding of localism is that, within any given country, there exist perceivable differences within localities and, with that, relative notions of *who belongs,* just as there exist perceivable differences in the United States between, say, the average local from Bertie County, North Carolina, and the one from Berkeley, California.

Thus, an issue common to both understandings of local is how this category completely obfuscates the fact that two locals are not necessarily equal, not even two people from Bertie County, since there exists a more clearly differentiating category, which is that of social class. This is a central point I make in this book.

In conclusion, "local" is a simplistic category, but it is still a central category in social design critique and promotion, and as such I must consider it. In this chapter, I will explore the question of localism by studying five cases of social design interventions carried out by so-called local designers as defined above. In terms of the location of the studied projects, these include rural, periurban, and core urban projects. I have also selected different types of projects (schools, libraries, housing, parks) in different countries of the world. This makes for a broad and diverse sample.

In order to strengthen my point, I am limiting my selection to only widely recognized projects and designers. The first is the Nueva Esperanza School by Al Borde Architects, located in Cabuyal, Ecuador. The second is the Makoko Floating School by Kunlé Adeyemi, located in Lagos, Nigeria. The third is the Torre David research and design project by Alfredo Brillembourg and Hubert Klumpner's Urban-Think Tank (U-TT) in Caracas, Venezuela. The fourth is the Biblioteca España ("Library of Spain"), by Giancarlo Mazzanti, as well as its umbrella project, social urbanism, both located in Medellín, Colombia. The fifth and last project is the Burrows Street Pocket Park by Architecture for Humanity, located in San Francisco, California, United States. All these projects are quite prominent in the social design world. They all have been and continue to be highly celebrated, and most of them have received some of the highest awards both in social design and the architectural design field as a whole. In fact, most of them have been exhibited at the highly prestigious Venice Biennale, which constitutes a pinnacle of achievement in the architectural design world. A couple of them have been conferred the highest awards at the Biennale.

Very importantly, in all these projects sustainability was invoked as a motivation, a goal, and/or an outcome of the project. Thus, these projects are relevant for my argument because their study allows for field-testing the outcome of social design's sustainability premises.

COLLAPSED SCHOOL IN ECUADOR

The Nueva Esperanza School is one of Latin America's most famous and highly celebrated social design projects (fig. 8). The school was designed by David Barragán and Pascual Gangotena, members of Al Borde, a team of four architects based in Quito, Ecuador. The school has been featured in prominent architectural magazines such as *Architectural Design* (see Leguía 2011) and *Architectural Record* (see Syrkett 2012), as well as influential online publications such as *Architizer* (see n.d.) and *ArchDaily,* where the project made its public debut (see ArchDaily 2010). It appears in several books, including Francesca Tatarella's *Natural Architecture* (2014), Elizabeth Golden's *Building from Tradition* (2018), and Andrea Griborio's *Al Borde: Less Is All* (2020). It has been displayed, too, in high-profile exhibitions, including the German Architecture Museum's Think Global Build Social in 2013, the Chicago Architecture Biennial in 2015, and the Venice Biennale in 2016. For their work in this school and two follow-up projects, in 2017 Al Borde was inducted as a Social Design Circle Honoree. This is a selective group of social design practitioners listed by the Curry Stone Foundation, a prestigious organization dedicated to promoting the practice of social design.

Fig. 8. Nueva Esperanza School in Puerto Cabuyal, Ecuador.

The school, whose name translates as "New Hope," is located in Puerto Cabuyal, a coastal village in Manabí, Ecuador. This village is the site of a contentious dispute that has pitted villagers against a Quito-based family that claims the village land as theirs. The school is run on a voluntary basis by a villagers' supporter, an urban self-exile who has endeavored to provide high-quality education to the children of the village. The structure, an elegy to rusticity and a pastoral way of life, serves its purpose in an endearing way. It is, as Al Borde describes it, "a school with a boat shape" (Al Borde n.d.a). In addition to its formal beauty, one of the school's most praised features is the fact that, according to Al Borde's own claim, the firm was presumably able to build it with a budget of only US$200 (e.g., ArchDaily 2010; Syrkett 2012; Kliwadenko and Novas 2017). As the school propelled the career of Al Borde, the firm made this project the main exemplar of its philosophy, which could be described as *arte povera* brought to architecture: no large budgets are required in order to produce great quality design. The secret, as Al Borde has widely argued, is using local resources and community participation, the result thus being "common-sense sustainability" (Kloppenburg n.d.).

The villagers' community participation in the project consisted of providing building materials such as timber and palm thatch, as well as providing their labor, which included building a raised platform for the architect-designed structure. Diagrams by Al Borde explain that this platform was supposed to be square-shaped, following the model of how villagers built their own houses: "The agreement was that the community will built [*sic*] the platform" (ArchDaily 2010, fig. 42). In order to metaphorize the boat shape, the architects designed an unconventional polyhedron-shaped structure

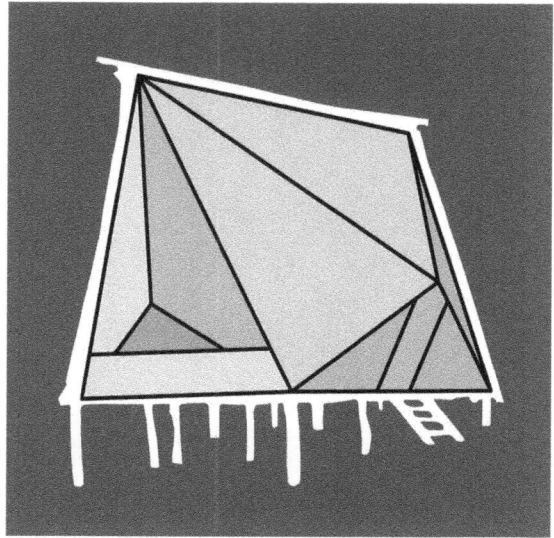

Fig. 9. Nueva Esperanza School, basic geometry.

formed by ten triangular sides; six of them constituted the roof, while the remaining four constituted the walls. This meant that the school walls were to be triangular in shape, and they were slanted, not vertical (fig. 9).

Overall, one of the most innovative features of the school was its ladder. As diagrams and photos from Al Borde show, it was a lift-up ladder like those in airplanes (2010, fig. 37). It was supposed to be lifted up to the level of the slanted walls with a string, and once it reached that position it would become in fact part of the wall. It would be made to stay in that position by tying the string to the framing (fig. 10). The idea of a lift-up ladder reinforced the metaphor that the school was a ship, in this case a spaceship for learning, as one of the Al Borde diagrams explains (2010, fig. 41).

According to reports from Puerto Cabuyal villagers I spoke to, the Nueva Esperanza School collapsed during the Pedernales earthquake of April 2016—although it is hard to determine the extent of the collapse, as I will explain later. The school was one of only a small number of structures that gave in to the earthquake in this village. Luckily, there were no children in it at that time, given that the earthquake struck on a Saturday evening during a vacation break.

Inexplicably, soon after the earthquake the Al Borde designers reported on Facebook that the school was fine (Al Borde 2016). Then, they traveled to the village and quietly rebuilt the school from scratch. The new structure was an almost exact replica of the original, and it was built quite close to the original site (fig. 11). Because of that, it is difficult to tell at a glance that

Fig. 10. The Nueva Esperanza School's lift-up ladder. (After Cadena [ArchDaily 2010])

Fig. 11. A composite image showing the silhouette of the original Nueva Esperanza School (*center right*) on the site where it used to stand, with the 2016 replica (*left*), and debris from the first building's unpublicized demolition (*lower left*).

anything actually happened. Indeed, neither the school collapse nor the rebuild were noticed by the media, and by the time I began to share the results
of my research (see, e.g., Arboleda 2020), this fact was still largely unknown
in architectural circles.

According to villagers, Al Borde completed the basic framing and roofing
of the new structure by the end of May 2016. This date in fact coincided with
the opening of the Venice Biennale, where the firm had been invited to exhibit its work. At the Biennale, Al Borde presented the school as if nothing
had happened. The firm displayed a photo of the by-then nonexistent original
school, and also projected images of that structure's design process. Those
images were in the background of an art installation aimed to demonstrate
Al Borde's point that low cost apparently does not have an impact on architectural quality. In addition to this art exhibition, the Al Borde presence at
the Biennale included the firm's participation in two colloquia. Just as with
the exhibit, in those colloquia the collapse of the school was never mentioned.
Then, a year after the Biennale, Al Borde co-produced a film titled *Do More
with Less,* which featured the school (see Kliwadenko and Novas 2017). Although the school displayed in this film is the new structure, the architects
failed to disclose this fact, and also in this case they did not mention the
original structure's collapse. Later on, in a 2020 Columbia University presentation of the firm's work, David Barragán went chronologically through the
history of the school project, and still bypassed any mentions to the collapse
of the structure and the construction of a replica. Instead, he declared with a
definitive tone: "The project was a success!" (2020, 13:15).

As for details about the collapse, it is very difficult to tell what exactly
happened to the school from a structural standpoint, given that Al Borde
so promptly removed all the evidence of failure from the site. Only a few
pictures of the village were published online in the days following the earthquake, so it is also very difficult to see how the school looked right after the
disaster. In fact, the picture used by Al Borde on Facebook to illustrate its
positive report about the school's condition was actually an old picture.
When I asked villagers to describe the structural failure, they did it using
terms such as *se viró* ("it toppled") or *se dobló* ("it bent"). On Twitter, a jour-
nalist who traveled through the area soon after the earthquake described the
school simply as having "fallen down" (Asar 2016). By most accounts, however, the school seemingly did not fully fall to the ground. One picture in a
GoFundMe donations campaign, which the campaign organizer confirmed
to me was a detail of the collapsed school, shows that the beneficiary-built
platform endured the earthquake with apparently no damage. I am thus
using "collapse" in the sense of collapsible, as in tending to fold into itself,
since it seems this is what might have happened at the very least, according

to some of the villagers' descriptions. However, some of the village leaders I spoke to minimized the situation by saying that the rebuild had been done just because it was a better decision than repairing the damaged structure. Yet, on the other hand, other villagers described the structure as having been too severely damaged to be used. A woman said that the architects had to tear it down "because it was soft," as in structurally weak. Other villagers added that some structural poles had broken, which might have caused the structure overall to give in.

In any case, all these descriptions suggest that the school's structural failure was fully attributable to its design. The Nueva Esperanza School design was such that the building had no columns as such, in the conventional sense of columns being vertical elements that transmit a given structure's loads down to the ground. The structure's few columns were actually part of the walls, and they were thus tilted toward the outside. Consequently, the big polyhedral roof was mostly self-supported. Furthermore, it had no internal bracing; the whole structure had been put together mostly with ties, and the timber joinery, when it existed, was also very basic. It is then easy to picture how, with the earth shaking, all those shortcomings might have led the structure to at the very least loosen or "soften," as the village woman described it.

The structure aside, other design issues made the Nueva Esperanza School in principle unsafe. One of the most serious issues was, indeed, its entrance. Although conceptually speaking, a lift-up ladder might seem like a great design idea, had the children been in the school at the time of the earthquake and had this ladder been lifted, the whole room would have been locked because in order to release the ladder, it had to be first untied. Thus, without a quick and safe exit, the children could have been trapped inside the building.

A question worth exploring is whether the Nueva Esperanza structural failure was partly due to the small monetary investment—that it was cheap construction. If this were the case, it would prove Al Borde's *arte povera* theory wrong. Indeed, it is necessary to invest a decent amount of funding in order to build structurally safe schools. However, as it turns out, the Nueva Esperanza School was far costlier than the bare US$200 claimed by Al Borde. Villagers I spoke with reported very different numbers. To begin with, the Al Borde figure only included the cost of lumber, bamboo, hardware, and "setbacks in construction" (see ArchDaily 2010, fig. 40). As villagers explained, just the thatch (budgeted by Al Borde as zero) and bamboo (listed as being only US$40) totaled US$400. Additionally, Al Borde budgeted the labor cost as zero because it was "self-construction" (ibid.). Villagers, by contrast, stressed that it took them about a week to build the structure. They estimated about thirty people participated in the construction, including ten parents and twenty outside volunteers. This is equivalent to 210 daily salaries. Considering that the average daily wage for a laborer in the village was US$15, then the labor costs alone were over US$3,000. In addition to the cost of labor, other costs that Al Borde excluded from its budget included transportation and food. The food item itself would have added over US$1,000, given that local contracting custom dictates the addition of US$5 to the laborers' daily wage for lunch.

Thus, Al Borde's widely publicized budget of only US$200 was evidently a partial report of expenses based on inaccurate numbers and on selectively excluding some items, most notably the labor costs. The structure was far more expensive, being actually closer to at least US$5,000. As for comparisons with the local cost of construction, some villagers estimated the cost of this type of construction, traditionalist construction in natural materials, to be actually higher than regular construction in concrete blocks. In general, there was the perception among villagers that the cost of building traditionalist thatch-roofed structures such as this school was higher than building the tin-roofed modernist structures that now constitute the majority of the housing in Puerto Cabuyal. Indeed, villagers often expressed to me how much they liked the aspect of the Nueva Esperanza School. However, when I asked why, if they liked it so much, they no longer built their houses using those traditional materials, their answer was that they could not afford them. The transportation cost of materials that are no longer locally available (such as thatch palm) or that grow too far away (such as bamboo), the cost of the materials themselves, the fact that those materials do not last for very long and thus they have to be constantly purchased and repurchased, the cost of hardware, including bolts to secure the normally feeble structures, and the labor costs, because traditional structures are more demanding to build; all these factors have made this type of construction affordable mostly to outside people of privilege. In fact, in the area around Puerto Cabuyal, traditionalist architecture built with thatch and bamboo like the Nueva Esperanza School is now more characteristic of luxurious eco-hostels than it is of regular villagers' housing.

Despite probably being costlier than regular modernist constructions, the Nueva Esperanza School was far less structurally resistant. If the school looked nice, it was not structurally firm—basically it was "eye candy" that seduced villagers and outsiders alike. By the own villagers' accounts, only about 20 percent of the Puerto Cabuyal constructions collapsed during the earthquake. The fact that the school was one of such a relatively small number of failing structures makes it evident that, comparatively speaking, it was structurally more vulnerable than the majority of the villagers' constructions. In fact, the housing structures that collapsed mostly did so because they were located on unstable land. Thus, the collapse of the school was arguably not due to low investment, since it was probably even higher than a regular investment, and also not due to unstable land conditions, since its site was unaffected. It is then safe to assume that the collapse was instead attributable to the formal and structural experimentation. Other constructions in Puerto Cabuyal are far more conservatively designed than this school—they are simply gabled structures—and most of them did not collapse.

It is important to note that the area of Puerto Cabuyal is well known in Ecuador for being located in a very active seismic zone. Indeed, it was in this area where most of the aftershocks following the April 2016 earthquake took place (IGEPN 2016). The land in Puerto Cabuyal is so unstable that, from long before the earthquake, landslides and earth fissures have caused great damage to the housing stock, as reported by the press (e.g., El Diario 2012). Considering this, it is to wonder why the Al Borde designers afforded themselves so much liberty to carry out formal and structural experimentations in this village. The answer is that experimentation is in fact at the core of Al Borde's practice. On the firm's own website, Al Borde is described first and foremost as a "collaborative and experimental studio" (n.d.b). Al Borde's David Barragán has explained the firm's vision in these terms: "If you are in your comfort zone, you will never try something different or know your limits" (quoted in Fixsen 2015, 49). That is indeed the meaning of *al borde* in the firm's name—to live "on the edge." As Al Borde's Esteban Benavides explained during the Venice Biennale to the architectural researcher Nicholas Anastasopoulos, "Al Borde symbolizes a condition of an unstable equilibrium, from which *one may fall at any moment*" (Anastasopoulos 2016, emphasis added).

However, *who falls?* Whose structures fall with those experiments? Al Borde's portfolio reveals just how frequently this firm experiments with unconventional architectural and structural design approaches in low-income communities throughout rural and urban Ecuador. The notion of taking risks and experimenting might be laudable as an abstract manifesto of innovation in architecture. However, it becomes quite perplexing if one considers the question of where and with/by whom those risks are taken. In the case of the Nueva Esperanza School, the Al Borde designers scorned a government program of school constructions on the grounds of their form (gabled structures), and their materials (cement and concrete blocks). They associated those constructions with prisons (see ArchDaily 2010). However, in that assessment they ignored the fact that such constructions are designed with codes in mind, and partly because of that, they tend to be formally conservative. The designers instead proposed a highly experimental and risky structure, blatantly disregarding building codes and basic safety design principles.

Al Borde's Nueva Esperanza School has been highly praised for its naturalism, presumed low cost, formal innovativeness, and beauty. However, this school was actually an expensive formal and structural experiment. Invoking the notion of sustainability, the Al Borde designers gave preference to conceptual musings while putting at risk the lives of children in a vulnerable community.

COLLAPSED SCHOOL IN NIGERIA

Located in Lagos, Nigeria, the Makoko Floating School was an iconic, triangular structure anchored in a lagoon that is crowded with thousands of stilt houses (fig. 12). They constitute the settlement of Makoko, "the world's biggest floating slum," whose estimated population is between 40,000 and 300,000 people (Ogunlesi 2016). The Makoko Floating School looked monumental in that environment; it was a calmly poetic piece that contrasted with the apparent chaos of countless houses, which looked tiny by comparison. The Floating School is perhaps Africa's most famous social design project. Its iconic aspect made it into one of the darlings of global media—most major outlets, from CNN to Al Jazeera, produced special reports on it. The school was designed by Kunlé Adeyemi, a Nigerian architect whose firm, NLÉ Works, is based in Amsterdam. The son of an architect, Adeyemi graduated from Princeton, and was later mentored by the prominent architect

Fig. 12. The Makoko Floating School in Lagos, Nigeria. (Photograph by Nathaniel Minor)

SUSTAINABILITY AND PRIVILEGE

Fig. 13. The many sustainability premises of the Makoko Floating School design, as described by Kunlé Adeyemi's firm, NLÉ (see NLÉ 2016a). These are indicated in a model of the school exhibited at the London Design Museum in 2014, and include (1) solar energy panels, (2) adaptability to different uses, (3) construction by local carpenters, (4) locally procured bamboo and wood, (5) promotion of low-carbon transportation forms, (6) natural climate-conditioning design, (7) waste-reduction technologies, (8) water and sewage treatment, and (9) recycled plastic barrels that create (10) a floating structure, which, according to the firm, is "invulnerable to flooding and storm surges" in an era of climate change. (Model photograph by B., Creative Commons, with author's designations added)

Rem Koolhaas. The school made Adeyemi a star in Euro-American architectural circles.

The Makoko School was intended to be an extension of another school, the Whanyinna Nursery and Primary School, which was established to provide children of Makoko with free education and was, at the time of Adeyemi's project, the only English-language school in the slum. The Whanyinna school was run by Noah Shemede, a fisherman and third-generation slum resident, and the only schooled child in a family of twenty-two. The funding for the school operations, including teachers' salaries, came from Shemede's own income and from outside donations. The school was physically deteriorated and flooded part of the year. This prompted Adeyemi to design a new school that floated, so it could also be used during the flooding season. On his firm's website, Adeyemi described the structure in these terms: "indigenous, ecological, local materials, self sustaining [sic], economical, adaptable, movable, safe" (NLÉ 2012, 9). Therefore, he concluded, the project "adheres to ideal standards of sustainable development" (2016a, 2) (fig. 13).

Speaking about the process of work, Adeyemi stated that the project was done "in collaboration with the Makoko Waterfront Community" (2016a, 2). As for the decision to build a school, he explained: "One of the first needs that the community expressed me was a school, and I volunteered to help design and build one" (Esiebo 2016). He added, with regard to the construction, "We started by working with the community, learning from the carpenters and local builders that have done most of the construction there" (2016).

The Floating School was finished in 2013. Soon after, the project began receiving awards. It was conferred the 2013 AR+D Award for Emerging Architecture, and it was shortlisted for the 2014 Design Museum's Design of the Year, as well as the 2016 Aga Khan Award for Architecture. Most notably, also in 2016 Adeyemi was awarded the Silver Lion Prize at the 15th Venice Biennale for the school—this was also the year in which Al Borde exhibited its Nueva Esperanza School at the Biennale.

Paradoxically, just as it was receiving praise in Venice, and as happened with Nueva Esperanza, the Makoko School collapsed (figs. 14 and 15). According to witnesses, it was a brutal crash that made the structure plummet within seconds. This was on a Tuesday morning, during class time. Fortunately, in this case also, there were no casualties among the children because the school was actually empty. In fact, throughout its existence, the Makoko Floating School had barely been used—some of the footage of classes being held in the school had been staged, a photographer would disclose later (Gaestel 2018). Interviewed after the collapse, Shemede, the head teacher, confirmed that the school had been used for only a few months and had then been vacated out of safety concerns (Fairs 2016; Gaestel 2018).

Fig. 14. The Makoko Floating School, before its collapse. (Photograph © Aga Khan Trust for Culture–Image ID: IAA120895)

Fig. 15. The Makoko Floating School, after its collapse. (Photograph by Allyn Gaestel, 2016)

Several reasons have been proposed to explain the collapse of the Makoko Floating School. In press interviews, the teacher and other residents argued that the school, including its foundation system, had not been strong enough (Fairs 2016; Okoroafor 2016). They observed how the structure would shake too violently when hit by seasonal storm winds (Oyewole 2016; Gaestel 2018). Because of that, they argued, the structure should have been only one story high, rather than three stories, as it was (Okoroafor 2016). Residents also pointed to the location of the school, which exposed it too frontally to windstorms (Oyewole 2016).

However, the main trigger of the collapse, both people inside and outside of Makoko tend to agree, was the mooring system. The mooring was insufficient to hold in place a structure that, because of its height, had a comparatively higher center of gravity and therefore wiggled too much, especially when it was frontally struck by the wind. Tomà Berlanda, an architect and educator who inspected the school when it was still standing and wrote a report for the Aga Khan Award nomination, observed that the mooring system had long been an issue (Berlanda 2016a). The system ultimately failed a few months prior to the collapse, which led the school to drift (2016b). Robert van Kats, a naval architect who had offered initial advice on the mooring, later told the press that his advice had been ignored. Furthermore, he explained, the school had been built on the basis of only general observations made by his firm during the conceptual phase, and without any detailed structural design work: "That is trial-and-error construction, in which you are taking a giant risk" (Van Zeijl 2016).

As for Adeyemi's response, he nonchalantly suggested that everything had been planned. In his version of the facts, the school had been "decommissioned" and had "come down" (NLÉ 2016b). Additionally, he said that moving the children out of the school had been planned as part of that "decommissioning" process (2016b). He also promised that an "upgraded" version would soon be built (2016b). Yet, as media outlets deepened their inquiry, a different picture emerged. Strongly disputing Adeyemi's version, the teacher said that it was he, not Adeyemi, who had made the decision to vacate the structure, acting on serious concerns from parents about their children's safety (Gaestel 2018). From the very beginning, as argued by both the teacher and his brother (a *baale* or traditional leader), people in Makoko had doubts about the safety and sturdiness of the Floating School (Van Zeijl 2016). In fact, the teacher said, he held classes there only because of the press, since journalists kept asking him why the school was not being used (2016). Still, the children were too scared and parents ended up warning the teacher "that they [would not] take it lightly with me" if the school collapsed (Oyewole 2016). It was acting on this warning that he decided to move the children out and back to Whanyinna, which was deteriorated but still operational. After the collapse, the teacher was relieved at having made the right decision: "If I had not, none of them would have escaped and I'm sure that I would currently be in jail" (2016).

Commenting on Adeyemi's plans to rebuild the Floating School, the teacher explained that the real need was instead to expand the existing school (2016). This was, in fact, the way in which the project had been initially envisioned—a simple, low-profile structure. This project had been initiated by Isi Etomi, another Nigerian architect; as she explained to the press, she had decided to partner with Adeyemi, but he ultimately took over the idea (Gaestel 2018). At some point in their collaborative drafting process, Adeyemi emerged with his artistic triangular design. As he became unwilling to compromise on a less elaborate and more affordable design, Etomi decided to step aside and no longer be involved with the project (Van Zeijl 2016; Gaestel 2018).

Referring to the ultimate fate of Adeyemi's project, the teacher vowed to rebuild the school on his own, stating that it would be just like the originally planned and much simpler structure. He emphasized: "One storey high" (Okoroafor 2016), and just like any other regular structure in Makoko: "We are turning to our centuries-long tradition of buildings on stilts. Not a single one of our huts was destroyed in the storm," he said (Welt 2016, slide 11). Additionally, the teacher said, his school would accommodate all of the students and not just some of them (Okoroafor 2016). Adeyemi's school accommodated only sixty children—less than a quarter of the Whanyinna school enrollment, which was over 250 (Oyewole 2016). Despite that, the Floating School was quite costly, roughly US$130,000 by Adeyemi's own estimate (Gaestel 2018). According to Etomi, that was about seven times the cost of the Whanyinna structure, while only accommodating such a small fraction of the student body (2018).

Responding to these charges, Adeyemi published a long piece providing his own explanation of the reasons for the collapse (NLÉ 2016b). Still short of accepting any responsibility, he actually blamed the teacher, arguing that the teacher had not performed any maintenance to the structure. Adeyemi also downplayed the teacher's criticism, arguing that the teacher was not the appropriate person to speak "for the community" (2016b, 5). This contradicted his earlier claims of having worked with "the community" as a unified group. Indeed, from press reports it is clear that there was a lack of consensus in Makoko about this project both before and after the collapse. When the school was still standing, some residents saw it as an individual initiative that had boosted the teacher's profile to the point that he had begun to conduct himself as "a local oga (boss)" (Gaestel 2018). This attitude presumably alienated some of the baales, who consequently did not feel compelled to participate in the project (2018). After the collapse, opinions also diverged; while parents, the teacher, and others opposed the school rebuilding, some of the baales favored the idea (Oyewole 2016). The reasons also differed; while, for instance, the teacher based his opposition on efficiency and safety, one magazine article suggests that the interest from one of the baales (the teacher's brother) in having the school rebuilt was possibly economic—to personally benefit from the small income brought in by tourists (Van Zeijl 2016).

Notably, the argument that Adeyemi made most strongly in his defense was that the Makoko School had only been a prototype, and as such it was not expected to last for too long (Okoroafor 2016; Goodell 2017). In fact, in early documents about the project Adeyemi had described it as a prototype (e.g., NLÉ 2012). However, Makoko residents apparently had not considered the project as such (Gaestel 2018). Just like in the Nueva Esperanza School, this case brings to light the problematic implications of experimenting on people in poverty. Papa Omotayo, a reputed Nigerian architect, observed that the Floating School "was supposed to be innovation, but now we're being told it was experimentation" (2018). Then he asked: "Can you experiment in a community like (Makoko) knowing things like budget, like social issues, and more importantly knowing that children are involved?" (2018).

In fact, if the Makoko Floating School was an experimental prototype, participants in this experiment were seemingly not given the opportunity to provide informed consent to be experimented upon. Referring to this issue, writer Allyn Gaestel made a chilling analogy between the Floating School and the historical resistance that Nigerians in poverty have had to being vaccinated, highlighting that such resistance comes from the fact that they have in the past been subject to experiments in which they have been the unknowing specimens (2018). Thus, in the end, also in this case the sore question that remains is: Why was a local designer carrying out untested construction experiments, and without informed consent, on members of a vulnerable community, prominently children?

EXPERIMENTING ON VENEZUELA'S INFORMAL RESIDENTS

Probably no social designer, local or otherwise, has offered more bluntly the rationale to justify experimenting on people in poverty than the Venezuelan Alfredo Brillembourg, one of the most celebrated social designers today. Brillembourg is the most visible figure of *Urban-Think Tank* (U-TT), a design practice he co-leads with the Austrian designer Hubert Klumpner. They won the Golden Lion Award for Best Project at the Venice Biennale in 2012.

U-TT's work focuses on slums, especially in South America, where these areas are called by various names, including *favelas* in Brazil and *barrios* in Venezuela. Some of the largest South American slums developed as land takeovers, mostly between the 1940s and 1970s. Because of that, even to this day residents regularly lack property titles, constructions are below code, and the neighborhoods as a whole lack proper public infrastructure, including water, roads, and community gathering areas. U-TT aims to address those issues with a focus on sustainability. They conduct community-based research to identify successful alternative technological strategies developed by slum residents. Brillembourg says: "Generally, we engage the community profoundly in discussions and meetings" (Navarro-Sertich 2011). On the basis of what they learn from this research, they propose a plethora of innovative solutions for those settlements, including green roofs, alternative water and sanitation technologies, and infrastructure for low-carbon transportation systems.

Brillembourg and Klumpner have explained these and many other ideas in a number of coauthored books and book chapters. These include a chapter in Marie Aquilino's book *Beyond Shelter,* where they report: "We are currently experimenting with using sections of a corrugated-metal roof as solar panels" (Brillembourg and Klumpner 2011, 132). In that chapter, they also describe one of their projects as exemplary of "a new experimental and empirical approach to architecture," given that it uses "simple solutions that *do not require engineering*" (139, emphasis added). Commenting on these and other innovative projects they have deployed in slums, they conclude: "Barrio cities are fertile ground for creative experimentation" (Brillembourg, Feireiss, and Klumpner 2005, 106).

A key question, however, is why? Why is it that architectural experiments like U-TT's are possible in spaces of poverty such as slums? Brillembourg confidently shared the key reason during the 14th Arquine conference in Mexico City just after having received the Venice Biennale's award. Explaining the origin and motivation of his work, he said:

I realized that the future of modern architecture, of experimentation, could be in the barrios, because barrios were blank zones in the city. These were zones with no land registration, cadaster, or zoning. That means, if you managed to intervene in a barrio, you could do *lo que te diera la gana*. (Arquine 2013, 2:20, emphasis added)[1]

The last sentence, which I have left partly without translation, is a complicated one. The expression "lo que te de la gana," which roughly translates as *whatever the hell you want*, is quite harsh, not only in English but also in Spanish. However, in the Spanish language it is both harsh and celebratory — it is a statement of daring. It is often used among people in privilege to celebrate the power they have to do anything whenever they want: *Voy a hacer lo que me de la gana.*

So, why is it that social designers, according to Brillembourg, can do "whatever the hell they want" in a slum? Why is it that slums can become zones of experimentation? As Brillembourg argues, it is because generally in those settlements people have no property titles or deeds that would give them legal standing if they were to oppose the architectural intervention.

Brillembourg formally stated this point in his best-known book, *Torre David* (2013), the bulk of which he cowrote with Klumpner. This book reports on a research project that earned U-TT the Venice Biennale award. The project is about the informal occupation of a 45-story building in Caracas popularly known as "Torre de David" (fig. 16). The name of this building, "David's Tower," refers to its original owner, David Brillembourg, a late relative of Alfredo Brillembourg. Construction of that building stopped in 1994 as a consequence of Venezuela's financial crisis, and in 2007 a group of about 750 homeless families saw in the unfinished structure an opportunity to provide housing for themselves and occupied it, deploying interesting systems of social organization and material resourcefulness to, for example, wall in

Fig. 16. The unfinished "Torre de David" (David's Tower), the site of the occupation documented by Alfredo Brillembourg and Hubert Klumpner in their 2013 book, *Torre David.* (Photograph by Eneas De Troya, Creative Commons)

the still open rooms and procure fresh water (fig. 17). Some of these families also started their own businesses such as small shops in the building (Brillembourg and Klumpner 2013).

In the book, Brillembourg and Klumpner highlight the Torre David occupants' resourcefulness, while paradoxically proposing their own innovative architectural designs for the occupied building. In fact, one of the most striking aspects of this book is how openly and explicitly Brillembourg and Klumpner advocate on behalf of using spaces of poverty such as this building occupation for architectural and other experimentations. Throughout the book they frequently invoke terms such as *experiment, laboratory,* and *test* to refer to the Torre David's setting. They explicitly describe the building occupation as "a laboratory for exploring and testing a utopian potential" (2013, 364), extending this observation to slums as whole, which they describe as "vibrant laboratories" (377).

Fig. 17. On the left, a view of the Torre David facade showing the residents' own built walls and finishes. (Photograph by Saul Briceño, Creative Commons)

Brillembourg and Klumpner's use of "laboratory" and related terminology is not limited to this book, but it is actually a staple of their work. They frequently use these terms in both their authored pieces (e.g., Brillembourg, Feireiss, and Klumpner 2005; Brillembourg and Klumpner 2010, 2011) and interviews (e.g., Frankfurt 2005; Ovink and Wierenga 2009; McGuirk 2014b; Frangie Mawad 2021). They have also published a magazine titled *SLUM Lab,* which was also the name of their former research project at Columbia University.

What type of "laboratory" are Brillembourg and Klumpner exactly referring to when they invoke this term? As made evident by the Torre David book, they are not using this term rhetorically. They specifically use "laboratory" in the sense of a place to carry out testing. They say: "Torre David affords architects and engineers a valuable context in which to test solutions that may prove appropriate for other projects in other parts of the world" (Brillembourg and Klumpner 2013, 350). Notably, in this book they extend an explicit invitation to architects, engineers, and companies to use the Torre David occupation to test approaches and products, explaining their rationale in these terms:

Torre David provides a setting for testing innovative solutions. It is a highly efficient laboratory, given its capacity to provide quick reactions and responses, revealing drawbacks or problems and enabling their on-site correction. (350–51)

Then, they explain that experimenting in the occupied building will afford companies the opportunity to emerge in the market with a fully developed product:

Rather than waiting for the marketplace to reveal the inadequacies of a new solution and, at best, having to issue a recall or, at worst, having their reputations and bottom-line eroded, private companies can take a system or product swiftly through development and enter the market with a proven solution. (351)

Thus, Brillembourg and Klumpner's laboratory proposal is unambiguous. In their view, the occupation of Torre David is a "highly efficient laboratory" for private companies to test innovative products because the occupants' reactions and responses to the tested products would quickly reveal these products' potential limitations and problems. Once those are identified, a private company would then be able to make changes and test its products, once again among the building occupants. Brillembourg and Klumpner continue by touting the advantages to companies in carrying out product testing and development in the Torre David setting: The companies would not risk entering the market with an inadequate product because all the defects would have already been identified through testing and retesting among the building's dwellers. In turn, this would spare these companies from the risk of having to issue a recall; it would then protect the companies' reputation and business, as the companies would emerge in the market with an already "proven solution."

To make their point even more unequivocal, Brillembourg and Klumpner go so far as to provide examples of companies that could carry out this type of product testing and development operations in Torre David. They volunteer the specific name of one company, the Schindler group, a Swiss manufacturer of elevators. They identify this company given that, at the time of the occupation, the building still had no elevators. Besides this example, they also express their "hope" that other kinds of companies will carry out product testing and development in Torre David, listing a few: "lighting, ventilation, security, plumbing, and other essential systems and fixtures" (350).

Thus, the message by Brillembourg and Klumpner in the Torre David book is clear to the point of bluntness: People in conditions of poverty can be experimented upon for the benefit of the construction industry. However, this is far from being the only public appeal that these designers have made for professionals and companies to experiment on people in poverty. In an interview for another book, they outline this idea in similar terms:

We propose that cities should designate areas of at least a square kilometre each that would serve as "laboratories" for testing dynamic zoning, programming, design, and construction. These zones could serve as well as educational and social incubators to motivate communities, and as centres of experimental design, with pilot projects and prototypes that represent best practices. (Ovink and Wierenga 2009, 222)

In light of these calls, Brillembourg and Klumpner's Torre David book reads as a celebration of these designers' having apparently found one of those laboratory zones ready-made for their use. In fact, the notion that the Torre David occupation was U-TT's own laboratory is clearly stated on the firm's project website: "Where some only see a failed development project, U-TT has conceived it as a laboratory for the study of informal vertical communities" (U-TT 2012). On the website, they also restate their appeal to professionals to experiment in sites of poverty: "U-TT issues a call to arms to their fellow architects to see in the informal settlements of the world a potential for innovation and experimentation" (2012).

Very interestingly, in that "call to arms" they invoke as the main justification that of sustainability, specifically, "with the goal of putting design in the service of a more equitable and sustainable future" (2012). Thus, the powerful notion of sustainability is here directly invoked to justify experimenting on people in poverty.

U-TT's Torre David was actually at the center of another major online debate on imperialism in social design following the one initiated by Bruce Nussbaum, which I described in chapter 1. In 2014, the writer Dan Hancox published in *The Architectural Review* a strongly worded critique of U-TT's work titled "Enough Slum Porn: The Global North's Fetishisation of Poverty Architecture Must End" (Hancox 2014). In this piece, Hancox focused on yet another aspect of U-TT's Torre David project, which is that of knowledge. He asked: If Torre David is a "research and design project" (as U-TT usually describes it), then whose design is it? (2014, 22)

In fact, as an architectural project Torre David is quite peculiar, insofar as U-TT did not take any part in the residents' occupation of the building. What they did was to document the occupation in such a way that, as Hancox notices, they virtually appropriated it, by producing plans, diagrams, and photographs (recruiting an award-winning architectural photographer for the task) and with that material producing not only the book, but also exhibits, conference presentations, and even a film (fig. 18). As a result, Torre David nowadays often appears more directly connected to the names of U-TT's Brillembourg and Klumpner than to those who conceived the

Fig. 18. Some of the material produced by Alfredo Brillembourg and Hubert Klumpner's U-TT about the Torre David occupation. From the top: the film *Torre David*, web site of TorreDavid .com, the book *Torre David: Informal Vertical Communities*, and Torre David installation at the 2012 Venice Biennale. (*Top:* U-TT, Creative Commons; *center left:* screenshot from Torre-David.com; *bottom:* Photograph by Nico Saieh, NicoSaieh.cl)

occupation—namely, the residents. In fact, Hancox notes, the firm went as far as to register the domain name TorreDavid.com, which they actively used during the time of the occupation to promote their own work. On the other hand, as the website shows, the residents, who were the primary authors of the ideas that U-TT was relying upon, were not given proper credit as such.

Thus, as Hancox's critique points out, Brillembourg and Klumpner appropriated the residents' work and the occupation ended up being more helpful to them than to the residents. Indeed, Torre David propelled these designers' careers to the very top of the social and architectural design scenes. The residents, on the other hand, were ultimately evicted from the building. The eviction took place in 2014, less than two years after Brillembourg and Klumpner had won the Biennale award for their Torre David project, and when they were still featuring this project in other exhibits and public presentations.

In his article, Hancox highlighted yet another term that Brillembourg and Klumpner frequently use to explain their work, *exploration,* equating it to the Spanish Empire's plundering of Venezuela's riches through its explorers in colonial times. Following this metaphor, just as the Spanish imperial troops did in the past, Brillembourg and Klumpner arguably capitalized on the results of their exploration by offering them as their own firm's design approach. In fact, they say: "We offer the kit—and the concept of incremental, individual improvement within the existing fabric of the slum" (Brillembourg and Klumpner 2011, 136). They add: "The kit can either be a product in itself . . . or a knowledge base" (136). Hancox concluded: "It's hard not to see this practice as fundamentally parasitical, feeding off the toil, risk and enterprise of the building's thousands of slum-dwellers—and devoicing them" (Hancox 2014, 22).

Just as in the case of the Nussbaum debate, strong rebuttals to Hancox's article and in support of Brillembourg and Klumpner soon poured out in architectural media. Among the most prominent was a letter to the magazine's editor written by the architectural critic Justin McGuirk, author of *Radical Cities* (2014b), a celebrated book that includes a chapter highly laudatory of Brillembourg. McGuirk was colisted as a winner of the U-TT Venice Biennale award for his role as the curator of the firm's exhibition. In his letter, McGuirk focused on an observation Hancox had also made about the predominance of white male viewpoints in U-TT's work. Calling this observation "knee-jerk political correctness of a simple-minded kind" (2014a), McGuirk aimed to disprove it by highlighting how Alfredo Brillembourg is a Venezuelan.

Another response came from the architect Charlotte Skene Catling, writing also in *The Architectural Review.* In her piece, called "Damned If You Do, Damned If You Don't: What Is the Moral Duty of the Architect?" (2014), Skene Catling pointed to the dilemma that architects often face: "Architects are ridiculed if they take a moral position, and attacked if they don't" (2014). After this sensible observation, Skene Catling embarked upon an impassioned defense of U-TT by targeting Hancox's main point, that of equating U-TT's exploration with imperial exploitation. To disprove this point, she, too, observed that perhaps Hancox was unaware "of the Venezuelan origins of U-TT" (2014).

Thus, Skene Catling implied, since Alfredo Brillembourg is a Venezuelan, he should be exempt from accusations of imperialism. For the sake of the argument this point is acceptable. However, the question remains: Does this make any difference? Does the fact that Alfredo Brillembourg is not an "imperialist" make any difference in how he regards the subjects of his research and design work? Alfredo Brillembourg's good intentions are beyond doubt. However, it is necessary to consider his bragging about being able to do whatever he wants in informal settlements because the residents of those settlements usually have no land titles. It is necessary to consider the way in which he insistently invites other building professionals and companies to experiment on those residents. Lastly, it is necessary to consider the extent to which Brillembourg's U-TT work relies upon the appropriation of knowledge that residents in poverty have developed for their own survival. By contrast, U-TT gives back to these residents comparatively little in exchange for their knowledge, and literally nothing in the case of Torre David. Thus, it is clear that also in this case being a local designer does not necessarily represent any advantage to the subjects of a social design intervention.

DISPLACEMENT OF INFORMAL RESIDENTS IN COLOMBIA

I will devote more space to the last two study cases because they are more complex. These are urban-scale projects that involved a higher degree of community engagement than those described above. The first is the Biblioteca España, a library in Medellín, Colombia (fig. 19). The Biblioteca España is located in the barrio of Santo Domingo in *Comuna 1,* a settlement formed by several barrios that originated as an expansive land occupation in the 1960s. Along with the similarly formed Comuna 2, Comuna 1 is located in the Zona Nororiental (Northeastern Zone), which concentrates the greatest levels of urban poverty in Medellín. Because of that, these two comunas were selected in 2004 as sites for a pilot project to implement an innovative urban and social development approach named *social urbanism.* The Northeastern Zone Project aimed to benefit about 150,000 residents of the barrios near the library and/or the transportation infrastructure that led to it. The library opened in 2007 and was given the name Biblioteca España ("Library

Fig. 19. The Biblioteca España, shortly after its opening in 2007. (Photograph by SajoR, Creative Commons)

of Spain"), to acknowledge some financial contribution from the Spanish government and also to honor the king and queen of Spain, who visited the barrio for the building's ribbon-cutting ceremony.

Social urbanism is based on the premise of using high architectural design as the driver of social improvement in slums. This approach takes social design to an urban scale through the building of a number of iconic architectural pieces in key points of slums, including sites that are highly visible, such as is the case with this library. These projects get roughly connected through innovative transportation systems such as cable cars and electric escalators in addition to a system of trains, trolley cars, and double-decker buses (fig. 20). Because of their comprehensiveness and scale, these projects are often referred to in Medellín as *mega-proyectos,* or megaprojects.

The main proponents of social urbanism were Sergio Fajardo, the mayor of Medellín between 2004 and 2007 (and whose father was a prominent local architect),[2] and Alejandro Echeverri, an architect who became Fajardo's director of urban projects and the person in charge of deploying the social urbanism project. The Biblioteca España, which spearheaded this program, was designed by another Colombian architect, Giancarlo Mazzanti, who won the commission in an open competition. Medellín's social urbanism project took place between 2004 and 2011, spanning the tenure of two mayors, Sergio Fajardo and Alonso Salazar. The latter had been Fajardo's secretary of

Fig. 20. The cable car line to the Biblioteca España, which is seen at the top-center.

government and continued his agenda of social design constructions while adding new structures. Although in later administrations social urbanism was renamed and received some (comparatively minor) changes to its focus, it became the city's overarching social and urban development approach.

Just as in the case of Brillembourg and Klumpner's U-TT, social urbanism relies heavily upon the notion that certain areas of the city are viable laboratories for experimentation. Mónica Guerra, a scholar of Medellín's social urbanism history, explains that this approach was conceived within the *Laboratorio de Arquitectura y Urbanismo* (Architecture and Urbanism Laboratory) at the Universidad Pontificia Bolivariana (UPB), one of the city's top private universities (Guerra 2014, 56). Alejandro Echeverri, who was then a professor at UPB, says that the urban analysis that yielded the information for the Northeastern Zone Project was done following the method of Barcelona's *Laboratorio de Urbanismo* (Urban Laboratory) at the Universitat Politècnica de Catalunya (Echeverri and Orsini 2010).

The notion that Medellín is a laboratory has since been widely invoked in official contexts. For instance, in 2011 the City of Medellín (as in the mayor's office)[3] published *Laboratorio Medellín* (Medellín Laboratory), a UN-Habitat-led study with lessons learned from ten areas of action in social urbanism (Alcaldía 2011b). Also, the City's International Cooperation Agency has a program named *Medellín Lab* (in English), which includes study visits for international academics, practitioners, and government officers. In one of the main events of that program, this office in 2017 organized along with the World Bank, USAID, and the Rockefeller Foundation a "living laboratory" for international experts to study Medellín's urban practices.

Unlike the other social design experiments I have referred to, the experiment emerging from the Medellín laboratory was far more exhaustive. It aimed to learn from previous experiments, in Barcelona, Rio, and Bogotá, and it approached its goals with great rigor. To materialize the experiment, the City of Medellín reshaped its planning office to operate as an independent company following a corporate business model. The company is called EDU, *Empresa de Desarrollo Urbano* (Urban Development Company), and it oversees the planning, design, and execution of the social urbanism project. (For convenience, I will still use "the City" when referring to this institution.) The City of Medellín also committed a huge amount of funding to make its experiment work. The construction alone of the Biblioteca España cost 15 billion Colombian pesos (roughly US$6.8 million in 2007). Attesting to the experiment's apparent success, in 2013 Medellín was named the world's most innovative city from a list of two hundred contenders drawn up by the Washington-based Urban Land Institute.

The Biblioteca España remains the most famous piece of Medellín's social urbanism. It is a monumental structure, striking because of its shape and size, which contrast with the much simpler and smaller structures around it (fig. 21). Similar principles of contrasting monumentality would later be employed by Kunlé Adeyemi in Makoko—Medellín's mayor, Sergio Fajardo, was, incidentally, a member of the jury that awarded Adeyemi the Venice

Fig. 21. The Biblioteca España in its context. Notice the contrast with the buildings surrounding it.

Biennale prize. Giancarlo Mazzanti describes his design, consisting of three different structures of irregular polyhedral shape, as "artificial rocks" that metaphorize the rocky mountainous landscape surrounding the city (Mazzanti 2009, 21). The structures have also been described as "three black sapphires" (Semana 2017). The library is a tremendously iconic project, and Mazzanti enthusiastically explained his rationale for this in *Maravillas de Colombia* (Wonders of Colombia) (Townsley 2013), a documentary about the project that was coproduced by the Discovery Channel. Mazzanti said: "This project is image. . . . The visual [part] is fundamental. It is what makes the community [want] to appropriate it" (2013, 31:37).

In addition to its innovative shape, one of the Biblioteca España's most attractive features is its facade. To emphasize its metaphorical association with the mineral realm, Mazzanti's design specified that it had to be built with black tiles from a very specific quarry, located about three hundred miles away. The tiles were affixed to a self-supporting envelope that was, in turn, attached to an internal cuboidal structure, as if it were floating around it.

For the social urbanism Northeastern Zone Project, and with a specific mention of the Biblioteca España, in 2009 Fajardo and Echeverri were awarded the Curry Stone Foundation's Design Prize, one of social design's highest honors. In 2013 Echeverri was awarded the Harvard University Green Prize in Urban Design, one of the foremost awards in that field. For the library design, in 2008 Mazzanti was awarded the First Prize in the Architectural Design Category at the Pan-American Architecture Biennial in Quito, and the Best Architectural Work Prize at the Ibero-American Architecture Biennial in Lisbon. In 2011, both the architectural model and a site sketch drawn by Mazzanti became part of the New York MoMA's permanent collection. Other material related to the library's design was later acquired by the Carnegie Museum of Art in Pittsburgh. Also, and just like the Nueva Esperanza and Makoko schools, this project was exhibited along with other work by Mazzanti at the 2016 Venice Biennale.

Notwithstanding its many awards and recognitions, in 2015 the library had to be closed due to construction problems. It was first closed partially and then, in 2016, it was cordoned off and the building was emptied. The closure was initially due to water leaks from the roof and walls, which were so serious that one resident hyperbolized to local newspaper *El Mundo* that on a rainy day being in the library felt like experiencing the biblical Flood (Zapata 2017). The water leaks weakened the supporting layers of the facade, causing portions of the tiling to fall off,[4] injuring residents as they passed by (2017) (figs. 22 and 23). To investigate this issue, in 2014 the City of Medellín commissioned a building assessment by the Universidad Nacional, Colombia's largest public research institution. On recommendation from the univer-

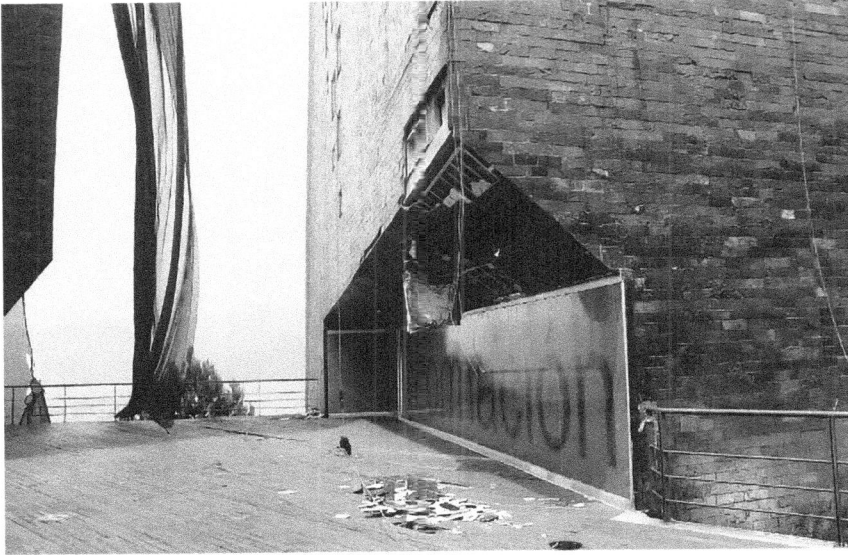

Fig. 22. The Biblioteca España's falling tiles in 2015. (Photograph by Jhon Alexander Chica Yara, Creative Commons)

Fig. 23. One of the library's three structures, closed and covered with tarp, 2015.

sity, all the tiles were removed in order to rebuild the facade. However, as this work was done, other construction defects emerged; they were so serious that ultimately one of the three polyhedral structures had to be fully demolished. As for the remaining two, they required such deep structural overhaul that they were poised to be demolished almost completely as well, according to the

Fig. 24. The Biblioteca España in 2008, a year after completion. (Photograph by Albeiror24, Creative Commons)

Fig. 25. The Biblioteca España, partially demolished a decade after completion.

City's secretary of infrastructure (Jiménez 2019). As of this writing (2021), the two structures were still standing, although half-demolished (figs. 24 and 25).

With regard to reconstruction costs, one of the university's engineers told the press that their evaluation had also suggested changing the stone of the facade to another material, but the City replied that the structure had to be rebuilt just as it was originally (Trujillo 2017). The reasons given were that the project had received many important awards and the building documents were already in museums. Thus, in the view of the City, in addition to a rebuild, the structure basically required the kind of restoration work needed for a work of art. The budgeted cost of the reconstruction turned more than twice as much as the original construction cost (see Alcaldía 2021)—this, despite the fact that the goal of rebuilding the structure exactly as it was originally was partially dropped.

Just as the library was crumbling, in the *Maravillas de Colombia* documentary Mazzanti passionately advocated taking the types of risks that led to the problematic outcomes. He said: "In the risk there is the possibility of building a better country" (Townsley 2013, 1:02). By making such an appeal, Mazzanti embodied the architectural designer's ideal—someone who is not afraid of taking risks by experimenting with forms. He took this ideal further by embracing the commendable goal of bettering his own country, thus further embodying the archetypal vision of a local social designer.

However, the question posed earlier becomes relevant also in this case: Who is supposed to bear the risks that the local designer decides to take? As I have discussed, children faced most of the risk in Al Borde's Nueva Esperanza and Adeyemi's Makoko, while entire families were unknowingly volunteered to be exposed to risk in Brillembourg's Torre David. The result of applying the latter's premise of capitalizing on the vulnerabilities of people in poverty in order to experiment on them is that, in the worst-case scenario, a structure can collapse as the result of such experiment, as was the case with Nueva Esperanza and Makoko. In the best-case scenario, exemplified by the Biblioteca España, it is a costly endeavor because those structures may end up being defective as a consequence of the experimentation—they may even have to be rebuilt, thus greatly increasing their already high economic cost.

The Human Cost of a Construction Experiment

However, in the case of the Biblioteca there was also considerable human cost. In the documentary, Mazzanti recounts how, after winning the competition and prior to breaking ground, he arrived in the barrio of Santo Domingo only to find that a group of residents had chained themselves to a utility pole at the construction site (Townsley 2013, 10:42). They were on a hunger strike to protest the library project. Mazzanti describes this event with a disdainful smile as if to emphasize how absurd it was that people were protesting the construction of a library.

But why were they protesting? Mazzanti continues: "Because five houses had been demolished to make the library" (2013, 10:52). This number is incorrect. In reality, a total of 118 houses were demolished for the construction, according to Adolfo Taborda, the leader of the residents' protest, in an interview for this book. Taborda's account is supported by a number of documents, including an official act by the City of Medellín that describes exactly the location of the plots required for the project (see Alcaldía 2004).

Such large-scale displacement of residents had a strong impact on social relationships in the barrio. In the *El Mundo* article, a resident is quoted as lamenting how "some of the neighbors from her whole life were forced to leave the barrio" in order to make room for the library (Zapata 2017). The article stresses that these residents did not have the option to decide whether they could stay. A story oft-repeated today in Santo Domingo is how, among those who were displaced, four elders died *de pena moral*—of depression, after having been forced to leave the neighborhood they had helped found.

Although the City of Medellín did offer to buy residents' properties rather than displace them outright for the construction, for the cost estimate it used an appraiser who valued the houses at an extremely low price. It was as little as one-fifth of the market value and in some cases even less, as Taborda explained to me. Furthermore, he added, during the negotiation some City officers threatened residents that if they refused to sell, their houses would be expropriated by eminent domain laws. Most people succumbed to this pressure and accepted the little money they were being offered. However, others resisted, and those included the ones who went on the hunger strike.

Notably, one of the aspects of the project that the hunger strikers and their supporters were protesting was that it constituted "imposition" (see Townsley 2013, 11:13). According to residents interviewed for a Universidad de Antioquia graduate research piece (Bornacelly and Rocha 2014), the library project was imposed on them despite the fact that their priorities were different. One of the interviewees, a well-respected elderly woman who was one of the barrio founders, said: "The administration has never really asked the community whether this library . . . could have been what the community needed" (2014, 4:39). Jorge Corrales, by then a member of the Junta de Acción Comunal,[5] the barrio's main community organization, added: "We were never asked what projects we wanted for the barrio, or in what way we wanted them to be [done]" (13:34).

This is surprising because one of the main claims that Fajardo and Echeverri have often made about social urbanism is that it is a highly participatory approach. However, it is possible to know from residents who partook in the library's participatory activities how participation was actually implemented in this project. For instance, a youth student leader interviewed for the *Maravillas* documentary explained that youth leaders were asked questions such as whether they wanted the library to have computers and books, and what colors and spaces would they like the library to have (Townsley 2013, 32:55). Thus, they seemingly participated, but about aspects that were either trivial or not decisive. In our interview, Adolfo Taborda rejoined: "Participation is when also the community has a *decisional* capacity; [when] there is no imposition. Here there was an imposition."

The decisional aspect Taborda referred to was whether the social infrastructure project that the City intended to build should be a library or something else. Although this question was asked of residents, the participatory process used by the City of Medellín's officers to arrive at an answer was actually quite constrained. Jorge Corrales explained how this was done in another interview for a community journalism report (Lara et al. [2011?]). City officers did consult residents about what type of project should be built, without specifically mentioning the library. However, the City had already decided unilaterally that it would be a library, so the officers conducted the participatory process in such a way that ensured residents would exactly say that they required a library. Corrales explained this process using a powerful metaphor:

They come with workshops basically tricking the community, saying: "What do you want that comes on a little stick and you lick it?" But I have to be the one who says it: "a popsicle." The EDU won't say it. So, the community said "a library": "A library is needed." ([2011?], 3:30)

That is, the City officers conducted the process in such a way that they progressively constrained the discussion until the only alternative left for residents was to say that they required the "popsicle"; that is, the library. However, the officers still made sure that residents were the ones who said the words, so as to officially claim that the library had been a request from residents.

As for the residents' priorities, not only was the library not their main priority but, in fact, a library was not even on their list of priorities. The reason was partly that there was already a system of community libraries working successfully in the comuna—the City could have helped strengthen those community-based initiatives rather than building a new gigantic structure. The residents' community development plan, which the City knew about, listed their priorities as: housing legalization and improvement, unemployment and income, health access, and addressing the high cost of utilities (Corporación Con-vivamos 2005).

According to Sergio Fajardo, the purpose of the hunger strike was to stop the construction of the library. The protest did not succeed, and that was the inauspicious beginning of an unequal struggle in Medellín's low-income comunas of residents trying to defend their housing rights in the face of social urbanism's advance. In fact, evictions to make room for social design infrastructure are presently the greatest threat that Medellín's low-income comunas face, according to Elkin Pérez, a planning professional who was raised and still lives in the Northeastern Zone. Pérez was the general coordinator of a 2005 comprehensive community-based development plan that identified the priority needs mentioned above. He said in a 2015 presentation: "The number one threat is mainly the intervention with megaprojects in the territory." This is a very serious assessment because these comunas face many threats, including gang violence related to drug trafficking. The megaprojects are a greater threat, he argued, "because it permanently expels and threatens [people]" (2015). In other words, none of the other threats displaces people as systematically and constantly as Medellín's social urbanism.

Displacement

It could be argued that displacing about six hundred people[6] for a social design project that aimed to benefit 150,000 amounts to little. However, the comuna residents' concern, as expressed by Pérez, comes from the fact that this was a displacement caused for the construction of only *one* building, while dozens of libraries, cable car stations, community centers, and other massive public infrastructure pieces have been built and continue to be built since the construction of the Biblioteca España. There exists a plethora of housing rights movements formed by residents of Comuna 1 and other low-income Medellín comunas, who seriously question this aggressive program of infrastructure construction in their settlements.[7] Even though among these movements there is a general appreciation for the social investment that the City of Medellín is making in the comunas, their main objection to social urbanism is its great focus on urban infrastructure at the cost of housing. First, huge investments are being made in that infrastructure while comparatively little is invested in housing, and second, these architectural megaprojects pose a great threat of displacement (fig. 26).

To understand these arguments, it is critical to consider that by the time of the Northeastern Zone Project, the two comunas where this project took place were faced with the greatest housing need in Medellín. According to a life quality survey carried out by the City of Medellín in 2006, the year when the construction of the library started, *all* of the housing in these comunas was either low- or very low-income housing (Alcaldía 2007). This area was

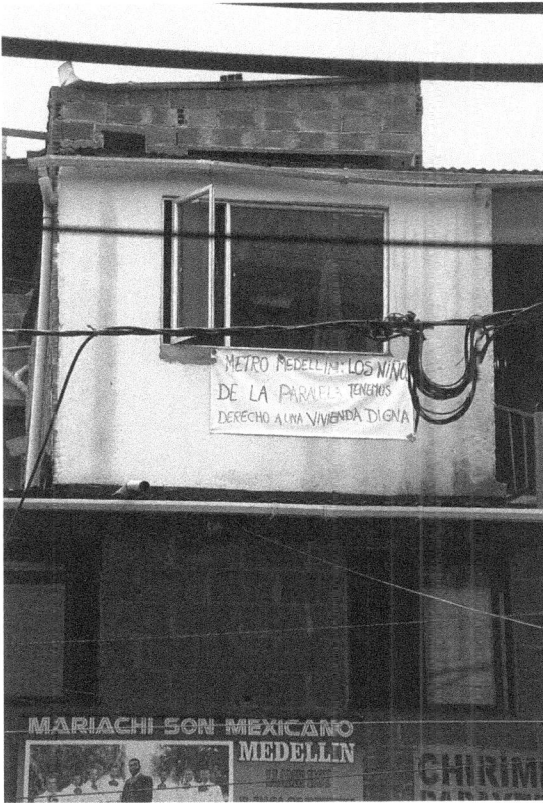

Fig. 26. A resident's sign near one of the cable car stations leading to the Biblioteca España, reminding the City about their children's right to dignified housing.

also among the most densely populated, and as such it had one of the highest indicators of overcrowding in Medellín—out of the roughly 56,000 housing units in the two comunas, over 11,000 units were occupied by between six and ten people or more. The conditions of some of the existing housing were also quite poor, which explains the "housing improvement" component of the residents' priorities mentioned above. A little over 1,000 houses in these comunas were shacks built out of materials such as mud, cane, or undressed wood, and 130 were built out of plain trash discard. In a little over 350 cases, people were living on the bare soil. Even more shocking, over five hundred families did not have a toilet at all. Granted, some of these numbers seem negligible when compared to the total housing units. However, when one imagines a sophisticated library being built in an environment where there could exist an overcrowded house made out of trash-collected materials with a bare soil floor and without a toilet, the outrageousness of this contrast to

Fig. 27. Low-income housing in the vicinity of the Biblioteca España. The houses right below the structure are built with recycled bamboo mats and discarded boards, which the residents also use to cover the bare soil floor.

the eyes of residents becomes quite understandable. In fact, as late as of 2018, over a decade after the construction of the library, there still existed houses in some of the conditions described above, right in the vicinity of the library (figs. 27 and 28).

Despite those dismaying levels of housing need, Fajardo and Echeverri's social urbanism project did not address the comunas' housing problem; social urbanism was largely about building public infrastructure. Out of the roughly twenty-six social urbanism interventions in the Northeastern Zone Project,[8] only *one* was a housing project, the rest being mostly public use buildings (like the library) and parks. Thus, disregarding the fact that the greatest need in the zone was housing, social urbanism did not aim to create more of it, but instead massively demolished houses to build public architectural and urban infrastructure. Fajardo says proudly that the Northeastern Zone Project "generated" 125,000 m² (30 acres) of public space (Escobar 2008, 174). However, this space was not generated out of nothing—it was

Fig. 28. This house, also in the vicinity of the Biblioteca España is built with discarded materials (tin, boards, pallets, plastic), with boards also covering the bare soil. Neither this nor the structures in fig. 27 are directly supplied with fresh water, so residents have resorted to attaching PVC tubes to their neighbors' pipes or to community piping.

generated out of the act of demolishing houses. To have an idea of the scale of that demolition, in these comunas the space so generated is equivalent to an area occupied by between 1,500 and 2,000 houses.[9]

In addition, on the comparatively few occasions in which Fajardo and Echeverri's social urbanism did concern housing, the greater focus was still on displacement. The two main housing-related projects in Fajardo and Echeverri's era of social urbanism were called Juan Bobo (the Northeastern Zone's only housing project) and Moravia. In both cases, families were resettled. After these resettlements, the first area was turned into a landscaped water stream, and the second became an urban garden with a few architectural art pieces like the library. Although social urbanism promoters claim to much fanfare that the families in Juan Bobo were resettled in situ (moved into apartments within the same barrio), this project included only about one hundred families. By comparison, in Moravia social urbanism ended up displacing 2,500 families far away, to the mountainous western periphery of Medellín (fig. 29). Notably, a number of academic pieces written by Medellín-based scholars has provided field-based evidence that, in both cases, these resettlements have made the displaced families actually poorer (see Mejía 2009, 2012; Mena 2011; Correa et al. 2013; Peláez 2013; Duque 2015).

The logic used by the City of Medellín to justify the Moravia displacement was that the land was unsafe for housing. Declaring slums high-risk areas for construction has been a frequently invoked justification in the social urbanism project of removing families to create parks and iconic architec-

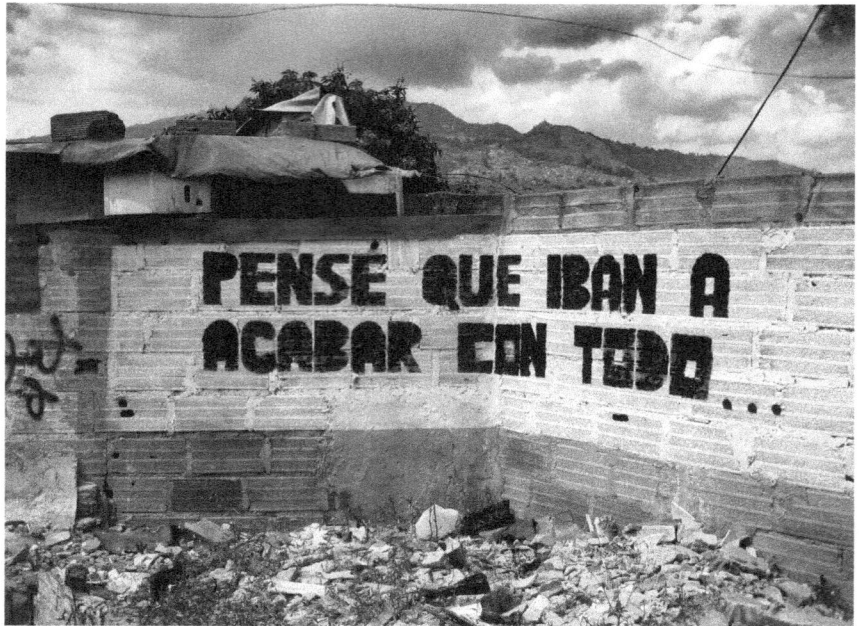

Fig. 29. A residents' mural protesting the demolition of houses for the construction of social urbanism infrastructure in Moravia, in 2010. The text reads, "I thought they were going to destroy everything": an ironic comment on a surviving wall. (Photograph by Adriana Navarro-Sertich)

tural infrastructure. As such, it was also invoked in the case of the Biblioteca España. One of the first arguments that the City made to justify the displacement of families for the construction of this project was that they were living in a high-risk zone—specifically, a geologically unstable zone that was prone to mudslides. It is true that mudslides are a common occurrence in Medellín's hillside comunas, and they do lead to the collapse of houses. However, as Adolfo Taborda highlighted in our interview, residents who were about to be displaced did notice the paradox that a gargantuan structure such as the Biblioteca España was to be built right on the same high-risk site as their houses. The City's response was that the issue of the site's unstable land would be solved by building an appropriate supporting infrastructure—in fact, a good portion of the multi-million-dollar investment in this library was used for the construction of deep foundations (see Townsley 2013). This response from the City prompted a remark that later became a central theme among the residents' housing rights movements: these areas are not high-risk as much as they are high-cost. The City of Medellín is willing to make a costly infrastructural investment for the construction of sophisticated architectural pieces, but not to help improve low-income residents' housing. In fact, some of the most upscale neighborhoods in Medellín are also located on those hillsides alongside barrios like those of the Northeastern Zone. However, mudslides are not a major issue in those upscale neighborhoods because they have actually received the required infrastructural investment.

Green Gentrification

In connection to these cost-related issues, the Northeastern Zone Project also triggered an issue of indirect displacement, since many of the barrios' poorest residents had to move out, given that they could no longer afford the rising cost of living in these physically improved neighborhoods. As the Medellín-based housing rights activist and researcher Juan Fernando Zapata observes, the construction of those architectural pieces significantly raises the cost of land and, with that, the cost of housing (Zapata 2014). The impact of those rising costs is greater on the most vulnerable families: "It must be considered that even the slightest increase in living costs means for these families to have to choose between paying [bills] or eating" (2014, 10). As Zapata also notices, the impact is not only on owners but also on renters, which in Medellín's low-income comunas are a considerable group. In the barrios of the Northeastern Zone Project, at the time of this project, about one-third of the families were renters (Alcalcía 2007). As their rent increased, many had to move out to Medellín's distant peripheries or to neighboring towns, which were the only places left with relatively affordable rents (Pérez 2015).

Thus, in addition to the direct displacement, the Northeastern Zone Project also unleashed a process of gentrification. This happened not only at the level of housing, but also of business. One of the key premises of social urbanism is that iconic architectural pieces such as the Biblioteca España economically reactivate neighborhoods. This seems apparent in the case of the Biblioteca España, since on the main street that leads to it, there exists now a quite active commercial zone. However, the narrative of economic success hides the fact that a significant number of those business owners are new to the neighborhood, according to Elkin Pérez (2015). The iconic architectural project actually attracted commercial entrepreneurs who bought residents out and established new businesses in the area. Today, the biggest businesses in that area are actually owned by newcomers, according to Adolfo Taborda. Thus, in the end the displacement from the Biblioteca España project went beyond only the direct displacement of construction; it was also indirect, since the project itself unleashed a process of gentrification at different levels.

Among Medellín's low-income comuna residents there remains great concern about the displacement caused by a vast program of social design constructions such as social urbanism. Presently, one of the greatest sources of anxiety among residents is an ecological restoration project called *The*

Green Belt. This is an ambitious project to surround Medellín's mountainous periphery with a network of natural preserves and parks that, by looking at renderings produced by the City of Medellín's architects, will feature even more iconic architectural pieces and no housing (see EDU 2012). Indeed, this megaproject is part of a strategy explicitly outlined in BIO 2030, the City of Medellín's master plan (overseen by Echeverri) to restrict the expansion of low-income hillside barrios (see Alcaldía 2011a, 136–42) (fig. 30).

Notably, in order to justify this containment project the master plan explicitly describes these barrios as *unsustainable* (34–36). The Green Belt has been presented by the City of Medellín as a project to protect the hills'

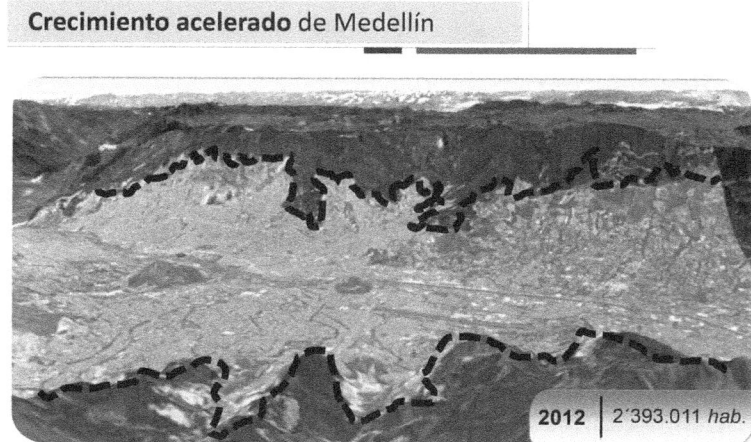

Crecimiento acelerado de Medellín

2012 | 2'393.011 *hab.*

Habitando laderas y quebradas de **alto riesgo**.

Jardín
Circunvalar de Medellín

edu
Medellín
todos por la vida
Alcaldía de Medellín

Fig. 30. *Top:* A slide from a City of Medellín's presentation about the Green Belt, indicating with bold strokes the purpose of this project, namely to contain the expansion of low-income hillside barrios. *Bottom:* A rendering, also from the City, showing how the "belt" containment is to be achieved: by building high architectural pieces and other infrastructure that excludes housing. (Illustrations by the City of Medellín)

SUSTAINABILITY AND PRIVILEGE

water resources, biodiversity, and forests because otherwise, the appeal continues, by 2030 Medellín will be unsustainable (EDU 2013). Sustainability was also presented as a "superior goal" in another urban plan from the City, the development plan for the period 2016–19 (Alcaldía 2016, 44). One of the focus areas of this plan was environmental stewardship, and it included a program called *Green Infrastructure: Generation, Conservation, and Upkeeping of Green Spaces* (346). The Green Belt project fell within that program component. Thus, the high ideal of environmental sustainability has been explicitly and widely invoked by the City of Medellín to justify the spatial containment of this city's poorest residents.

"What is the worth of a park, if those of us who have lived around here for so long are being kicked out, and thus we cannot enjoy it?" This question, formulated in a community assessment of the Green Belt carried out by the sociologist and comuna leader Carlos Velásquez (2014, 626), reflects the main concern among Medellín's comuna housing rights movements. Their concern is that the infrastructure for social urbanism might have been created with other people in mind. There was undoubtedly a great sense of commitment in Medellín's social urbanism project, which was carefully planned and supported with an outpouring of funding. However, social urbanism's emphasis on iconic architecture in principle ignored the residents' own priorities. The project, although aiming to address poverty, privileged an elite vision of the issue, one that advocated for *beautification* as the first step to overcome poverty. This view radically contrasted to that of the people experiencing poverty. They instead requested that the City of Medellín directly deal with key markers of poverty such as housing quality and tenure. It must be noticed, of course, that a simple project of housing improvement and legalization probably would not have become part of the MoMA collection. As Giancarlo Mazzanti enthusiastically celebrated, the visual impact was essential to the Biblioteca España, as it was for the whole Northeastern Zone Project. Thus, privileging the logic of museums and image, an extraordinary amount of money was invested (and, in the case of the library, wasted) on iconic architectural pieces while not really addressing the comunas' main issue—namely, housing. Rather, the housing situation became worse in these comunas, as thousands of families ended up being displaced in order to make room for infrastructure that brought about a vision of social improvement that might make sense, although mostly in the eyes of outside people in privilege.

In theory then, Medellín is a better example than the previous three of an appropriate engagement of local designers with local subalterns. However, from the perspective of comuna housing rights movements, in the careful planning and financial backing of this project, there might have been a different agenda at play. These residents' rights movements generally see social urbanism as a project of territorial encroachment and control orchestrated by Medellín's elites, a project to progressively take over the residents' land by pushing them out by means of direct removal (either negotiated or forceful) and gentrification. Thus, in these residents' view, the ultimate goal of social urbanism is to upgrade low-income comunas for the benefit of a higher income class. According to this view, social urbanism is then ultimately a project of expropriation and generalized displacement. Notably, this project relies highly upon the invocation of the logic of public space and environmental sustainability as central to its goal.

The case of Medellín's social urbanism reveals just how wide the gap in determining the goals and priorities of a local social design project can be. In this case, the gap is evident in the purpose of a huge investment in social development, in whose priorities that investment represents, and in whom, in the end, the social design infrastructure might be built to benefit. This gap becomes even more troubling considering that the City ultimately decided to rebuild the structure at an even higher cost, once again ignoring the calls from residents to prioritize housing and related social issues.

Thus, even in the best-case scenario, when there is more preparation, sustained commitment, and funding behind a social design intervention, and even when at least in theory the project invites more community participation, it can still reflect a deep social disconnection. Local designers might regard the priorities differently than the subjects of their benevolence do. Thus, it cannot be assumed even in those cases that being a local designer immediately ensures a better outcome for local subalterns.

ANTIHOMELESS DESIGN IN THE UNITED STATES

I will close this chapter's interrogation of the role of local designers by studying a project from Architecture for Humanity, the highest-profile social design organization in the history of this practice, and the one that made social design mainstream in the early 2000s.

As mentioned in chapter 1, Cameron Sinclair, cofounder of Architecture for Humanity, mounted a fierce defense of localism during the Nussbaum controversy. Sinclair highlighted all the great work that local designers affiliated with his organization did in their own communities, addressing, for example, issues of homelessness. However, in order to understand the scope of Sinclair's statement, it is necessary to place it within the context of the decentralized nature of Architecture for Humanity. Designers working independently in a given place could indeed have done the type of work that

Sinclair described, although with little to no involvement or even funding from the organization's main office in San Francisco, California. That was part of the "laissez-faire" nature of Architecture for Humanity, which made it possible for this organization to recruit hundreds of independent designers worldwide for its cause and, in exchange, list what these designers did as part of its own portfolio.

This model of work, explained by Sinclair in a talk I attended at the University of California at Berkeley, was as simple as it was clever in terms of the synergy it created. A group of local designers in, say, South Africa, could become a de facto "local chapter" of Architecture for Humanity by starting a humanitarian venture on their own. "We just tore the organization apart and became this . . . matrix of organizations" (Sinclair 2007, 21:28). Given how renowned Architecture for Humanity was, if designers could claim that they were part of the organization, then their work would be easier in terms of dissemination and fundraising. By the same token, once those designers presented themselves as local chapters of Architecture for Humanity, then Architecture for Humanity could also claim their projects as its own. This is how, Sinclair explained, the organization's portfolio of projects suddenly grew from five in 2004 to 104 in 2007 (21:00). Thus, this model allowed for Architecture for Humanity to rapidly appear to have a huge international presence. The model also explains the big claims that the organization often made about its reach: 75,000 designers, over two thousand structures, two million beneficiaries (e.g., TEDx Vienna 2011; AFH 2012a, 2013b; Lincoln 2013b; Sinclair 2019).

In terms of budget, the claims to such large numbers also allowed Architecture for Humanity to grow substantially. These numbers were often invoked in Sinclair's pitch for funding to big donors, including financial groups, large corporations, and global nonprofits. As a result of cash donations from these and other sources, Architecture for Humanity's revenues grew impressively. As its tax filings show, in just one decade (2003–13), the organization's assets went from less than US$10,000 to over US$12 million. This apparent success notwithstanding, only a couple of years later it filed for bankruptcy. A lawsuit that was brought in 2016 against Sinclair and other members of the board alleged funds mismanagement. The lawsuit was later settled out of court.

For the purposes of critical research, Architecture for Humanity's decentralized and organic model of self-creation of local chapters poses a difficulty because it confuses observers. For example, the model allowed Sinclair to make broad claims of localism during the Nussbaum controversy. However, what "Architecture for Humanity" exactly was Sinclair talking about? In practical terms, this was not just a single organization (that is, the San Francisco "headquarters," as they were known in the organization's parlance), but instead dozens of them, if we also consider the independently run local chapters. Addressing this difficulty, I am careful here to limit my analysis to only one project by the organization, and one that was carried out in the city of San Francisco. Thus, I am exploring the localism of Architecture for Humanity through a project carried out in the place where the organization was based. This project involved both the organization's San Francisco headquarters and the San Francisco local chapter. Therefore, when I refer to "Architecture for Humanity" in my descriptions of this case, I mean the San Francisco-based designers affiliated with the organization and acting locally in this specific project.

A Local Project by Architecture for Humanity

The Burrows Street Pocket Park is located in a cul-de-sac at the meeting point between Burrows Street and US Highway 101 in San Francisco's Portola district. It was designed by Architecture for Humanity and completed in 2014. The organization described this project as a "pocket park" or "parklet." This is an innovative urban form developed in San Francisco in 2005, after an initiative by the public design organization Rebar to take over public parking spots and transform them into minimal-size parks (see Merker 2010). Pocket parks are nowadays a hugely popular form of urban design across cities, especially in the United States.

Architecture for Humanity's Burrows Street Pocket Park project sought to transform a buffer piece of highway land into a pleasing little park that included a tiny footbridge, a garden with strategically placed rocks, a "minilibrary" cabinet, and an evocative mural with flowers and symbols of the Native American people who first inhabited the area. In addition, sidewalk pavement was resurfaced with tiles, and public benches—which I will describe later—were installed on one of the sidewalks. Also as part of this project, an upscale café was invited to open a location by the garden (fig. 31).

On the surface, this was a commendable idea: beautification was supposed to meet business development while also meeting environmental sustainability through the greening of a space. Because of that, the project became highly celebrated in design-related media and architectural literature. For instance, it appears described in Adam Wilmes's *Altruism by Design* as exemplary of how "morality and financial accumulation" can work together in a social design project (2015, 216). The project was also offered as exemplary of how "participatory design [can] save the world" in an *Architectural Digest* article (Keskeys 2018).[10]

Fig. 31. San Francisco's Burrows Street Pocket Park. (Photograph: Google Earth)

Of the many praiseful mentions of Burrows Street Pocket Park in the design literature and popular media, some of the most prominent were featured in several promotional videos and press releases produced by the luxury car company Lincoln. The reason is that Lincoln provided most of the funding for this project and actively used it in its own advertising. As part of a campaign called the "Lincoln Reimagine Project," the company showcased the pocket park as an example of its commitment to reimagining "design, innovation and building a community" (Lincoln 2013b). Cameron Sinclair is prominently featured in the Lincoln material on the park. Describing the significance of the project, he says in one of the videos: "What's really great about the Lincoln Reimagine Project is that it has brought together both community groups, nonprofit organizations, and corporate philanthropy to look at a kind of grassroots approach to social impact" (2015, 2:57). Architecture for Humanity is also widely mentioned in the Lincoln material, and two of the videos even show one of Architecture for Humanity's project designers driving a Lincoln vehicle (see 2014, 2015). Lincoln presented this as an example of how the vehicle model had provided the designers with inspiration: the park benches actually mimic the curves of a Lincoln MKZ sedan (see 2013c, 1:00; 2014, 0:41; Tittmann 2014a, 41–44) (fig. 32).

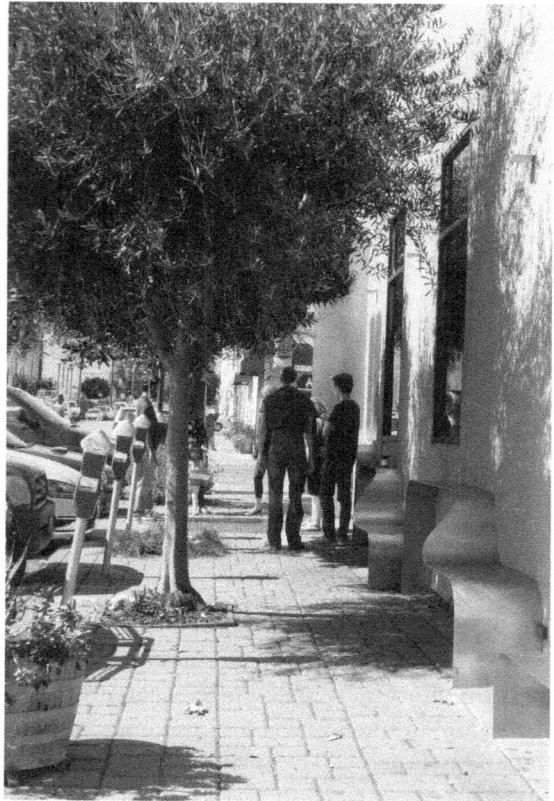

Fig. 32. On the right, the Burrows Street Pocket Park benches, designed to mimic the curves of a Lincoln MKZ sedan.

Questions on Design

The Burrows Street Pocket Park project is highly regarded as exemplary of good practices in social design. Granted, unlike the other projects I have studied in this chapter, this one was well-built and was, at the time of my fieldwork (2018), in relatively good physical condition. However, considering the process that led to this project, it is relevant to ask to what extent a nicely designed and well-built social design project might still represent the interests of people in privilege, with local social designers honoring these interests above those of the most vulnerable populations.

In fact, one issue that the laudatory mentions of Burrows Street Pocket Park consistently ignore is the past history of this site and the reasons that motivated the project. To begin, it is necessary to consider Architecture for Humanity's own description of the project site as "an underutilized and abused corner" (AFH 2013e), and also the organization's description of the original condition of this site as "a dumping ground and gathering spot for vandals and illicit activity" (2012b).

The question is, who were those vandals? Homeless people were the only group explicitly identified by the Portola Neighborhood Association, the group of residents that commissioned Architecture for Humanity for the design of the park. In a number of public statements, members of the Portola Association described the site in terms similar to those employed by Architecture for Humanity. For example, the leading member of the association's committee in charge of the project described the site as having been "a dumping ground and occasional homeless encampment" (Wallace 2012). Such a connection between trash and homeless people was constant in descriptions of the project made both by Architecture of Humanity and the Portola Neighborhood Association, and was used to justify the project's emphasis on beautification.

The issue of homelessness in the Portola district has been a contentious one for a few years. Attesting to this, during the planning phase of Burrows Street Pocket Park, the association's chair reported a residents' meeting where the creation of the park was being debated (Waddling 2011). Speaking of the reaction by owners of the two properties adjacent to the site, the chair described how one of them vehemently complained that the pocket park could potentially attract homeless people, while the other "respectfully pointed out that there already is homelessness, dumping, and other criminal activity in the location . . . and suggested that it really couldn't get much worse" (2011). The chair also reported that, in addition to the park, the association's committee in charge was "also going to be installing surveillance cameras in the area to try to deter homeless encampments and help police catch bad-guys" (2011). After the project, the association celebrated: "The PNA has reclaimed the neglected dead end that was a site of frequent homeless encampments" (Waddling 2013).

How was the Burrows Street Pocket Park designed to push homeless people away from the site? This was done through the implementation of strategies of so-called *defensive design*. Such is the name given to the practice of using subtle design gestures to produce a space that, although nominally public, displaces certain demographics that are deemed undesirable. There is public consensus that the main goal of defensive design is to push homeless people away (see Hohenadel 2014; Staff and Agencies 2014; Andreou 2015; Atkinson and While 2015; Savić 2015; The Spectator 2015; Wallace 2018). Because of that, I will be referring to this design approach using the more direct term *antihomeless design*.

In fact, as praised as Burrows Street Pocket Park has been, this project is actually a textbook example of antihomeless design strategies at play. Cer-

Fig. 33. Antihomeless strategies in the Burrows Street Pocket Park, including (1) large windows, (2) increased lighting, (3) antihomeless benches, (4 and 8) surveillance cameras, (5) direct visual control, (6) lack of seating within park, (7) area crowded with plants, (9) warning signs, (10) spotlights, (11) upscale café, with (12) proprietary seating placed in public space, suggesting that the garden is part of the business, (13) removable seating, (14) small bridge and path leading nowhere, thus (15) visitors must turn around and leave.

tain elements that make the park an endearing piece of urban design actually have a strong effect upon how people can use it. First, the garden cannot be actually used as a public space, insofar as there is no actual place to be. The minimal-sized bridge leads to a narrow path that in turn leads to nowhere— it simply ends after a few steps. It is not possible to stray away from this path because the area around is crowded with vegetation. Additionally, there is no seating within that space, so the most that a user can do is to stand, or turn around and leave. The only other option would be to break into the plants and damage them, thereby reaffirming the project's initial premise, which linked the use of the space to vandalism.

As part of the park design, one of the adjoining buildings (the one on the north side of the street, which received most of the design intervention) was converted into a full business-use structure. The upscale café is on the first floor, while on the second, and directly overlooking the pocket park, are the offices of the Portola Neighborhood Association, which conceived the idea of the park. The design of the second-floor facade included considerably enlarging the existing windows for more visual control over the park. Although that part of the design was not realized in the end, windows were still installed on the previously windowless side facade of the corner business. As a mechanism of social control, the idea of adding many windows, in addition to the association's initiative of installing surveillance cameras (complete with caution signs such as "WARNING. Security cameras in use"), sought to ensure visual control from inside the buildings of the park area, and to convey to users of that space the impression that they were being watched.

Deterred from staying in the garden both because of the lack of space and the surveillance measures in place, users of the park are then naturally pushed toward the only other public area outside of the garden. However, this second area is primarily designated for the use of the café's patrons. The cues for the user that this is a private space come from symbolic landmarks of territoriality such as the occasional placement of the café's sign well within the public space and even past the entrance to the garden, which suggests that the garden is also part of the business. However, the most prominent indicator of private property is the fact that the café places its own proprietary seating in that public space. This seating is removed after the business closes so it cannot be used by homeless people at night (fig. 33).

Antihomeless Benches

Granted, in addition to the café's private seating, the design included public seating; however, it was a very peculiar type of seating. Among the existing repertoire of antihomeless design strategies, seating is often the design focus, and thus it is one of the most prominent elements in so-called pocket parks. The high focus on seating is due to the fact that homeless people might use it to sleep in the nights. Given that an upscale business is usually the main element that ensures the control of a pocket park, once this business closes, the space becomes inhabitable again by those people whom the business might deter during the day. Although the seating is often privately owned and, just as in the Burrows Street Pocket Park, is put away when the business closes, pocket parks generally also include public seating that might be nicely designed, yet intentionally designed to be uncomfortable, under the pretense of being an art piece.

Such is the case with Burrows Street Pocket Park, where the public benches are the most overtly designed element of the entire project. They look like a wall decoration or an artistic attachment—they are "sculptural tables and seats," as cheerfully described by the design publication *Inhabitat* (Chino 2014). They have been described by their designers as having a "ribbon" form (MoreLab 2014); that is, they have undulating forms that, depending on their height and width, can be used as either tables or benches (fig. 34). Although this sculptural arrangement covers a good length of the sidewalk (approx. 18 m or 60 ft), it actually does not include too many benches. The ribbon-like undulations mean that much of this space is taken up by other uses, including not only the tables but also an information panel where the

Fig. 34. View of the Burrows Street Pocket Park benches showing their "ribbon" form. This was in 2014, right after the project conclusion. (Photograph by Hester Tittmann)

name of Architecture for Humanity is prominently displayed along with those of the project sponsors. There is space for only four benches, as such, and they are not designed for comfort. Since the benches are attached to the wall of one of the properties, they have full upright backs, and, only about two of them are the standard height for a bench. None of these benches is long enough to fully lie on. The design of the benches, then, is such that it makes it difficult for anyone to sit for too long, much less sleep. This was made even more difficult a few years after the park opened, when the wooden boards that originally covered the metal seating were removed, so the seating surface became bare metal. During the normally cold San Francisco nights, sitting or lying on this surface became even more uncomfortable, as it gets too cold and moist (fig. 35).

The lighting design of the park also contributes to making sitting or sleeping comfortless, as it ensures that the space remains fully illuminated during the nights. First, the windows that were installed on the corner business allow for direct visual control from inside the building of those who are on the benches, and at night these windows shed a great deal of light directly onto the benches and the people using them (fig. 36). Even when this business closes, there is still plenty of light shed on the benches. The project also included the placement of light fixtures right above each bench. In addition to an independently added strong street lamp and spotlights on the facade of one of the properties, the lighting features of this project thus ensure that the night users of the park would be quite visible and exposed.

Evidence of the explicitly antihomeless purpose of the Burrows Street Pocket Park benches was provided by ethnographic research carried out by

Fig. 35. The bare metal benches in 2018.

Hester Tittmann during the design phase of the park (Tittmann 2014a, b). A Hampshire College architectural studies graduate, Tittmann wrote a thesis on small-scale urban design using the case of Burrows Street and another pocket park in neighboring Oakland (2014a). I was one of the advisors for Tittmann's thesis. As part of their field research, Tittmann carried out an ethnography of practice by enrolling as an apprentice at Rebar, the organization that developed the notion of pocket parks, which was founded and directed by the landscape designer and artist Matthew Passmore. Tittmann joined Rebar for an academic semester during the time when the Burrows Street Pocket Park benches were being designed. As part of their apprenticeship, Tittmann helped with design, fabrication, and other tasks at Rebar while documenting day-to-day work at the office. The purpose of this research was to assess, through studying the work approach of one of the leaders in the field and comparing it to community members' voices, the impact of small-scale urban design on a city's public space. This research was fully disclosed to Passmore, who authorized it. He and other members of Rebar, as well as members of Architecture for Humanity involved in the Burrows Street Pocket Park project, agreed to go on the record about the design process of the park's benches, and some of them talked openly about the antihomeless nature of the design.

In their thesis, Tittmann explains how Architecture for Humanity hired

Fig. 36. The Burrows Street Pocket Park benches in the night. Different light sources ensure that these benches remain illuminated even at night time.

Rebar to design the Burrows Street Pocket Park benches (2014a, 37). A 2014 resume by Passmore confirms this: "I designed the bench system" (2014). Passmore's MoreLab studio (Rebar's later incarnation) provides more detail: "We designed two key elements of the Park, the 'ribbon' bench and table system that runs along the wall of a private building, and a custom gate and integrated bench" (MoreLab 2014). Additionally, in that project description Architecture for Humanity is listed as the client.

Tittmann explains that Rebar was specifically tasked with further developing seating concept designs created by Architecture for Humanity (2014a, 37). In fact, an early sketch by Architecture for Humanity indicates "removable chairs + tables" for the location where the ribbon benches now are (AFH n.d.). As part of their role as a Rebar apprentice, Tittmann participated in the design development of the bench model under the supervision of Passmore and other Rebar designers. Once the basic "ribbon" form of the bench was defined at Rebar, the design was completed through a back-and-forth

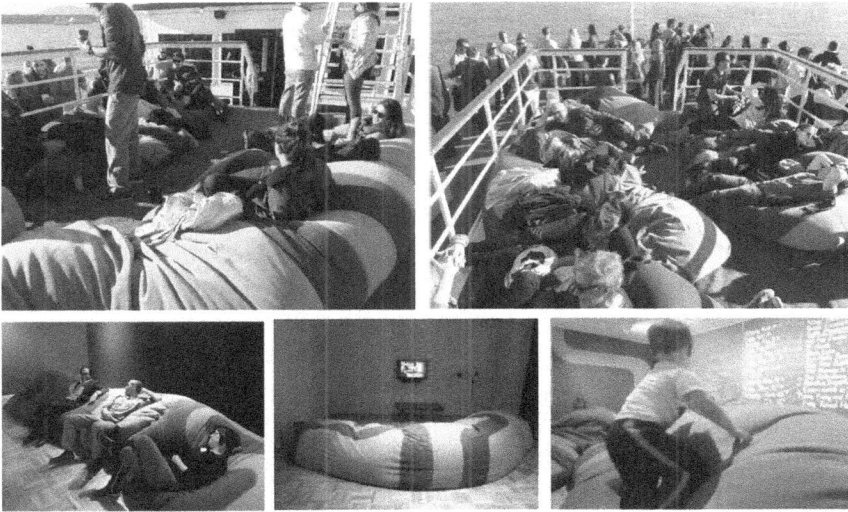

Upper row: Yelp! private party on Hornblower cruise ship
Bottom row: Vinyl exhibition at the Oakland Museum of California

2

Fig. 37. The contrast between two seating arrangements simultaneously designed by the same firm, Rebar, later MoreLab. *Top:* advertising from the firm showing people enjoying the *Groove Grove; bottom:* a homeless man rough-sleeping in one of the Burrows Street Pocket Park benches. (*Top image:* screenshot from the MoreLab website; *bottom image:* Google Earth)

communication between Rebar and Architecture for Humanity. In fact, one of the Lincoln videos shows Architecture for Humanity's project coordinator working on a small model of the bench (Lincoln 2013c).

Very importantly, Tittmann also states that it was Architecture for Humanity that made the request to Rebar regarding the "defensive" nature of the benches, and that "removing houseless individuals, as well as prohibiting other 'undesirable' users" was part of the bench design process from beginning to end (Tittmann 2014a, 40). Indeed, Reaz Haque, the Architecture for Humanity designer who initiated the project, stated this explicitly as he introduced the project's goals: "This proposed project will beautify the area, cut down on refuse dumping, graffiti and homeless encampments" (Haque n.d.). The result, then, was "a design that would work structurally, aesthetically, and make sleeping difficult or impossible" (Tittmann 2014a, 41). Tittmann stresses: "This bench was specifically designed so that no one could lie down on it; and no one could sleep on it. No one can sit on it comfortably for a really long period of time" (2015).

Discussing the project with the Rebar designers, Tittmann explicitly asked them about their position on antihomeless design. Tittmann noticed how, paradoxically, although none of the designers found it "morally acceptable to design spaces that exclude homeless people, they often do because of client demand" (2014a, 40). Evidently, it was client demand that led the Rebar designers to limit the level of comfort of the seating they were designing. There is a great contrast between the Burrows Street Pocket Park's benches and another seating design project by Rebar called the *Groove Grove*. Designed for the Oakland Museum of California, this is a cozy and welcoming set of "bean bag modules that can be reconfigured for a variety of inhabitation options" (MoreLab n.d.). Remarkably, the Groove Grove was designed simultaneously as the Burrows Street's benches. These were two seating arrangements designed at the same time by the same design office; one was a comfortless and limited one, and the other one invited not only sitting but also lying down, in full relaxation. Clearly then, Rebar was designing differently, depending on the client and the intended use of the seating (fig. 37).

On Community

Describing the aims of the Burrows Street Pocket Park project, Architecture for Humanity stated that the design would foster "stewardship, beautification and humanization of the surrounding area" (AFH 2012b). Such an invocation of humanization is paradoxical, as it prompts the question of why Architecture for Humanity, which was once called "one of the foremost humanitarian building initiatives in history" (Winter 2015), was suddenly advocating for such a conspicuously inhumane practice as antihomeless design. According to Hester Tittmann, the organization was simply acting on the wishes of the Portola Neighborhood Association's representatives: "The Portola Neighborhood Association initiated the redesign in order to push out houseless people, and requested uninhabitable furniture" (Tittmann 2014b, 7). In fact, in his description of this project, the Architecture for Humanity's designer Garrett Jacobs explained that it had started as a "grassroots, community-driven desire" (Lincoln 2013c, 0:45), and that it had been "a community driven pilot" (OAC 2017). The Portola Neighborhood Association's project leader stressed: "So we decided that we would *take the space back* and make it a shared community space" (Lincoln 2015, 1:37, emphasis added). According to Tittmann, during the design process, Architecture for Humanity was in constant communication with the Portola Neighborhood Association. They would bring the association the design proposals being developed with Rebar, and the association would provide input (Tittmann 2014a, 41).[11]

Thus, the situation for Architecture for Humanity was complicated because the organization intended to tackle this project using a community participation approach, but pushing homeless people out was what "the community" desired. However, what "community" was that? It is important to look at the notion of community in this project because it was central to its narrative. A good example is how fondly Wilmes's book describes the project as an ode to community:

This enclave known as 1 Burrows is more than a simple high-design pocket park. It is an effort to incorporate the voice of the surrounding community, to understand their vision of what the space could include. Through public as well as private stakeholder presentations, the design solution evolved to speak for the community, not just to it. It is only a matter of time until the silence—that only a community-driven pocket park can provide—is heard vociferously once and for all. (Wilmes 2015, 214)

Indeed, the notion of community was widely invoked by Architecture for Humanity throughout the whole design process. First, in online publications about the project, the organization described it as a "run-down cul-de-sac turned community park" (AFH 2014b), and cited as one of the goals that of "building community pride and empowerment" (OAN n.d.). Invoking the "reimagine" theme of Lincoln's campaign, the organization also celebrated: "Reimagining community spaces takes the entire community" (AFH 2013c). Garrett Jacobs also explained that "when the community decided what it wanted in the park, it decided a mural" (Lincoln 2013c, 1:35) and that "the end result is going to be very special, because everyone believes in the importance of engaging the community" (2013c, 2:41). Cameron Sinclair concluded: "Transforming *unused* public spaces around the world into functional, valuable resources greatly benefits local communities" (Lincoln 2013a, emphasis added).

It is also important to note Sinclair's characterization of spaces such as Burrows Street as "unused." This characterization immediately makes the homeless users of those spaces invisible. Thus, the answer to the question of to whom all those mentions of community referred, is that they referred to only the *housed* residents of the neighborhood, who defined themselves as "the community" in opposition to the homeless residents. Indeed, not all the community stakeholders were part of the project's community planning and design process—no homeless people rights' organizations or advocacy groups were invited (see Tittmann 2014a, 41–42). This means that, although Architecture for Humanity intended to use a community participation approach, the "community" they were working with was a self-selected group that excluded the community members in greatest poverty. Consequently, and going back to the popular assessment that the Burrows Street Pocket Park project was highly participatory, this would be accurate only if we consider that those who participated were a subgroup of the community— namely, the ones in more relative privilege. Burrows Street Pocket Park is then an example of a key limitation of participatory design: The demographics of those who participate can be easily restricted, and when that happens the results of the participatory process then benefit only the interests of a subgroup.

Burrows Street Pocket Park in Context

In a larger context, the case of Burrows Street Pocket Park illustrates the drastic housing situation presently experienced by people in poverty in the United States. Indeed, this case was not simply about a few "vandals," as the homeless users of the site were often characterized. Since the 2008 housing crisis, the scale of homelessness in the United States has grown to a degree hardly seen before. Homelessness has become a common condition of life for an increasingly large social group, beset by decreasing job stability and salaries. They have been left without access to public housing because of the intentional shrinkage of public housing stocks; more than 100,000 public housing units were demolished in the United States in the 1990s (Vale 2002), and the trend has continued since. This situation is exacerbated by the rapid privatization of remaining public housing under the label of "affordable housing"—affordable for whom is always an open question. These practices have been pushing people out of what used to be low-income housing into poverty accommodations such as trailer parks, which are just one step from living on the streets. This process has been powerfully described by the sociologist Matthew Desmond in *Evicted* (2016).

Consequently, homelessness today affects not only individuals but also entire family groups. Often these families have no other option than to live in vehicles, which they constantly have to move from one parking spot to another in order to avoid parking enforcement. Those vehicles are commonly seen throughout the city of San Francisco, including the Portola district. In fact, as of 2018, the presence of these vehicles in the Portola was a source of irate complaints to the City of San Francisco by the more entitled Portola residents (see Hobbs 2018; Sparling 2013; Swan 2018).

The case of homelessness in San Francisco is particularly critical because this city has experienced some of the most vertiginous advances of gentrification in the United States. The reason is that some of the largest and also wealthiest information technology companies in the world are headquartered in the San Francisco Bay Area, including Apple, Facebook, and Google. The fact that thousands of highly paid professionals working for these industries have moved into the area has meant the displacement of a large number of people who have been priced out of the housing market. This displacement, of course, has happened first and on a larger scale among those who are in greatest poverty. Such rapid burst of gentrification has, consequently, contributed directly to the increase of homelessness in San Francisco. In their need of a place to live, homeless people often congregate in parks and other public spaces. However, not long after that, they might be removed from those spaces by the City. In order to ensure that they do not return, remaking the spaces with gardens and design interventions has become an increasingly popular strategy. It includes the creation of pocket parks, which have become a propeller of gentrification (see Douglas 2014, 2019; Hubbard 2016; Wilson 2018) (fig. 38).

This, then, is the Burrows Street Pocket Park in a larger context. In Architecture of Humanity's material about the project, the Portola is described as a working-class neighborhood (e.g., OAN n.d.). However, just like the rest of the city, it is clearly undergoing a process of gentrification. This is particularly evident in the presence of the upscale café in the Pocket Park. Literature on gentrification mostly focuses on housing, but the gentrification of business, as in the new businesses that open catering to newcomers, is what makes gentrification most visible to the naked eye. I have referred to new businesses as indicators of gentrification in the case of Medellín; we see this also in the Portola. At the time of my fieldwork, in the area along San Bruno Avenue near Burrows Street Pocket Park, most businesses still catered to the socioeconomic status of the majority of residents. There were

Fig. 38. McCoppin Hub, a homeless people's gathering space in San Francisco that was converted into a pocket park.

Asian and Latin American fresh produce stores and takeout restaurants, as well as coin laundries, beauty parlors, and nonprofit social support centers. There was a Subway fast food restaurant—which was the business on the corner of Burrows that had the windows added as part of the pocket park project—as well as a Walgreens pharmacy. That is, most of the urban landscape still looked like the one commonly associated with an American working-class neighborhood. However, other businesses had also begun to appear. The café at Burrows Street Pocket Park was one of them, a sophisticated café where the cost of a cup of coffee was between twice and four times that of the Subway next door. There was also an artisanal beer place, as well as a breakfast restaurant. The latter was on a second cul-de-sac that the Open Architecture Collaborative (the reincarnation of Architecture for Humanity after the latter's demise), also endeavored to design as a pocket park just like Burrows Street's. Given the nature and/or pricing scheme of these businesses, they were mostly patronized by people who were ostensibly different from the majority of those circulating along San Bruno Avenue (fig. 39).

These and other changes then taking place in the Portola appear described in a 2017 *San Francisco Chronicle* article: "San Bruno Avenue and more broadly the Portola district, known as San Francisco's Garden District, is experiencing a level of interest not seen since the corridor went into decline in the 1970s" (Dineen 2017). Pointing to the actors spearheading what it calls the revitalization of this area, the article continues: "The Portola Neighborhood Association has emerged as a strong voice for revitalization,

Fig. 39. Gentrification in the Portola District, evident in the changing nature of business along San Bruno Avenue, around the corner from Burrows Street Pocket Park

pushing for pocket parks and the redevelopment of abandoned greenhouses on Woolsey Street" (2017). It is worth noting that the most active members of this association, the ones who championed the Burrows Street Pocket Park project, were comparatively recent arrivals to the Portola. The *Chronicle* article also cites a resident enthusiastically describing new amenities in the area: "We have incredible cuisine. We have coffees shops [*sic*]. We have several breakfast joints. We have a banquet hall" (2017). In the article, this resident is quoted as advocating now for the establishment of an arts venue in a long-vacated 1920s theater whose neon sign had recently been restored. The article also mentions the brewery's owner, as she commented on how the theater's owners had "attempted to bring in a CVS pharmacy a few years ago, exactly the sort of tenant she doesn't want to see" (2017).

Now, gentrifiers are not bad people per se. Even human rights advocates or public interest attorneys could be gentrifiers. Probably they do not see themselves as gentrifiers; they simply happened to move into a new place. They might be middle-class people who see an opportunity for good affordable housing, albeit in a run-down neighborhood. Since this is what they can afford, they buy, and then they start improving the neighborhood with small and poetic acts of urban design such as murals and pocket parks. This ends up increasing the value of their property and incidentally also that of the properties around it. This, in turn, unleashes the forces of gentrification.

Very importantly, though, and as mentioned in the previous chapter's literature review, sustainability is nowadays often invoked as the purported goal of a gentrification process. This was the case with Burrows Street Pocket Park, since the goal of making the cul-de-sac "green" was a central driver of this project. Architecture for Humanity described the project as one that "will transform an underutilized cul-de-sac into an attractive, green public plaza" (OAN n.d.). The organization also envisioned that as a result of the project, "the Portola neighborhood in San Francisco will be a little bit greener and a whole lot safer" (AFH 2013c). Upon the project's conclusion, the organization celebrated: "[A] neglected urban space has transformed into a lush, productive, and activated mini park" (AFH 2013d). As for the green features that the organization was referring to, publications often and enthusiastically highlight the runoff water management system and other environmental measures implemented in the site. They talk about the creation of a garden with drought-tolerant plants and the planting of trees on the sidewalk. They also highlight the installation of solar panels and a composting toilet in the café. They highlight the idea of economic sustainability—making a business (the café) interested in occupying that "underutilized" space. Thus, invoking the discourse of sustainability in a gentrification process ultimately helps to obscure this process, since it makes it sound like the right thing to do: it is not gentrification—it is sustainability.

Cameron Sinclair's final assessment of the Burrows Street Pocket Park project was celebratory: "It helps other community groups and architects and civic activists see a very tangible solution they can replicate, like the parklets, which have been incredibly successful" (Lincoln 2015, 2:43). The question, again, is, successful for whom? Contrasting Sinclair's assessment, Garrett Jacobs reflected on one of the key lessons he had learned from his engagement with Architecture for Humanity:

Don't compromise values for money. Even if it's a large sum of money for one project, make sure you understand what your base values are, what your base principles are when you want to approach that project. (Jacobs 2017, 7:13)

Jacobs's earnest reflection offers a note of caution on how, in their desire to do a good job, social designers might end up unintentionally betraying their own principles and playing along with other contrary interests. This brings back the question of whether local designers are actually better equipped to address the social needs of local people in poverty. The answer, as learned from this case, is that even if one is a local social designer, the challenge is not simpler, and the outcome is no less prone to be problematic. In the design of Burrows Street Pocket Park, Architecture for Humanity aimed to use a strong community participation approach. However, only the group with more relative privilege regarded itself as "the community," and thus the organization ended up only honoring the interests of that group in pushing homeless residents out of public space. Thus, in the case of this project, Architecture for Humanity ultimately ended up taking the side of privilege, unwittingly supporting a gentrification process. The park design reveals a series of antihomeless design strategies that restrict the possibility of people staying in the space unless they are in the private business area of the park. Most visibly and catering to the wishes of its client group, the organization specified the design of a bench that would restrict seating and would make sleeping comfortless. Notably, the larger goal invoked to justify this project was that of environmental and economic sustainability: making the space "green" and activating business. With this, the line between greenification and gentrification in this project became all too tenuous.

Thus, not even in this, a project from the world's highest-profile social design organization, did the fact of being a local social design necessarily represent an improvement for local subalterns.

CONCLUSION: ON LOCAL DESIGNERS

In this chapter, I have explored the first localism premise advocated for by both critics and apologists as the solution to what it is broadly considered to be the main challenge of social design, namely, imperialism. The premise is that local issues should be tackled primarily by local designers. I have studied a number of representative local designers' projects, all of them paradigmatic of social design practice; these are highly recognized projects that have garnered the highest awards and honors and have been widely celebrated in exhibits and the literature. As it turns out, the outcome of local designers' projects can be quite perplexing: structures that collapse because of experimentation, calls to experiment on vulnerable populations, celebrations of taking risks while the designers are not the ones living with the consequences of those risks, and designers' support of processes of gentrification that directly or indirectly displace vulnerable populations in the name of beautification and/or by implementing strategies of antihomeless design. Notably, despite all these troubling outcomes, in the cases I have presented designers were still able to make strong claims of sustainability in their projects; they were able to invoke sustainability as the motivation, the goal, and even the outcome of their projects.

Thus, the outcomes of these cases suggest that localism, as in leaving matters to local designers, is not necessarily the solution to the main issues faced by social design practice. Also in the cases in which the project is in the hands of a local social designer there can be very detrimental outcomes that severely affect vulnerable populations. This happens even in the United States, where there exists more oversight, and therefore social designers tend to be more self-restrained in their work. Thus, as we learn from these cases, the fact that a project is run by a local designer might not really make a major difference, since the abuse that is usually attributed only to imperialism can still persist. Local designers can unintentionally engage in problematic practices just as much as foreign designers do. Consequently, there exist grounds to believe that, as much as imperialism is a very serious issue, the challenge of social design goes beyond imperialism.

In the next chapter I will carry out my exploration of the second premise of localism, which concerns involving community participation.

CHAPTER 3

Localism

On Community Participation

In chapter 2, I began to explore *localism,* the paradigm proposed by both critics and supporters of social design to address the issues of imperialism that currently affect this practice. The idea of localism involves two basic premises: first, that local social design practice should be carried out by local designers, and second, that designers should carry out their work by involving community participation. To begin my exploration of this proposition, I interrogated the first premise, that of leaving local matters to local designers. Demonstrating the limitations of such a premise was a relatively easy task. I examined a number of representative examples that demonstrate that being a local social designer does not by default offer any advantage, whether economic, technological, or social, to the subjects of the intervention.

I will now explore the second premise—namely, that the solutions proposed by designers should be carried out with community participation. This is a far more complicated premise to test for a number of reasons. First, the bar as to what qualifies as participation in a social design project can be very low, as some of the cases I studied in the previous chapter demonstrate. In fact, in all of those cases the designers made passionate claims of having involved community participation in their projects. However, participation in the majority of those projects was quite limited, since participants were normally limited to providing labor or information, or to participating only on nonessential matters such as the color of a wall. Second, in the case of projects that have presumably involved a higher degree of community participation, it is often difficult to tell the actual extent of participation beyond what is self-reported by the project designers or promoters. Take the case of Medellín, whose social urbanism project was touted by its designers and promoters as highly participatory, but, according to residents' reports, the participatory process was in fact highly controlled, and in some cases even manipulated. Third, in the case of projects in which there has been a deeper consideration for community participation, the outcome of those projects can be unexpected. This was the case with San Francisco's Burrows Street

Pocket Park, where Architecture for Humanity engaged in a community participation process that, in comparison to the other cases, gave more decision-making power to participants. Surprisingly, however, that process set the tone for the dehumanizing nature of the project in how it targeted homeless people.

In sum, the reasons that make studying community participation more difficult are, first, that often just very basic forms of community engagement are deemed participation; second, it is crucial to establish in the field how exactly a given participatory process was carried out because the findings from the field might radically contrast with the descriptions made by the project designers or promoters; and third, whenever there is a deeper participatory process, its outcome might still be surprising. It is for these reasons that I explore community participation in great detail in this book, and in this chapter I will do so through one paradigmatic example: that of *ethnoengineering*.

THE ETHNOENGINEERING PROJECT

"Ethnoengineering" is the name of a participatory development method conceptualized by Carlos Perafán, an anthropologist at the Inter-American Development Bank (IDB) (see Perafán 2001). It was later formulated as a construction method by the Intermediate Technology Development Group (ITDG) (see Perafán et al. 2005).[1] The construction method was tested in a large-scale social design project in rural Ecuador between 2002 and 2010. The project catered to the communities in greatest poverty in the country, which happened to be mostly indigenous, Afro-Ecuadorian, and other traditional communities settled in distant rural areas of the country. Perafán's method was specifically formulated to carry out infrastructure work in the settlement areas of ethnic minority populations. This explains its application in this project and also the "ethno" part of its name, which refers to *ethnicity,* specifically to ethnic minorities (see Perafán 2001, 1).

The project, which I will refer to as "the ethnoengineering project," was part of a US$45 million government construction program called FISE III,[2] whose initial aim was to use the ethnoengineering method to build nearly one thousand constructions in Ecuador's five hundred poorest communities. The constructions included classrooms, health and day care facilities, community kitchens and meeting centers, as well as toilets and bridges.

The Ecuador ethnoengineering project is paradigmatic of the practice of social design, given that it was carefully planned by social development experts, and the designs were created by some of the most experienced and best prepared architects working in poverty alleviation, sustainable construction, and/or culturally appropriate construction in Ecuador at the time—all of them local designers. The architects were Grace Almeida, Edinson Benítez, Luis Gallegos, Jorge Morán, and Bolívar Romero. The project design and execution was overseen by Bayardo Ramírez, a civil engineer. Another professional, the architect Miguel Camino, also designed buildings for this project, although unlike the architects just named he did not participate in the development of the project's design guidelines.

The Ecuadorian ethnoengineering project was then far from the model of amateurism[3] that is so highly praised in social design, and which often ends in the kind of problematic outcomes we see in projects such as those of Adeyemi, Al Borde, and Architecture for Humanity, examined in the previous chapter. This project was a completely different case—a rigorously planned and designed project that was well backed economically and organizationally. It thus offers an ideal scenario to study community participation in social design, because its shortcomings cannot be attributed to simple deficiencies in the project's conception or execution.

The ethnoengineering project is particularly relevant to explore participation because of the very comprehensive way in which the project embraced this principle. Participation was the project's keystone, since it was supposed to permeate all the phases, from planning to construction to maintenance. The project beneficiaries were in charge of everything, from identifying and prioritizing their infrastructural needs to managing the budget (US$72,000 on average per community).[4] The beneficiaries procured the materials, hired the project accountants, architects, and building contractors, supervised and participated in the construction, and carried out maintenance and repairs. They performed these tasks through villagers' committees called CEJAs[5] (project administration and execution committees) and with the training support of government-organized teams called UCATs[6] (training and technical support units), formed by professional advisors including architects.

The second aspect of ethnoengineering that is relevant for the purposes of this book is its understanding of sustainability. The Ecuadorian project followed social design's predominant understanding of this notion, namely the Brundtland Report's idea of permanence toward the future. However, the project also strongly connected sustainability to the notion of *traditionalism*. As mentioned in the introduction and chapter 1, traditionalism is a rebuke to modernism in that it advocates the use of nonindustrial construction materials and the recovery of traditional architectural languages and material culture. The key architectural premises of the ethnoengineering project were, first, that traditional people, like those catered to by the project, by default live in harmony with nature; second, that traditionalist construction in materials such as thatch and mud is by default more climate-efficient than modernist infrastructure in concrete; and third, that traditionalist construction is in principle more affordable than its modernist counterpart.

The latter premise, affordability, was directly connected to the project's main goal, poverty alleviation. According to the ethnoengineering method, traditionalist construction is more affordable for two main reasons: it uses local materials and involves community participation (see, e.g., Perafán et al. 2005, 1). First, local materials are presumably more affordable because in theory they can be gathered from the villagers' own land. Therefore, as Bayardo Ramírez reasoned in one of our interviews, the construction of a *choza,* an Andean traditional hut, "does not cost anything" because people can make adobe bricks using mud from their own land for the walls, and gather thatch grass in the moors for the roofing. Second, for the ethnoengineering method, community participation lowers construction cost also due to two factors: First, beneficiaries are supposed to build the project at no cost, because traditional labor, according to this method, normally does not involve a monetary exchange (9, 114); and second, when villagers participate in a project's construction, the project in theory lasts longer because villagers develop a sense of ownership or appropriation, and thus are more willing to perform the maintenance and repairs required to keep it standing.

The premises of harmony with nature, climate efficiency, and affordability ruled the designs of the Ecuadorian ethnoengineering project. First, the project constructions were built with local materials, especially bamboo, mud, and palm thatch and wood. These are prevalent materials in the traditional construction of each of Ecuador's three major geographic regions (Pacific Coast, Andes, and Amazon, respectively). Second, traditional construction technologies were partially modernized with the addition of industrial materials and processes, though in a restrained form, and only to make them more efficient and durable. Third, in order to ensure the affordability of the constructions, the ethnoengineering project required villagers to provide free labor for the construction, as well as cost-free locally available construction materials, the collection of which had to be also provided cost-free by villagers.

The main design and technological premise of the ethnoengineering project was to combine what people usually know about their own needs, existing alternatives, and best local practices with what professionals know from a design and technical standpoint. According to the method, this combination should result in an addition of advantages that would make a social design project more efficient in terms of cultural appropriateness, lower en-

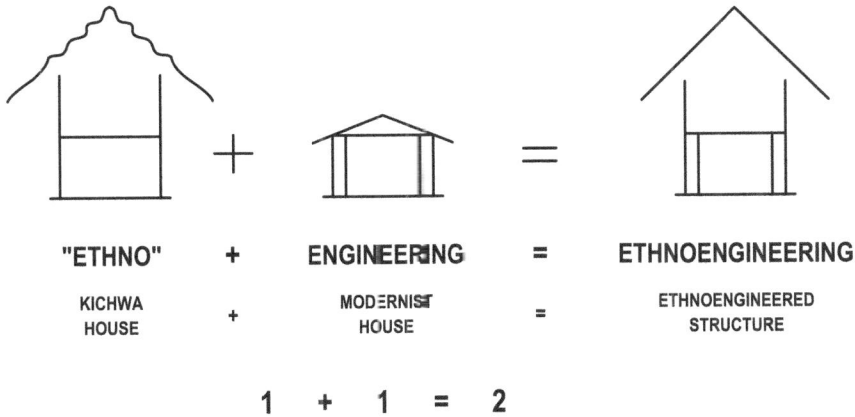

"ETHNO"   +   ENGINEERING   =   ETHNOENGINEERING

KICHWA   +   MODERNIST   =   ETHNOENGINEERED
HOUSE   HOUSE   STRUCTURE

$$1 \quad + \quad 1 \quad = \quad 2$$

Fig. 40. The design and technological rationale of ethnoengineering.

vironmental impact, climate comfort, and affordability. Figure 40 illustrates the design and technological rationale of the approach. On the left, there is a traditional structure like the Kichwa house of the Upper Amazon, which is raised on stilts, making it more resilient to floods, and covered by a steep thatched roof that makes it more comfortable with regard to temperature. Those features make this construction environmentally appropriate, but the fact that the materials used are in their entirety natural means that there would be an environmental impact in their overuse. By contrast, the structure in the middle is a typical modernist structure like the ones commonly built today also in the Upper Amazon. The walls are built with concrete, and the roof is made of metal or fiber-cement sheets. These materials offer durability, but the design lacks the environmental advantages of the traditional structure on the left. However, if the durability of these industrial materials were to be combined with the design advantages of the traditional structure, then the final, "ethnoengineered" structure would be in theory far better than any of its constitutive structures separately. Therefore:

"ethno" + engineering

=

twice as good

traditional knowledge + professional knowledge

$$1 + 1 = 2$$

The final designs resulting from the application of this premise are illustrated in figure 41. The image shows traditional structures from the Pacific

	MODERNIST INFRASTRUCTURE	TRADITIONAL CONSTRUCTION	ETHNOENGINEERING
COAST	Classroom in Tacole, Esmeraldas	House in Súbere, Esmeraldas	Classroom in Taquísquele, Esmeraldas
ANDES	Classroom in Azabí del Mortiñal, Imbabura	House in Guantopolo, Cotopaxi	Day care center in Michacalá, Cotopaxi
AMAZON	Classroom in Ñucanchi Allpa, Napo	House in Puyo, Pastaza	Classroom in Ñucanchi Allpa, Napo

Fig. 41. The ethnoengineering project's design rationale. The Tacole and Puyo images are digitally rotated in order to make the formal connections more evident.

Coast, the Andes, and the Amazon along with modernist standard ones, and the resulting formal combination between both. That last type, the combination, constituted the three base ethnoengineering models for the project. The traditional structures originating those models were, first, a gabled structure using bamboo mats that is the most typical traditional housing form of the Ecuadorian Pacific Coast (fig. 42). Jorge Morán reengineered this house as a bamboo pole structure, with a tin roof and concrete-layered mats for the walls (fig. 43). The second model was based on a veranda house in mud that is the most widespread traditional housing type of the Ecuadorian Andes (fig. 44). Bolívar Romero reworked this house by adding concrete reinforcements, while keeping its general form and the traditional grass thatch roof, as well as

Fig. 42. A traditional gabled bamboo-mat house from the Ecuadorian Pacific Coast. This housing type was the base model for Jorge Morán's ethno-engineering designs for the Pacific Coast.

Fig. 43. Jorge Morán's ethnoengineering prototype in the village of Tacole, Esmeraldas province. Notice the bamboo pole framing and the paneled and concrete-layered bamboo walls. To the left of this structure there is a modernist FISE preethnoengineering classroom.

the walling material. He built the prototype using *tapial,* an ancient pressed-earth technique (fig. 45).

The third model was more complex as a technological-traditionalist proposal. It was based on the traditional house of the Amazonian Saparoan people, a rectangular structure with rounded endings that is built with

Fig. 44. The traditional housing type that formed the basis of Bolívar Romero's ethnoengineering designs.

Fig. 45. Bolívar Romero's ethnoengineering prototype for the Andes in Michacalá, Cotopaxi province.

chonta palm (*Socratea durissima*) and other woods from the Amazon (fig. 46). Edinson Benítez kept this house's general form (fig. 47), emphasizing its most peculiar structural feature: the ridge beam is not supported by any internal columns—it rests only on the two columns that support it at its end points. The fact that the house's internal space is column-free allows for an open plan and a free flow of movement (fig. 48). Due to the house's elongated

SUSTAINABILITY AND PRIVILEGE

Fig. 46. A traditional house from the Amazonian Pastaza province. This is an uninhabited model for display in the town of Puyo, capital of the province.

Fig. 47. The general form of the traditional Saparoan house as reinterpreted in Edinson Benítez's ethnoengineering designs for the Amazon. These structures were built in Ñukanchi Llacta, Napo province.

shape, the ridge beam is long (5–7 m or 16–24 ft). However, it does not bend despite the lack of internal supports, for two reasons. First, the wood used is remarkably strong. Second, the palm roofing is comparatively light and the roof is very steep (approximately 45°), so its weight naturally carries toward the periphery rather than to the center of the structure (fig. 49).

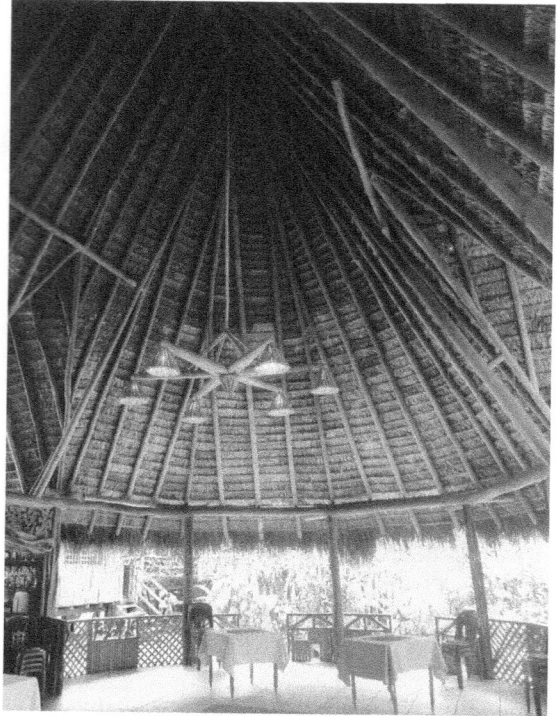

Fig. 48. A monumental, trussless Saparoan-style roof built on commission by traditional builders in an ecohostel in Puyo.

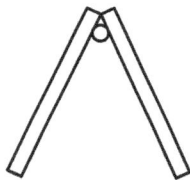

Fig. 49. Basic section of a Saparoan roof structure and the regular outcome of that framing logic, which explains the conventional trussed framing on the right.

SAPAROAN
ROOF
STRUCTURE

REGULAR OUTCOME
OF BUILDING
WITHOUT BRACING

COMMON
ROOF
STRUCTURE

PARTICIPATION AND SURPRISE

Ethnoengineering's design premise of combining the advantages of both traditional and professional knowledge makes great sense from a sustainability perspective because of its cultural, environmental, and economic postulates. In fact, it makes so much sense that both the planners and designers of the FISE III program took for granted that the result of the community participation process would be the villagers' wholesale embrace of the approach.

The deeply participatory nature of the program included the stipulation that villagers themselves were the ones to decide how the infrastructure should be built; that is, whether the ethnoengineering approach would be used, with its traditionalist stance, or a conventional functionalist modernism approach, with, say, concrete blocks and fiber-cement roofs. Surprisingly for the program's planners and designers, not one single community or *comunidad* where ethnoengineering was proposed was in favor of implementing the approach, according to Bayardo Ramírez's reports, a finding that I confirmed through my field research.

The ethnoengineering approach was proposed in about 196 *comunidades*,[7] "comunidades" being the administrative division term used in Ecuador for rural villages, and translating into English as "communities." (In order to avoid confusing the sociological term "community" with this administrative term, from this point on I will use the Spanish "comunidad" for the latter.) In the end, the ethnoengineering project was implemented in only thirty-one comunidades, and, even in those, the villagers' opposition to the project still subsisted during and after the project's implementation.

The extent of the villagers' opposition was such that it was a challenge getting just two comunidades to accept the building of the ethnoengineering prototypes. For instance, although Jorge Morán's construction of the coastal prototype was supposed to take only seven months, it took almost four years. Most of the delay was accountable to the fact that FISE, the government office that ran the ethnoengineering project, was unable to find a comunidad where people accepted the approach. The most iconic case of rejection of ethnoengineering was Telembí, which had been selected as the prototype site until villagers unexpectedly changed their minds, something that Morán realized only after having traveled to this site with his bamboo carpenters on unpaved roads and rivers for many days. In one of our interviews, Morán mentioned how happy and relieved he was to finally get started with the project after so much incertitude. However, not long after arriving in the village, he found himself in the middle of a community meeting where the village's CEJA president surprisingly announced that Morán's contract had been reassigned to another architect, who would be using "reinforced concrete, steel, [and] concrete blocks, because bamboo was worthless" (Morán 2004, 1).

Something similar happened with the Andean prototype. FISE fruitlessly searched for over a year for a comunidad where people would be interested in the project. Bolívar Romero, the designer of the Andean model, told me that he had to caution the office that if by a given date they had not selected a comunidad, his contract would no longer be valid, given that it would be well past the deadline. Only three days before that date FISE found such a comunidad: Michacalá. Later, just like Morán in Telembí (and later also in

Tacole), Romero found that the Michacalá villagers were ultimately unsure about the approach. Such hesitance, if not simply outright refusal, would become a recurrent theme throughout the entire execution of the ethnoengineering project. In Taquísquele, for example, after being presented with the ethnoengineering bamboo designs, villagers "screamed to the heavens," as Bayardo Ramírez told me. Similarly, Ramírez added, when Miguel Camino's team began its work in three Manabí villages, "people did not want anything to do with bamboo, but they wanted concrete poured in."

These examples offer an idea of the tremendous resistance among villagers to ethnoengineering's traditionalist proposition. This refusal occurred because the project had encountered a completely transformed rural society in Ecuador, where villagers already shared a deep connection with the modernist ethos. "The modern is good" was like a mantra that I heard from village to village as I carried out my field research. For example, referring to outside infrastructural interventions, a Ñukanchi Allpa woman I interviewed explained: "If you want to give something, give something that is good." A member of the local CEJA explained that they had objected to ethnoengineering's traditionalist proposition "because we live with that, with wood. In that [sense], we wanted to see good building, as in to be permanent." The woman concluded: "With those [previous] experiences, we can ask for good things."

As for the type of modernist construction that villagers favored, it was a very simple structure: a small gabled house, normally roofed in metal or fiber cement sheets, with walls built with wood boards or concrete blocks (fig. 50). Its aspect encompasses the core characteristics of modernist functionalism. Beyond its formal simplicity and the fact that it is built with industrially processed materials—tin, fiber cement, iron, concrete, sawn and dressed boards—it is very easy and quick to build, relatively affordable, and of relatively long durability with little maintenance. It is also spatially flexible, as it allows for easy subdivisions or additions. Thus, it has all the characteristics, and for rural villagers all the advantages, of modernist architecture. Such a simple gabled structure in no way looks like a clean Corbusian volume, but in principle it is all about the functionalist paradigm of modernist Corbusianism.

This type of house is omnipresent in Ecuador, from the high Andes to the Amazonian lowlands and the Pacific Coast. It is a very popular housing type among lower-income rural Ecuadorians, including those from indigenous and other ethnicities. Indeed, its popularity is such that when one travels through rural Ecuador, a bursting movement can be witnessed everywhere— rural dwellers doing anything they can do in order to materialize this aspiration, a modernist little house. For example, in a field visit to Michacalá, I saw

Fig. 50. Guanto Polo, Cotopaxi province: a typical modernist house in concrete block and tin roofing (*left*) contrasting with a traditional mud-and-thatch house (*right*).

Fig. 51. View of a llama caravan passing by the village of Michacalá Cotopaxi. The llamas carry concrete blocks for the construction of a modernist house high up in the Andes mountains.

a caravan of twenty llamas pass by carrying concrete blocks for the construction of a modernist house high up in the mountains (fig. 51). The owners had purchased these blocks in the city of Latacunga, hours away, and had transported the material by truck as far as the vehicle could reach, where the road ended. At that point they transferred the blocks to the llamas and continued on the journey for several more hours, up to a place located more than twelve thousand feet above sea level.

When they cannot afford to hire a truck, villagers simply use public transportation to move the industrial materials. In another sighting during my fieldwork, two rural dwellers (fig. 52) waited in the city of Tena for the bus to Chonta Punta, in the Napo province. Once the bus arrived, they checked over a half a ton of cement as their luggage. The fact that villagers go to such great lengths in order to bring those materials to distant areas reveals the extent to which modernist construction is appreciated in Ecuadorian rural settlements. In these settlements, as the ethnoengineering designers correctly observed, building materials are indeed usually available within easy reach—bamboo, mud, thatching palms, and so on. However, villagers prefer to travel afar and bring industrial materials by any possible means, such as llamas or the bus.

Such appreciation for the modern often surfaced in what villagers expected from the ethnoengineering project. In a consultation workshop with

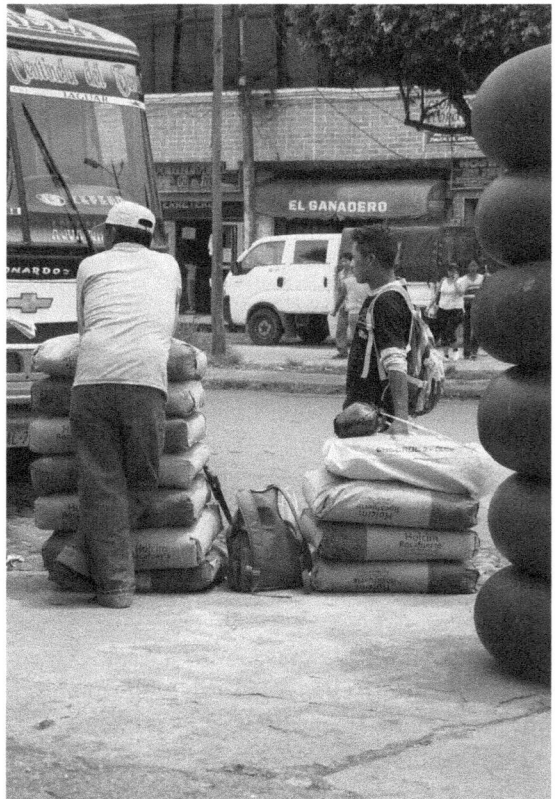

Fig. 52. Two villagers wait in the city of Tena for the bus to Chonta Punta, in the Napo province. They intend to check over a half a ton of cement as their luggage.

Fig. 53. A view of the Andean village of Apahua, which is populated mostly by Kichwa indigenous people. The majority of the housing in this village is now modernist housing built with concrete block walls and fiber-cement roofs. There remains only a very small number of traditional tapial mud houses.

Saparoan villagers, who were the most aboriginal group catered to by the project, Edinson Benítez asked them about their expectations for a school to be built as part of it. Their answer was: "We want zinc roofing so it lasts, and so it is a good modern school" (n.d., slide 72). Thus, as it turns out, the many sensible traditionalist design ideas that the ethnoengineering designers had relied upon were based on how these people had lived in the past. In Apahua, for example, the ethnoengineering construction was supposed to be in the tapial pressed earth technique. Yet, in this village, there remained only a handful of tapial houses—no more than three, as far as I could tell—as the majority of the construction was now done in concrete blocks (fig. 53).

Indeed, although no-nonsense from the viewpoint of the designers, the traditionalist notions espoused by ethnoengineering were now perceived as very exotic in the villages. Villagers now tended to identify traditional architecture as the housing of other people, in particular the wealthy people of cities. "These houses are not for us," a Tacole leader told me bluntly, then observing, "but for you, it is good," highlighting my position as a researcher of a higher social standing for whom traditional housing would therefore be more fitting. In fact, by the time of my fieldwork, the ethnoengineering structures stood as exceptional buildings in most of the villages, different from everything else around them (fig. 54). Pointing to the uniqueness of these designs, the Bejuco CEJA president said that people from other villages "have visited it [the project] here, and have realized this work is not [seen] everywhere." The visitors, he added, "say: 'If we ever had any money, we would build a house

Fig. 54. Ethnoengineering classroom unit in El Desquite (*right*), compared to a regular modernist classroom (*center*), and the typical housing (*left*).

like this to live in.'" A similar association between bamboo pole construction and the housing of the wealthy was also common in Los Colorados, where, in referring to the bamboo school, the CEJA president noted that "people get here and [say]: 'This belongs to a rich man.'"

The notion that traditional architecture is most fitting for people in privilege was often invoked in my interviews in both urban centers and rural areas. For example, a former FISE driver based in the city of Portoviejo mused, "If I had any money, that would be my house." A Domingo villager mentioned that their ethnoengineering bamboo school had been visited by a millionaire from the town of Santa Ana, who wanted to build a house for himself following its model. "The [technology] transfer was done for something else," Jorge Morán himself reflected with a tone of resignation. He trained two Tacole villagers in bamboo pole construction, and the first job they were offered was to build a beach house for a World Bank employee. The technology transfer had been done for the leisure building of a wealthy client, since there was no demand for these builders' new skills in their own village.

The amount of craft involved in the construction of these traditionalist structures, which makes them almost like fine art pieces, partly explains why they could be so desirable among people of privilege. The Huasicashca CEJA president said that people from other villages visited their ethnoengineering building and were impressed by the traditionalist effect of the walls, to which a texture had been added to emphasize the unevenness of handicraft work. The craft required for these structures was usually of a very high level. In Manabí, the bamboo structures designed by Miguel Camino were so intricate that it was not in fact possible to train villagers in their construction, as it would have been too time-consuming. Also, villagers with a mastery of traditional technologies were generally in short supply. The Manabí master builder was a master in the full sense of the term; he was a unique bamboo artist who had to juggle the Domingo, Los Colorados, and El Desquite contracts all at the same time because there was no other bamboo pole builder available. He also had to work fast because he was already committed to more work, for wealthy clients, elsewhere.

In Michacalá, Bolívar Romero found that traditional builders were now so familiar with reinforced concrete that, in order to secure good carpentry for his construction in this remote Cotopaxi village, he had to bring carpenters from the city. But even the local knowledge of traditional methods to procure wood was now scarce in the comunidades. The timber for the Apahua construction was also procured from the city, because only people in the city knew how to cut the wood during the appropriate moon phase for this task, according to the village's CEJA president. As for mud construction, tapial was now so rare that Romero mentioned to me an old builder he had employed in a previous project in Pujilí who was, he guessed, "perhaps the last *tapialero*." He worked with untrained villagers in the construction of the Michacalá walls, and they produced defective work. Also in Apahua, the local CEJA faced great difficulties in trying to find a master builder familiar with mud technology. After thirty years of widespread adoption of concrete, all the builders that applied for the job were reinforced concrete specialists; "The majority are *hormigoneros* [concrete builders]," Luis Gallegos commented. One by one, they withdrew from applying after learning that the project would be built with mud. Not only they did not know the traditional technology, but they were also not interested in learning it. Gallegos said that his organization, Funhabit, did offer them training, but they saw mud work as lowly and dirty. They said things like, "I am not going to get muddy with that other thing; I [do] go to Quito and work with concrete," thus demanding respect because they worked in concrete construction in the city. Only one finally agreed to undertake the work on the basis of having some experience with mud, though not much, as the constant rebuilding of defective work would eventually demonstrate.

IMPOSITION VIA PARTICIPATION

A relevant question is why, if the entire group of comunidades where the ethnoengineering approach was proposed rejected it, the project still ended up building in thirty-one of them? The answer, in fact, lies in participation. Some of the people in charge of running the participatory process, including FISE personnel, UCAT technical support professionals, and also, sadly, some of the project designers, used a series of techniques to manipulate participation that are worth examining. Understanding these techniques will help us to understand how participation works in the case of social design projects like this Ecuadorian ethnoengineering one and also the Medellín Biblioteca project described in chapter 2, projects that claim to be highly participatory but whose outcomes actually betray the participants' own interests. How exactly, despite partaking in an engaged participatory process, do people end up making decisions detrimental to their own interests?

According to what villagers described to me, most of the project's traditionalism advocates (FISE staff, UCAT members, and some designers) were ready to press for the adoption of ethnoengineering at all costs. Thus, they used a number of techniques to achieve this goal, ranging from progressively enforcing adoption, to providing inaccurate information about the project, to the more disruptive divide-and-conquer approach. In the midst of a generalized opposition, a project that was supposed to be participatory was indeed imposed, yet in such a way that it could still technically be called participatory. Just as in Medellín, in the Ecuadorian ethnoengineering project the beneficiaries were the ones who made decisions, but in making them, they were reacting to a series of imposition-via-participation techniques employed by advocates of the project's traditionalist stance. In the next three sections I will describe the most commonly used of these techniques.

From "Inducing" to "Implanting" the Approach

Sometimes, the ethnoengineering project's traditionalist agenda directly conflicted with the real priority identified in a given comunidad. Ethnoengineering was a priority-based project, so FISE was supposed to build only those types of constructions that were identified as such in the comunidades. This was not the case with the coastal prototype in the village of Tacole; the prioritization process in this village indicated that the most urgent need was the construction of a bridge. However, FISE had planned that the prototypes of the project should be buildings, and not any other type of infrastructure. Given that there had already been too many rejections, FISE did not want to lose the opportunity to finally build the prototype in a place where some interest had finally been expressed. In order to make this possible, the office then made the decision to grant the Tacole comunidad the requested bridge, but it added to its offer also a building—a bamboo structure to be used as a school kitchen. The villagers accepted the offer, but requested that this building be constructed in a conventionally modernist way, using concrete blocks rather than bamboo. The local leader quoted earlier explained to me how he talked frequently to Jorge Morán, the project designer, to explain the simple logic of their preference: "It [concrete] lasts longer than this [bamboo]. To me that's better."

This was a puzzling issue for FISE, because the goal of having offered a building was precisely to have it built with bamboo. As villagers persisted with their request, FISE staff and UCAT members decided to run several workshops to restate the advantages of ethnoengineering's traditionalism, with the expectation that villagers would be left with no valid reasons to reject the approach. However, the villagers stayed firm in their request; consequently, FISE and UCAT personnel then tried other approaches. First, as the leader put it, "They induced it [the project]. They said it was a government project, and that the government had said these types of classrooms shall be built." They also told villagers that they were unable to grant the villagers' request for concrete construction because "it was an order that they had to follow, and they could not [change it]." The leader added that later on, Morán himself appealed to the villagers' sympathies, pleading with them to allow him to fulfill his contract: "He had to pay an insurance policy of I don't know how much, because he had not done the work on time." Morán's situation was difficult because the construction work was stalled in the debate, and FISE was charging him onerous penalties for being past the deadline.

When the Tacole villagers' request for a construction in concrete remained undeterred, they were finally told that if they did not accept the ethnoengineering construction, then no construction at all would be done in their comunidad. "They said, 'Well, if it is not done [in that way] then we will look for another pilot comunidad,'" the leader said. Categorically, he added: "They *implanted* it on us! Of course! They said that was the order they had; that if not, the funding would go away."

Besides Tacole, villagers from other comunidades also received such pressure. It also happened, for instance, during the construction of the second prototype of the project, the Andean structure in Michacalá.[8] There, villagers explained to me that from the very beginning they had wanted to build the project using concrete blocks. They reasoned that blocks make the work easier and are more affordable, thus allowing them to build more infrastructure with the assigned budget.

Just as in Tacole, when the Michacalá villagers stood by their request, they were met with a variety of reasons why it was not possible. For example, one villager said they were told that their request could not be fulfilled because the project was an experiment: "Of course; we requested [concrete] blocks. We wanted blocks. But then, the engineers said that because of an experiment, they made us do it [in mud]." In fact, all the options that villagers were given were traditionalist, as confirmed by Bolívar Romero—following his design specifications, villagers were supposed to choose only between mud bricks, rammed earth, and pressed earth (tapial). As Romero explained to me, when the villagers insisted that they would prefer a modernist approach, they were warned by FISE staff and UCAT advisors that they would then have to reapply for the FISE III program—a slow, lengthy, and ultimately uncertain process because the comunidad might or might not be selected. This put pressure on villagers, who faced the risk of losing an investment that had already been granted to them.

Still, the villagers insisted that the construction would be more affordable using concrete blocks. Finally, they were told by FISE and the UCAT that the budget had been approved only for mud construction and nothing else:

M3:[9] We wanted to work with blocks. If it had been with blocks, with all that huge amount of money, we would have made such a tremendous house; three stories, two stories.

GA: Is it more expensive like this [using tapial] than with blocks?

M3: It was more expensive like this. The labor; it was expensive, expensive.

GA: More labor. And you said no, and they said yes?

M5: "No; not blocks."[10]

M3: "No." They said that the tapial was in the budget.

M4: That [in the budget] there was tapial, and that the budget was already [decided].

Thus, according to village participants in the two ethnoengineering prototype projects, the construction of these traditionalist structures resulted from the application of a number of techniques to progressively impose traditionalism through participation, from "inducing" to "implanting" the approach, as described by the Tacole leader. The project's traditionalism advocates at FISE and the UCAT became progressively stricter, shifting from trying to persuade villagers through workshops, to telling them it was a mandatory government experiment and they could not change anything, to finally arguing that the budget had been approved only for traditionalist construction. When all of these arguments failed, they bluntly told villagers that if they did not accept ethnoengineering, either no infrastructure would be built at all, or they would have to reapply for the program and might not be selected.

Misleading Information

Another argument that ethnoengineering's traditionalism advocates frequently used to impose the approach was that the available budget would be insufficient to build a modernist infrastructure. However, the US$72,000 funding would surely have been enough because that was also the budget assigned to the majority of the many other FISE III projects that ended up built as modernist structures with concrete blocks, and it was sufficient in those cases. It is then obvious that villagers were being misled about the cost of construction with concrete. This occurred, for example, in Chisulchi Chico, where a woman who participated in the construction told me that among other reasons, "they also said that the money is not enough,[11] so mostly [because] of that it was made with adobe." Speaking along with another woman, she explained:

CHC1: They did tell us that there are also [concrete] blocks, that we can do it with blocks, but it is not convenient. I mean, it is not warm [inside], and things like that.
CHC2: FISE didn't allow it.
CHC1: And because it was better if we make it with materials from right here.
GA: Of course. Did they say that FISE did not allow it?
CHC1: Yes.
GA: OK. How did they say that?
CHC2: That they didn't allow it. I mean, that the money was not enough. And they said that the adobe, we had to make it. That from our side we had to provide that.
GA: I see. So as to make the money last.
CHC2: Yes.
CHC1: Yes.
GA: OK. But, how much money did they tell you there was [available]?
CHC1: They said US$72,000.

According to the two women, Chisulchi Chico villagers were told that if they used concrete blocks, the constructions would not be as warm inside—this was another routine line that the project's traditionalism advocates often used. Then the villagers were told that FISE did not allow the use of concrete for the project, and also that the budget was not enough and therefore the villagers had to manufacture the adobe bricks on their own as the comunidad's economic contribution. The villagers were indeed made aware of the available budget, yet they were misled into believing that this amount would be insufficient for concrete block construction.

Similar situations occurred in Domingo and Los Colorados. Having hired Miguel Camino well in advance of the community participation process meant that FISE had decided beforehand to build with bamboo, since this is Camino's specialty. However, during the participation process, it became clear also in these villages that the main priority was not a building but instead another type of infrastructure, in this case a road. In order to lead villagers to disregard this priority and opt instead for a bamboo structure, the UCAT technical advisors argued that the budget would not be sufficient for the construction of a road. A woman who was part of the process explained:

When they came to have the meeting we talked about the road, because we have no access road; that was it. Then, they said, those from the UCAT, those that were walking around, that the money was not enough for a road. But looking again, now we say: I know that the school is beautiful; it is perfect. But we do have a stone quarry over here; it is so close! If they could not [afford the complete road], at least they could have done some [of it]. But anyway, since they said it was not enough, then we chose the little schoolhouse.

The Domingo villagers were pressed into selecting a building and not a road, also with the argument that the budget would not be enough for another type of infrastructure. As the woman expressed it, while they appreciated what they had received, the villagers still reasoned that with a quarry onsite, the budget could have been used to at least get the road project started (as in, say, an unpaved road) even if it was not enough for a fully finished road. However, also in this case, and just like in Tacole, after agreeing to the construction of a building, the Domingo villagers still expected a regular building with reinforced concrete, one "made of iron," as several of them described it to me. The UCAT professionals then countered with a plethora of arguments in favor of traditionalism, including also the climate efficiency claim that a bamboo construction would be cooler inside. Nonetheless, the villagers still insisted on reinforced concrete.

They did not succeed. When I carried out my interviews about a year after the project conclusion, villagers spoke about those events with a tone of resignation. However, Bayardo Ramírez said that at the time of the discussions, they had reacted so furiously that the work was stalled. Given that it was not possible to settle the differences between villagers and UCAT members, representatives from both the central and regional FISE offices had to travel and personally appeal to villagers to let the project continue. FISE ultimately carried out the Domingo project as a conventional architectural project with no input whatsoever from villagers. As one villager described it, "just as the design came, that's how they built it." Not only the design but also the specialized labor was brought from outside. This top-down attitude permeated the whole intervention in this village. In the case of Domingo (as well as the other two Camino-designed Manabí projects), basically none of ethnoengineering's participation claims were followed during project execution. Villagers were left out of every major decision, from budgeting to design to contracting.

In Los Colorados, too, villagers had identified a road as their main priority. It was an even more pressing need here, as this was the most isolated among the Manabí ethnoengineering comunidades. The local CEJA president explained:

LC1: Of course, it gets ugly here, because this path gets tremendously [muddy], from here to Pueblo Nuevo. From here to Pueblo Nuevo, the mud gets awful.
GA: Muddy . . .
LC1: Yes, deep. Horses get stuck, they fall in the fields, entering [the village] . . .
GA: And what do you do when there is an emergency, for example a medical emergency or something like that?
LC1: Here, let's say, [we do it] with our shoulders. In the winter [the rainy season], we do it ourselves, the comunidad. [If there is] illness, we have to look for a hammock, a bamboo pole, and off we go, shouldering [the patient] from here to there.

The village of Los Colorados becomes so hard to access during the rainy season that, during medical emergencies, people are carried out by foot by fellow villagers who must deal with the deep mud, in which even horses get stuck and fall. Thus, it was expectable that the villagers identified a road as their main priority. Yet, refusing this request, the UCAT members also in this case told them that the program funding was not enough. The CEJA president explained: "They say that the money was not enough for the road." The villagers had no other option than to accept this justification; however, since the issue was supposedly one of cost, they countered that FISE should then build a concrete block structure that, they reasoned, would be more affordable than a bamboo one. As the CEJA president explained:

Because of the expense, I told them: "Why don't you just do it with cement only, so it is faster." Not much is spent, and whatever was left could have been put [into] let's say, the fencing, a good fencing.

This was clearly a well-founded rationale to save expenses: They could use a conventional reinforced concrete approach, and with the savings they could build a good quality fence for the school. In response, the UCAT members also resorted to a wide variety of arguments. The CEJA president said they were told that classrooms are noisier when built with concrete than with bamboo, and that "cement has a chemical [product]," an argument apparently meant to instill fears among villagers about the impact of concrete construction on human health. Regardless of that, the villagers insisted on concrete. Thus, being left with no arguments, the UCAT architect finally admitted that FISE had decided beforehand to build a bamboo structure and thus put an end to the discussion. The CEJA president explained:

LC1: So he says, "This is what the study [ethnoengineering] was about, and this is how it is going [to be]."
GA: Who told you that?
LC1: I mean, that, let's say, [this came] from, from FISE itself. Since we were left alone with the UCAT . . . Really, it was a UCAT architect. We asked him why it wasn't possible [to use concrete], and "this is how it [the project] is going [to be]; this is how they gave it." [He said that] FISE had given him the order that it be made in that way, and that was it.

This is how the traditionalist approach ended up being bluntly imposed in the village of Los Colorados. Saying that FISE had mandated that the projects be traditionalist and that this order could not be changed was another argument used by UCAT members to manipulate participation throughout the project. It was also applied in the village of Huasicashca, although apparently not in a consistent way, which led to confusion among the villagers. As the local CEJA president described it, villagers received mixed messages about what they could and could not do regarding the project. While some UCAT members told villagers that they were not supposed to change anything in the architectural plans, others (correctly) told them that they could in fact do so. In response to these contradictory messages, the villagers decided to play safe by adhering to the original design plans: "So we said, 'Whom to believe, the one, the other, the one? Let's just do it as it is there [in the plans], so as not to have any problem later on." Per FISE III's regulations, villagers were contractually committed with the government to conclude the project, so in order to avoid any liability issues, the Huasicashca villagers opted for the first (and, to them, safer) option of not changing anything, thus accepting the traditionalist proposal in full. Yet, reflecting another form of pressure that villagers were receiving, the Huasicashca CEJA president added that they also felt pressed for time. Villagers, she said, had spent a long time debating the adoption of the traditionalist proposal, and at some point they became afraid that if they delayed their decision for too much longer, FISE could take away the funding and assign it to another comunidad; she said this had happened elsewhere. Thus, the villagers' logic was that accepting the traditionalist proposal in full would help them avoid further debate among themselves.

Dividing and Conquering

The last technique of imposition-via-participation I will describe was a divide-and-conquer approach, in which some of the project's traditionalism advocates decided to capitalize on the comunidades' normal internal fragmentation, siding with the local supporters of traditionalism and pitting them against those who opposed it. The most striking example is that of Yanaturo. In this village, Grace Almeida doubled as a UCAT member and a project designer, so she was essentially in charge of persuading villagers to accept her own designs. For quite some time, Almeida had upheld the idea of developing self-sustainable villages, communities that generate everything from within (e.g., food, clothing, electricity) "in a way that is adequate to the place, which does not harm the environment" (Asamblea 2010, 6:42). Before Almeida's participation in the ethnoengineering project, this was only an unrealized idea. However, the fact that it largely coincided with ethnoengineering's overall sustainability goal became the decisive factor that led FISE to hire her, despite the fact that she had no field experience. Yet, once she tried to materialize this idea through the project, Almeida met great opposition from villagers.

For the design of a classroom in Yanaturo, Almeida proposed to use the villagers' own traditional housing form, a hipped-roof structure that villagers call "four corners." They staunchly opposed this plan, expressing instead a predilection for the little modernist gabled house described earlier:

Y1: We wanted to do it like this little house [the villager points to the modernist gabled house in concrete pictured in fig. 55].
Y2: Not like [the] four corners. Only with a roof, nothing more. Simply that.
Y1: It would have been faster. Now, because it has four corners, you see, it is made of concrete, wood, cement, all that is wasted. For example, doing it like these houses, the thing would have been done faster; it would have been less expensive, you see?

This quote clearly reflects the villagers' disapproval of their own traditional housing, which they argued uses more material, and their preference for the modernist house type that has a conventional gabled roof.

As a way to overcome this opposition, Almeida decided to side with a few villagers who agreed with her proposal, marginalizing the many who did not. In our interviews, villagers contended that she had expelled the dissenters from the participatory process, while others simply felt discouraged and left on their own:

Fig. 55. The modernist house that Yanaturo villagers identified as the model they had intended to follow for their ethnoengineering project.

Y2: When one criticized, "Let's do it like this; with other things [materials] like that"

Y1: Just with concrete blocks.

Y2: They didn't want to know anything, and one—

Y5: Was taken out; was expelled.

Y2: One was commanded to get out. The ones who stayed were those who—

Y1: Those who were obedient to the architect; they stayed. . . . Since she was the builder, the boss, [she would say,] "You go away; he comes here."

GA: What's that?

Y1: She was the head of the [construction] works, right?

GA: Yes.

Y1: If we talked back to her or said, "Let's do it in concrete blocks," then [she would respond,] "Nothing with you; go there. Those who want it with adobe, you stay." That was it.

GA: Did she separate you?

Y1: "Separate them!"

Y4: Only eleven of us stayed.

Y1: That is why; that is why this construction went so badly.

As the villagers explained, anyone who suggested building the structure in concrete blocks was expelled from the participatory process, and only those who were "obedient" and agreed to a mud construction were invited to stay. According to the villagers' recollection of the events, marginalizing opponents became a common practice throughout the whole project. Whenever someone else raised objections, that person was also expelled. Consequently, most people lost interest and left on their own:

Y1: [Talking about Y2] He was also part of that group. Those who stopped, saying, "Let's do it in concrete blocks," which the architect did not want. Because of that, she ordered to have him expelled from the group. She kept expelling people. People didn't want that anymore. They then didn't pay attention to the architect anymore. Now go screw yourselves.

Y2: We quit, then.

Thus, the villagers explained, the people who remained became tired of Almeida's practice of expelling those who proposed concrete blocks. As a result, they lost interest in the project and quit.

Grace Almeida's tough approach reflects her philosophy of ruling with an iron fist as the best way to work with Ecuadorian indigenous people. This is Almeida's response to what she argues is a paternalistic approach that has done them no good. Just as her ethnoengineering constructions were in progress, Almeida was elected as a member of Ecuador's Congress, the National Assembly. She made this philosophy clear in her opening statement as a congresswoman, as she observed, playing with words, that "our indigenous people used to ask for *abono* [fertilizer], not for a *bono* [welfare check]" (Asamblea 2009, 6:40). She criticized in these terms a cash transfer program established by the government. The program is officially called "the human development bonus," although popular use gives it the cruder label "poverty bonus." It is a small welfare program that, by the time of Almeida's speech, provided a meager US$35 a month—16 percent of the minimum wage—to Ecuador's poorest citizens, particularly unemployed mothers, elderly people, and people with disabilities. Given the high levels of poverty among indigenous populations, a considerable part of the program funding goes to these populations.

Almeida reaffirmed her position when I interviewed her. Although agreeing that the Ecuadorian indigenous poor suffer under current economic conditions, she argued, "We cannot fall into the paternalism of giving them thirty dollars every month and that's it." Then she volunteered that "self-sufficiency will precisely aim for them not to depend on anything but themselves." This might make sense, but it was her idea that she had tried to impose at any cost in Yanaturo—the villagers had a different vision of their own future.

According to the villagers' descriptions, after they removed themselves or were expelled from the building process, Almeida turned to another segment of the comunidad: young, schooled people. She subscribed to the notion of young versus old, praising the youth for their open minds while chastising as obsolete the elderly leaders, including the current and former comunidad presidents. Addressing this charge, Almeida reasoned in our interview that there always exist dividing factors and groups in a community, and it is not always possible to work with everyone at once. Although this is also a sensible observation, her apparent efforts to capitalize on that social division ultimately deepened it to such an extent that this division became central in a dispute among villagers about the project. In the end, a group of five young members of the comunidad took over the Yanaturo CEJA, undertaking the execution of the ethnoengineering project on their own and ignoring the opposition from the older members. It did not end up well, since they were unable to complete the project, as I will explain in the next section.

THE OUTCOMES OF THE IMPOSITION

Thus, the ways in which traditionalism advocates set out to impose ethnoengineering by means of controlling participation were many and varied. As for the outcomes of such imposition, first there were some situations in which the buildings were abandoned midway through the construction, and one of them even collapsed. Second, in the majority of cases the work was completed, but it was structurally defective and/or problematic from a social standpoint. Third, there were a few but significant positive outcomes, those of projects that were successful even despite the imposition.

These varied outcomes are explained by the fact that villagers still resisted even after the traditionalist projects were imposed. Although in the most problematic cases their resistance slowed down and in some cases even stalled the projects, in the successful cases the villagers managed to strategically tweak the projects and make them still work in their interests. I will explain how these situations played out with the examples of Yanaturo and Pilchipamba (demonstrating the first outcome, of abandoned projects), Michacalá and Azabí del Mortiñal (the second outcome, of completed but problematic projects), and Apahua, Ñukanchi Allpa, and Chibuleo San Luis (the third outcome, of successful projects).

Abandoned Projects: Yanaturo and Pilchipamba

As explained above, Grace Almeida decided to deal with the rejection of traditionalism in Yanaturo by capitalizing on social divisions, pitting the more educated youth against the older generation of mostly illiterate villagers, and favoring the former in a way in which they ended up taking over the project by running the local CEJA. However, this group was unable to complete the project due to poor monitoring of construction, misuse of material, bad procurement practices, bad accounting, conflicts of interest in contracting, and overall corruption. As a consequence of these malpractices, the available funding quickly ran out. The construction stopped after beneficiaries—who, as mentioned, were committed by the terms of the program to make an economic contribution in labor (that is, to provide free labor)—completed this contribution, and when the paid workers quit because their payments were not being honored by the CEJA. The project was officially suspended after FISE's monitoring visits found the work to be far behind schedule; the office decided to freeze any further funding disbursements until the *contraloría,* the government comptroller's office, clarified the situation.

The Yanaturo project consisted of a classroom and nearly one hundred toilets. With respect to the classroom, the CEJA managed to complete only the external walls with adobe bricks of very poor quality. An upper beam ring in concrete was cast with only a few very thin iron rods; being structurally substandard, it quickly bent over the window framing. Moreover, the concrete mix, which had been prepared with too much sand and too little cement, easily crumbled. Fundraising on their own and outside of the project's budget, villagers managed to procure some fiber-cement roofing in order to protect the mud walls, which were at risk of collapse after prolonged exposure to the rain. However, they could not afford all of the required roofing, so portions of the building still remained exposed. The structure was then an unusable building at risk of collapse, with incomplete walls, an incomplete roof, and very poorly built overall. It had no windows, no doors, no electrical or water installations, and on the bare soil floor lay a pile of unused—and now, after so much time, unusable—cement. A woman of the comunidad summarized the building's condition with a sad joke: "This will work to raise the pigs." It would certainly be more fitting for pigs than as a place to educate their children (fig. 56).

With regard to the toilets, dozens of unfinished outhouses crowded the village landscape upon the project suspension. As several villagers argued, these toilets were originally conceived as little houses with thatched roofs, but most people objected to the roofs by saying they were not sheep, implying that the tiny thatch-roofed structures looked more like corrals for animals than like structures for human use. They were successful in opposing the thatch, but instead obtained flat roofs that, in a rainy and humid area like this, meant that the water often did not drain off but simply stayed on the roof, exposing it to leaks. In the end, the roofs leaked not only because of their flat form, but also due to the poor-quality concrete mix (fig. 57).

Fig. 56. The condition of the Yanaturo ethnoengineering classroom unit upon the project conclusion.

Time passed, and the project remained suspended by FISE. Uncertain as to whether it would ever be resumed, some villagers gradually began to work individually, with each family building their own toilet using their own labor and money. This effort led to several toilets that appeared finished, although most did not actually work, given that the issue of water provision had yet to be addressed. During the dry season, Yanaturo villagers face difficulty in procuring even the minimal amount of water for their farming activities, and spending hundreds of gallons every day to flush toilets was certain to strain the availability of an already scarce resource. Still, according to villagers, the CEJA-appointed outside contractor dishonestly claimed that the work that villagers had done was his own, and he was paid for it. After that, FISE decided to close the incomplete toilets project, reporting it as complete in its control database. As for the classroom, by partially covering the crumbling walls with the fiber-cement roofing, the villagers had managed to keep the building from fully collapsing, but this was as much as they could do with their meager funding. The structure remained in that condition—an empty, incomplete, and crumbling shell—when FISE decided to also declare it complete.

Unfortunately, similarly problematic was Almeida's project in Pilchipamba. This was an even more ambitious project that included the construction of a bridle path and toilets for the existing housing, as well as the construction of a full boarding school. The goal of the latter was to have children in this distant and dispersed high Andean village live in the facilities during the week, thus reducing their long walks between home and school to only the weekends. Almeida designed this school to have all the necessary amenities, so as to make the children's life away from home comfortable. In addition to classrooms and bedrooms, as well as a kitchen and dining hall, the school was to be furnished with composting toilets, an icon of the sustainable life that Almeida envisioned. Also iconic was her proposal that the school be built

Fig. 57. A villager scratches concrete off a leaking ceiling in one of the Yanaturo toilets.

with *cob,* a European rammed earth building technology that she had learned in France. However, she did not succeed with the experiment of importing this technology into the high Andes. After too much trouble and impossibly slow and expensive work, the in-progress ethnoengineering mud structure collapsed in the excess humidity during the construction process. Not only was the environment too humid for the mud walls to stand before there was any chance to protect them with any roofing, but also the technology demanded too much work to be carried out in a place that was too distant and hard to access. Almeida could not be as constantly present as she needed to be for the technology to be implemented by local contractors, who were unfamiliar with it, and by villagers, who, as in Yanaturo, had disagreed with its implementation. As the cob walls collapsed, the Pilchipamba project was abandoned altogether (fig. 58). Eventually, FISE quietly closed it with the simple note: "contract concluded, work not finished" (FISE 2009, 2).

Remarkably, and despite this outcome, Almeida later refashioned the

Fig. 58. View of the ethnoengineering construction in Pilchipamba as it stood when the project was abandoned.

troubling story of Pilchipamba as an exemplary sustainability project. In her first congressional speech, she made an impassioned call to foster economic sustainability and invoked her own work to show how it was possible:

With US$72,000 I was able to build a school [of] 360 square meters, a four- or five-kilometer bridle path, [and] basic [toilet] units. Because that money was used [for] local materials from the area, labor from the area, it was reinvested, and they were able to build their own woodshop. And because they sold to the same building project the doors, windows, and floors, and everything else that is in wood, we have been able to buy alpacas for them to be able to produce fiber, natural fiber for clothing. That means these are resources that can rotate on top of each other. It is just a matter of wisdom, and knowing how to use the money. (Asamblea 2009, 7:08)

In this speech, Almeida described a self-sustainable project she claims to have built, in which villagers were ostensibly hired to build their own public infrastructure. In doing so, she claims, they earned money that they reinvested by building a woodworking workshop; the workshop generated income, which in turn was used to buy alpacas. Almeida's speech is curious because the project she described precisely fits the description of the ethnoengineering project. Not only was US$72,000 the standard budget per comunidad, but Almeida was, in fact, describing the architectural program of Pilchipamba.

In her speech, Almeida did not identify the name or location of the project. In fact, she described the process in a very passionate and poetic yet vague Spanish style. To clarify, I asked Almeida herself, and she confirmed that she was referring to the Pilchipamba project. It is hard to understand how this project could be presented in such terms when all that was left was a ruin of mud and, as in Yanaturo, a comunidad was left with nothing but problems after the whole project crumbled before their eyes. Almeida had created a fictional account about the successful outcome of an ambitious social infrastructure initiative. That initiative was based on a great idea, that of economic self-sustainability by the means of reembracing traditionalism. However, this was not an idea coming from those people for whom the project had been conceived, since the majority of them had objected to it as they had their own ideas of improvement. Through a nominally participatory process, the project had been imposed despite the villagers' refusal with very troubling outcomes, both socially and materially. The fact that Almeida still opted for presenting the project's outcome as a story of unqualified success recalls two of the projects described in the previous chapter, Al Borde Architects' Nueva Esperanza School and Kunlé Adeyemi's Makoko School. In those cases, too, the designers brushed off the collapse of their structures as trivial events, and they continued to uphold them as exemplars of sustainability even after their collapse.

Completed but Problematic Projects: Michacalá and Azabí del Mortiñal

The ethnoengineering designers, and other traditionalism advocates, frequently offered an argument based on the assumption that traditional life in rural Ecuador was originally in essence self-sufficient. They further argued that, in order to help villagers return to that primeval condition of self-sufficiency, it was necessary to recover traditional construction practices as accurately as possible, with the ultimate goal of reimplanting these practices in the comunidades. The best example of this endeavor is Bolívar Romero's Andean ethnoengineering prototype, a day care structure built in the village of Michacalá. Among the forty-eight structures of the ethnoengineering project, this was the one that most closely resembled a traditional house (see

Fig. 59. Bolívar Romero's ethnoengineering prototype in Michacalá.

fig. 59). As mentioned, the walls were built with the now rare tapial, and the roofing was in thatched grass.

For this design, Romero followed ancient Inka architectural practices such as the *hanan/urin* binary space division, the symbiotic integration between house and natural environment, and a solar orientation that made certain facades and corners point to the position of the sun during certain times of the year. In Romero's view, only such a design would provide Ecuadorian indigenous people a way to reclaim their own cosmovision and to prevail over the hegemonic history and symbols. Thus, Romero was proposing for indigenous people "a space that replicates their identity, and not the white-mestizo idea of nationality, homeland, order, and socio-political hierarchy that is definitely outside their own cultural behavior" (2004, 12). This was the reason that he set out to create what he called "a replica of the traditional rural house of the Sierra" (6). In his proposal, this traditional architectural object was meant to lead Andean indigenous people back to a traditional life, which he argued was being lost. Critical of his own "white-mestizo" ancestry (6), Romero proposed keeping indigenous people from accessing "Western modern culture" (6), which he saw as detrimental to their traditions.

However, as I have explained, Romero's proposal met with strong opposition from the very people on whose behalf he believed it was made. Also, from the basic standpoint of function, the building ultimately did not work as expected. The decision to orient the structure in the solar Inkan way exposed the central corridor to a cross-ventilation that, in this snowy environment, made the building—intended as a day care center—unbearably cold for children. One of the villagers who participated in the process explained to me that after Romero had "produced his decision," the villagers commenced the construction work during the warm season, so they did not foresee this could happen. Otherwise, the villager said, "we would have done it like this," gesturing with his hands to indicate the exact opposite to the solar orientation. In other words, the villagers would have freely dispensed with cultural symbolism and radically changed the orientation of the design for the sake of function so that the building would be warmer.

Highlighting those contradictions of cultural restoration, a FISE project consultant sympathetic to the villagers' plea described to me her impressions after an official visit to the village, ironically observing that the building had been designed "supposedly using all the elements of a Sierra indigenous house: tiny, dark, windowless, cold, ugly, uninhabitable." She also observed that "the kitchen had no ventilation and it was very narrow, tiny." Because of that, when women cooked in their traditional way with wood, smoke soon accumulated inside the structure just as it did in traditional houses. This description is interesting because it highlights another side of traditionalism: life has changed in traditional communities, and certain nuisances that were perhaps inevitable in the past such as darkness, overcrowding, cold, and smoke can now be perceived differently.

When I interviewed Romero, he earnestly conceded those and other project's shortcomings. By that time, he had already become deeply critical of his own and other designers' engagement with ethnoengineering, categorically asserting that the project had failed, "and we all [those who carried out the project] are to blame."

In the case of Azabí del Mortiñal, the villagers, seeing that they had been left with no other option than a traditionalist model, decided to select one even though it was meant for a different ethnicity, simply because they liked how it looked. Although they knew that the ethnoengineering project's architectural designs were specific to each ethnocultural zone of the country, they told Bayardo Ramírez of their intention to explore the designs for the other zones as well, despite the fact that those were not part of the package of options that FISE offered for Andean comunidades. The villagers ended up selecting a design for the Amazon, and there now exists a building modeled on a lowland Amazonian house high up in the Andes mountains (fig. 60).

There was a problem, however. Acting upon their interest in modernism, the Azabí villagers discarded the traditional elements of the Amazon Saparoan house by applying materials that did not originally correspond to it. For the roofing, they did away with thatch and instead selected an industrially manufactured glazed tile. The rationale for this choice was functionalist:

The villagers were seeking a durable type of tile so that reroofing would not be necessary for a while.[12] The change in the roofing material presented a structural problem because the roof became much heavier than a traditional thatch Saparoan framing, with only two supporting columns, could bear. In addition, the fact that the villagers had chosen ceramic tiles meant that the high pitch of the traditional structure had to be lowered in order to keep the tiles from falling. This created a higher load to be countered toward the center of the structure.

There was a simple solution to this structural issue: add internal columns. This would disrupt the beauty of the Saparoan house's free spatial flow, but the structure would be sound (fig. 61). This was what the project's master builder,

Fig. 60. In the distance, to the left of the building complex, a distinctive Amazonian roof in the middle of the Andes mountains. This is the ethnoengineering structure in the village of Azabí del Mortiñal.

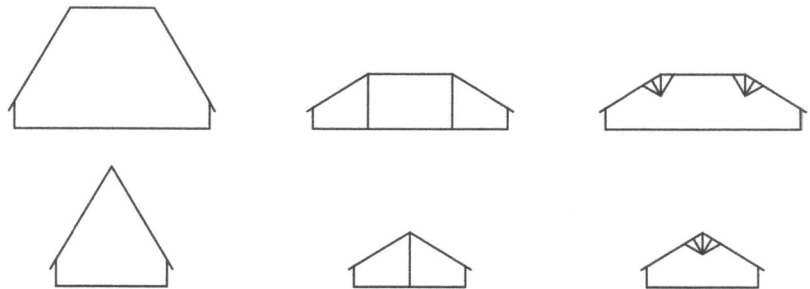

Fig. 61. The middle and the right columns of the diagram show two contrasting visions on how to reinterpret the structure in the left column.

TRADITIONAL STRUCTURE   VILLAGERS' STRUCTURE   DESIGNER'S STRUCTURE

SUSTAINABILITY AND PRIVILEGE

Fig. 62. Experimental roof structure in the ethnoengineering project of Azabí del Mortiñal.

a villager, recommended. However, the technical director, an engineer and landowner who had retired to the village, decided to take on the intellectual challenge of still faithfully replicating the column-free Saparoan structural arrangement despite the change in materials. This led to the development of an experimental framing that, in order to do away with internal columns, is self-supported through a system of diagonals that neutralize the roof loads by coming together to a single point (fig. 62). The structural knot hangs from the roof, as opposed to supporting it. It looks very elegant as a piece of structural design. However, villagers raised serious concerns, which were downplayed by the engineer. A teacher from the school confided to me that she felt "there was great danger that the building fell, that it fell down." She explained:

Another fellow [villager] came, a *maestro* [master builder], and said that this, rather than building an educational center, they are building a graveyard. Because this, with the weight, is going to fall down; it does not have [any columns] to rest on.

As quoted by the teacher, the builder's assessment does make sense. The system looks very stable, but if there happened to be any sudden lateral movement disturbing the perfect system of counterbearing loads, there would indeed be a risk of the roof collapsing on the children. In this area of the Andes, lateral movements from earth tremors are very common. Azabí is located in a very active earthquake zone, to the extent that, by the time of my fieldwork, the most recent tremor had occurred only a few months earlier. As I noticed in the previous chapter when referring to similar structural experiments by Al Borde, it is common construction wisdom that in earthquake-prone areas, more conservative, less experimental structural designs are safest. The Azabí villagers were well aware of the risks that such a structural experiment posed in their case, and they were anxious about it. The teacher said:

We thought everything was going to [collapse]. . . . I mean, seeing it in this way, due to the great weight of the tiles, I think that was dangerous with a seismic movement.

She added that the builder insistently pleaded with the engineer against proceeding with such an unusual structure:

He said no, and talked back to the engineer a lot. He said: "No, engineer. This makes me afraid; this is up in the air, and with a great weight from the tiles. This, if we climb up and this opens up . . . we are going to 'fly,'" he said.

The villagers' concerns fell on deaf ears. In an attempt to break their opposition, the engineer apparently told them that the system had already been tried with success elsewhere:

The engineer assures [us] that . . . there will not be any problem because this construction is a model that is already in the *Oriente,* and that as of today nothing has happened.

The engineer was likely referring to the structural system of the ethnoengineering project of Ñukanchi Allpa, which I will describe later. This project was also inspired by the Saparoan house and its distinctive long beam with no internal supports. However, the construction was being carried out at about the same time as Azabí's, so there was no evidence yet that the system was going to work. More important, although the concept of an unsupported long beam was similar, the structural demands were different. In Ñukanchi Allpa, located in the Amazon, hard and long pieces of timber were indeed available, while trees in the Andes are generally less resistant and shorter.

Also, the Ñukanchi Allpa's zinc roofing was far lighter than the ceramic roofing used in Azabí.

In the end, the Azabí villagers managed to persuade the engineer to allow them to install at least some bracing. The teacher said that finally, "after we demanded it so much, because the engineer did not want [it], we had those timbers put up there." However, as figure 62 shows, the experimental part of roofing structure still remained with sectioned-off columns suspended in the air. During my time in the village, a general anxiety remained about the soundness of this structure, as well as the issue of what would happen once the inefficient structural timbers began to deteriorate. Granted, the villagers themselves had selected the building form, but evidently they were only interested in the innovativeness of this form, not in the traditional elements of its structure. Following the teacher's description, they instead proposed a simple, tried-and-true, conventional system of bracing and columns. However, in the interest of honoring the traditional structure, the engineer had ended up imposing on villagers a risky structural experiment. The villagers were left with that unsafe structure to maintain and repair on their own. They endured their concerns mostly in silence; the teacher, who was the most vocal in opposing the project, lamented that the other villagers only privately agreed with her. However, as a state worker whose salary did not depend on the village's main employers—who happened to be the engineer and her husband—she was freer to speak than the other villagers.

Successful Projects: Apahua, Chibuleo San Luis, and Ñukanchi Allpa

The ethnoengineering project's imposition-via-participation had in a few rare cases a more positive outcome. Those were cases in which villagers were able to negotiate their visions of the project and/or they had supporters in privilege (e.g., designers and project managers) who either directly helped them or indirectly allowed them to materialize their own visions of the project.

One such successful case is the ethnoengineering construction of Apahua, also a school structure. In this village, the focus of the most opposition was the tapial mud technology specified in the ethnoengineering base designs. The tipping point of this opposition was the collapse of a tapial wall after a long and frustrating process of work using this technology. Since none of the villagers who participated in the construction had expertise in tapial construction, they had to learn as they went, and tapial has a steep learning curve. Not once but several times, they had to demolish the work they had already done and start again because the walls would crack. When the wall fell down, the structure was almost completely finished; the roof had even been installed. Infuriated, the villagers refused to continue working with mud.

Seeing this opposition, Luis Gallegos, the school's designer and technical director, decided to take a different approach from the norm that had operated throughout the implementation of the ethnoengineering project. Rather than continuing to press for traditionalism, he agreed to halt construction and offered villagers the possibility of changing the project's specification of materials. They took this opportunity as far as they could. They switched from mud to cement and burnt bricks, which they procured in the city of Latacunga. Gallegos fully supported them in this change, which is apparent in how only a portion of the building is built in tapial and the rest is in bricks and cement (see fig. 63). Encouraged by Gallegos's support, the villagers took their modernist escapade even further, and requested a change also in the roofing material. The roof was originally designed to be in clay tiles, which the villagers were concerned could fly off the roof in the strong Andean winds. Gallegos then agreed to install an asphalt-coated roofing fabric on top of a layer of concrete. As he told me, villagers were "delighted" with this change because the industrial roof saved them time in construction and relieved them of future maintenance issues.

Thanks to Gallegos's support of the villagers' desire to modernize the structure, the project continued with no further issues and was successfully completed. A decisive factor behind this successful outcome was that Gallegos managed to navigate the Ecuadorian government politics on behalf

Fig. 63. The ethno-engineering structure in Apahua. The left, buttressed portion is built with tapial, while the right is built with bricks. The roof is in reinforced concrete covered with an asphalt-coated fabric.

of the villagers. He was able to convince FISE to accept the redesign of the Apahua project in the terms proposed by the villagers, without his becoming legally liable for not delivering the design in the traditionalist way it had been originally contracted.

In two other cases, Chibuleo San Luis and Ñukanchi Allpa, villagers were able to oppose traditionalism by strategically negotiating their own views of modernity. They decided to appeal to the FISE managers who made the final decisions about the project, thus bypassing the UCAT and FISE field staff.

The ethnoengineering construction for Chibuleo San Luis had been originally designed as an "educational module in wood" (Ramírez 2009). However, villagers refused this proposal, which led to a redesign, undertaken also by Luis Gallegos. Following the project's base design specifications, he proposed mud construction, adobe bricks, and a timber framing. However, villagers refused that option too, on the grounds of durability, arguing that they had the evidence of adobe houses in their own comunidad that were highly deteriorated. Seeing that opposition, Gallegos then developed a third option, which used burnt bricks. FISE, however, decided to go with his mud construction option and gave the commission for this construction to a Riobamba civil engineer.

When the construction process began, the villagers again challenged this traditionalist proposal and ultimately managed to build a conventional structure in burnt bricks and reinforced concrete. They did this by directly involving a FISE manager in the decisions and bypassing the UCAT and FISE staff. To sell their proposal, they sought approval only for partial changes, but they did this several times; thus, progressively, they were able to completely transform the traditionalist proposal. They started by objecting to the mud bricks. After the manager approved the switch to burnt bricks, villagers then objected to the wood columns, expressing concerns that this material would deteriorate too rapidly in the copious rains. Once the villagers obtained approval for that change as well, they targeted the roof, which in the FISE proposal was supposed to be of thatch. FISE then counterproposed a roof slab type that they also did not like. Thus, villagers engaged in the negotiation process once again and finally achieved what they had set out to do from the beginning. As one of the villagers explained to me, "Then again, we talked to the engineer, we went to talk to the director, and then he opted for it to be as it is now, which is what we had [initially] asked for."

The Chibuleo San Luis villagers were finally able to undertake a construction with columns in reinforced concrete, burnt bricks, and a glazed tile roof: a nontraditionalist construction, as they had envisioned from the beginning. Significantly, little by little the members of this mostly Chibuleo Kichwa indigenous comunidad disposed of all the indigenous folk elements of the

Fig. 64. The ethnoengineering project of Chibuleo San Luis, redesigned by villagers.

ethnoengineering design—walls, columns, and roof—until they completely *deindigenized* the building. The end result was a regionalist modernism structure that visually is clearly more related to a Spanish colonial building than to the indigenous structures the designers had envisioned on behalf of the villagers (fig. 64).

The fact that the Chibuleo San Luis villagers succeeded with these changes prompted a series of processes of appropriation during and after construction. The villagers tackled the construction project as a fully em-powered group. In terms of the program, this was a complex project, more so than many of those that did not succeed, such as Yanaturo. However, the villagers accomplished it without any major issues, producing construction work of great quality, carried out mostly by the villagers themselves, including specialized labor; the only outside workers in this project were the technical director and the master builder. The construction was finished before the deadline, even though they faced disbursement delays from FISE. The local CEJA managed the budget in such a way that there was even enough funding left to fully furnish the classrooms, and there were still funds left over afterward. CEJA members went on to become actively involved with the functioning of the school, lobbying the province's board of education[13] to have three additional teachers assigned, which made it possible for the school to accommodate a greater number of children. Also, as of the time of my fieldwork, school parents were duly contributing fifty cents a year for the building maintenance.

The Chibuleo school project was realized by a group of villagers who strategically and successfully negotiated their vision of the project. A woman who participated in the project celebrated: "It was almost like, say, a community design. . . . We tried to subject it [the project] to our ideals." She concluded that "neither the engineers nor anyone else did it, but we did." With that, the villagers were able to reclaim their right to materialize their own vision of themselves, overcoming the static image of traditionalism that the project promoters had conferred upon them.

A change in Ecuador's national educational policy resulted in the closure, years later, of this school as well as other schools from the Juan Benigno Vela parish that the Chibuleo San Luis comunidad belongs to. All of the students from this area were brought to a newly built "megaschool." However, the quality of the villagers' construction had been such that a 2017 study from the Ambato Technical University found the ethnoengineering classrooms to be still in great condition despite having been empty and unmaintained for years. The study found this to be different than the other classrooms of the school, which had been built by contractors, and which were by then very deteriorated (see Cabrera, Coral, and Moya 2017).

A third and last example of success is that of Ñukanchi Allpa. The ethnoengineering project for this village consisted of a day care center and a classroom unit. As in all of the other cases, the Ñukanchi Allpa villagers were told during the participatory process that for these constructions they had no other choice but to use traditional materials. Seeing that, they decided to also directly contact the project's managers. "We phoned the very same ones from outside, the ones from FISE," a woman told me. A CEJA member added, "We phoned them again to change that [material]." The villagers insisted, and the office finally gave up its attempt to press for a traditionalist approach in this comunidad.

I asked the Ñukanchi Allpa villagers what had to happen for people to effectively resist the imposition of a viewpoint that is against their interests, in this case traditionalism. A leader responded: "Conversation [and] dialogue with those from the organization" in other words, the negotiation of their viewpoints. Explaining what would happen if they did not engage in such negotiation, the leader observed: "Otherwise, they will come with their [building] plans"; that is, the traditionalist building plans would be imposed.

The original building plans for the Ñukanchi Allpa project had, indeed, been highly traditionalist. They were based upon Edinson Benítez's palm-based designs that so closely evoked the traditional Saparoan house and that, as mentioned, were also used in Azabí del Mortiñal. FISE had decided to use these plans in Ñukanchi Allpa even though this betrayed the project's cultural appropriateness premise—this was, after all, a predominantly Canelos Kichwa comunidad, a completely different ethnocultural group. However, just as in Azabí, the Ñukanchi Allpa villagers saw no problem in adopting the Saparoan plan, despite its not being part of their cultural traditions. They did this because in their case, too, they liked its exotic semioctagonal-capped rectangular shape. However, and just like the villagers in Azabí, they did not intend to fully embrace Benítez's traditionalist proposal beyond its general plan design.

Free to make changes after their successful insistence at FISE, the Ñukanchi Allpa villagers fully modernized Benítez's design, combining aesthetic and functional considerations. They changed the columns from raw chonta palm to square-section sawn and lacquered hardwood, the walls from chonta strips to cement-bound stones, and the roofs from palm thatch to plain metallic sheets. The villagers adopted these materials because they found them to be more visually appealing than traditional materials. However, there was also a strong component of functionalism in their decisions: They were looking for durability and also for materials that would make the building easier to clean. As a result of the material changes they implemented, the villagers' redesigned building became an intriguingly eclectic postmodernized version of a foreign traditional architectural language (figs. 65 and 66).

Fig. 65. Detail of the villagers' selection of materials in the Ñukanchi Allpa ethnoengineering project: stone, lacquered wood, cement, and glazed tiles.

Fig. 66. The ethno-engineering classroom unit in Ñukanchi Allpa, showing the villagers' selection of materials.

In the construction of Ñukanchi Allpa's two structures, the villagers worked fast. They completed the whole construction project in only one year, finishing it also in this case before the deadline, and despite the project's scale and the fact that it was a complex project because of its use of polar as opposed to Cartesian geometries. This stands in great contrast with the cases in which traditionalism advocates imposed the traditionalist approach, and where the construction process (if the project was in fact completed) took up to four times as long.

As in Chibuleo San Luis, and in contrast to the bulk of the ethnoengineering project's participating comunidades, in Ñukanchi Allpa there was a general satisfaction after the project's conclusion. The woman cited above celebrated: "This is a joy." The leader added: "It is a joy to have this house." They expressed themselves as proud of their creation, which they considered to be special in comparison to other buildings in the area: "This model, we have not seen it [here]." Although modernist houses are now very common in Ñukanchi Allpa, theirs is a special model, the villagers said, because it is a special type of modernist building not the kind that is typical where they live. It looks modernist because of the materials, but it has an innovative shape that comes from the building language of other indigenous people. It is the modern, negotiated and materialized on the villagers' own terms.

TRADITIONALISM AND SUSTAINABILITY

What do these different outcomes say about ethnoengineering's sustainability premise, which was so deeply linked to traditionalism? With their rejection of traditionalism, villagers everywhere demonstrated that the sustainability principles behind the project's advocacy of traditionalism were either inconclusive or inaccurate. As mentioned, those principles were first, that traditional people live by default in harmony with nature; second, that traditionalist constructions are more climate-efficient; and third, that traditionalist constructions are more affordable and as such contribute more effectively to the goal of liberating villagers from economic dependency.

With regard to the first premise, of living in harmony with nature, if one follows this assumption, it should be expected that as a result of such harmonious relationship traditional environments as a whole should be very well preserved. In reality, however, there was already considerable environmental degradation in the comunidades participating in the ethnoengineering project. In our interviews, villagers constantly reported problems that were either a consequence of, or had been magnified by, environmental depletion: water scarcity, floods, mudslides, windstorms, extreme rainfall, and so on. In fact, according to the Apahua CEJA president, the collapse of the mud wall that triggered the villagers' ultimate refusal to the traditionalist project was partly due to the fact that there had been an unusually strong rainstorm during that week. In other places, drought was a common situation during the project. I have mentioned the difficulties that the Yanaturo villagers faced to procure water for their crops. In other villages, such as Huasicashca, the villagers had difficulty making adobe bricks because of water scarcity. These are examples of how people who were assumed to be living examples of harmonious coexistence with nature were in fact already dealing with harsh environmental conditions on a day-to-day basis.

With regard to the second premise, of climate efficiency, the notion that traditional housing is per se more responsive to changing temperature conditions strongly motivated the designers' advocacy on behalf of traditionalism. However, modernist construction can be also well adapted to climate—villagers who succeeded in fully changing the traditional material specifications reported feeling similarly comfortable in their modernist constructions. That was the case of Ñukanchi Allpa, a hot and humid lowland settlement where villagers noted that their modernist classrooms felt just as cool inside as their traditional palm buildings. It was also the case in the opposite environment, Chibuleo San Luis, a cold village in the mountains where villagers reported a warm thermal sensation similar to being in a traditional mud building. Thus, defying the common narrative of the climate responsiveness of traditionalist buildings, modernist buildings were apparently performing fairly well in terms of climate comfort in the villagers' own perception. Thus, the designers might have been incorrectly ascribing climate responsiveness solely to traditional construction.

As for affordability, the notion that traditionalist constructions are more affordable was the most important sustainability premise of the ethnoengineering project, insofar as it was the one most directly connected to the project's goal of poverty alleviation. Yet, during the project's execution, a recurring topic of debate between designers and villagers was precisely about the accuracy of the former's assessment that traditionalist construction is low-cost. This assessment had been based upon the assumption that local materials were affordable; as mentioned, some designers had argued that local materials such as earth for adobe bricks were free, since they could be gathered from the villagers' own land. Villagers, on the other hand, objected that these materials were actually not free; the land had an owner, and the owner still had to be paid for the earth. "There is no way to simply grab and make," the Huasicashca CEJA president expressively observed in our interview.

However, that was not the only incorrect assumption made during the ethnoengineering project about the presumed affordability of traditionalist construction. I have mentioned another key argument put forward by the ethnoengineering method in support of this premise, namely, that the traditionalist constructions of an ethnoengineering project should be more affordable as a consequence of community participation in labor. This argument demands greater attention because it directly involves the notion of participation, which is the central concern of this chapter. I will then devote the next two sections to analyzing it.

Participation and Affordability: Construction Labor

The most important argument offered by the ethnoengineering method in support of the affordability of traditionalist construction is that community participation in the construction allows for savings in labor expenses. As mentioned, one of the key participatory principles of the method is that villagers have to provide their labor force at no cost because they are working on infrastructure for their own use, and doing so would help them to develop a sense of ownership of the constructions.

The ethnoengineering project relied heavily upon this participation-via-labor premise. Indeed, the reliance upon a mandatory unpaid labor contribution in the project was so crucial that in the budget for Apahua, for instance, the community labor contribution was as high as 50 percent of the total labor cost. This was a very steep contribution for a place where every single day villagers spent working for free on the project was one in which they were unable to provide for their own basic needs. The project budget did not consider those needs either, as it ignored the fact that even when the contribution was about the local materials, in addition to the materials' cost the villagers also had to pay for their own food and transportation expenses to procure the materials.

Another problematic assumption of the project was that villagers were ready and able to provide free labor, as if they were just sitting around waiting to be put to work. In reality, of course, they were tremendously busy providing for their own sustenance. For example, in Apahua, which largely remains a patriarchal community, men usually had to travel outside the village to procure money for the household, so most of the labor for the project was provided by women, and sometimes even by their children as well. This put a tremendous burden on the Apahua women, whose workloads doubled since they had to work on construction while continuing their household work and farming. This situation was upsetting to Vinicio Gallardo, the senior builder of Funhabit, Luis Gallegos's nonprofit. In our interview, Gallardo lamented that he had expected more commitment from the men, but he also acknowledged that the most they could do was to work on the project during the weekends.

The inability of villagers to afford the great building demands of traditionalist construction was partly the reason they insisted on building the project using an orthodox modernist approach. They reasoned that if they were to make a great effort by working for free, their labor investment should be spent as frugally as possible, and this would be possible only by adopting modernism, which allowed for rapid construction. Not only in Apahua, but virtually everywhere, I heard stories from villagers who had argued to impervious traditionalism advocates that the traditionalist approach required more labor. In Huasicashca, the CEJA president remarked: "To make adobes it is necessary to work hard, a lot." In Ñukanchi Allpa, the woman cited earlier explained that the continuous repair of traditional structures meant that people had to work twice as much. In Yanaturo, more labor was among the reasons behind the villagers' rejection of Grace Almeida's proposal to build using their own traditional house form. They argued that a modernist gabled house was faster to build and more affordable overall. They made a handy comparison between concrete block and mud brick construction, observing that each mud brick only covered an area equivalent to half a concrete block. Thus, they concluded, not only they had to lay twice as many bricks but the cost of mud bricks themselves was over two and a half times that of the concrete blocks (US$0.18 vs. US$0.07).

The same was the case for bamboo construction, the other structural focus of the ethnoengineering project. As mentioned, in Domingo the UCAT members' argument for traditionalism was that the construction of a road was expensive, and thus the available funding would not be enough. However, this funding was not actually enough to complete the bamboo structure, contrary to what the UCAT advisors had argued. Parts of the structure, most visibly in the staircase area, were left unfinished. I asked Domingo villagers what made bamboo construction so expensive. One of them explained that it was the amount of labor involved: "Bamboo canes are not expensive, but labor is." The villager referred to a long and strenuous process that Jorge Morán had prescribed in his proposal as the only possible way to extend the durability of bamboo. The process started from the very moment of harvesting the bamboo pieces, which had to be done only during the waning phase of the moon, and covered many other steps. One of those steps even included drilling dozens of small perforations on each pole in order to inject a chemical solution for preservation, and then covering the perforations again so as to prevent wood-boring bugs from dwelling inside the poles. All the care required to prepare the bamboo poles was due to the fact that, under normal circumstances, bamboo is only a temporary building material that does not last longer than a few years.

Consequently, according to Bayardo Ramírez, the time required to make the bamboo poles construction-ready and to train villagers in that process added three extra months to the construction process. However, besides the preparation, the construction itself with bamboo turned out to be very demanding as well, since it had to start with the casting of reinforced concrete supports for the bamboo poles, which cannot be dug directly into the ground because humidity rapidly causes them to rot. The framing itself of the bamboo structures was also tremendously demanding, as it entailed complicated carpentry with specialized cuts for the joints. Still, the work was not supposed to stop with the finished construction, since the structures basically had to be kept alive by performing maintenance on a constant basis. Given that bamboo poles naturally split over time, splitting poles had to be routinely replaced. The new poles had to be prepared following the same careful process used for the original ones. Normally, the process of replacing the poles is more demanding than installing the original ones, given that in addition to having to prepare the material and redo the joints, it is necessary to partially disassemble the structure for the removal and reattachment of poles. Sometimes the carpentry of those structures is so intricate, as I have mentioned was the case with Miguel Camino's designs, that the disassembly is not a simple matter.

With all those complications, the construction of the average ethnoengineering bamboo structures, even without including all the subsequent and

Fig. 67. The Los Colorados ethnoengineering bamboo structure, finished by villagers with steel.

continuous maintenance and repair work, ended up taking two-and-a-half times as long as similar constructions using concrete. The extra cost of paid labor required for this long and demanding construction process meant that in Los Colorados, just as in Domingo, the budget was ultimately insufficient to complete the construction. Given that in the case of Los Colorados there was no funding left to build a staircase and that this was a raised structure, in order to be able to actually use the building, villagers had to fundraise on their own, and provide even more of their unpaid labor force to finish the construction. However, with the project now in their own hands, they decided to drop the traditionalist approach altogether and proceeded to build the staircase with steel (fig. 67).

To explain the magnitude of the cost difference between bamboo and concrete, the Tacole leader quoted earlier observed that the final construction cost of the bamboo structure in this village was about US$30,000, three times the local cost of concrete block construction. FISE's initial estimation of the affordability of bamboo had been based on the cost of the raw material—US$1.50 per cane, for a total of only about US$1,000 for a structure like Tacole's, per Bayardo Ramírez's estimate. However, this estimate excluded both labor costs and other materials required for the construction, including specialized materials. With regard to the latter, the Tacole leader observed that "people sometimes do not have the capital" to purchase specialized materials required for the bamboo preparation and continuous maintenance, such as linseed oil, which is a material commonly used in the fine arts. Moreover, the leader noted that these materials are unavailable locally and thus have to be purchased in distant places like the Andean city of Santo Domingo. This increases the transportation costs and time expenditure involved in procurement.

When I inquired, both Jorge Morán and Bayardo Ramírez disputed the idea that bamboo construction was more expensive. Morán estimated that the total cost of building a structure like Tacole's should have been only between US$1,500 and US$2,500. The reason, he said, is that "cane [bamboo] does not cost anything; people provide the cane." With this argument, he too disregarded the investments that villagers made in labor, food, the materials cost, and the transportation cost of those materials. Moreover, in the case of Tacole, villagers had to work three times as long as FISE's already long initial estimation because they were not gathering the bamboo in the appropriate way. Since they were not familiar with the traditionalist techniques, the villagers were not following the careful harvesting process prescribed by Morán, and therefore they had to repeat this task several times, thus having to multiply their "free" labor and other investments in the project.

However, the issue that most upset villagers about having to spend their unpaid labor force and other assets was that they were spending these in traditionalist construction. In great contrast, in those places where villagers were able to tweak the project to build conventionally modernist structures, they did not seem too bothered by providing unpaid labor. In fact, in Ñukanchi Allpa, villagers did so much unpaid work that once they finished, the FISE accountants realized the villagers' labor economic contribution had been much higher than they were expected to provide. In Chibuleo San Luis, villagers were even required to make a cash contribution to procure stone for the foundations. Given that local materials were not free, as the project's traditionalism advocates had assumed, the Chibuleo villagers had to purchase them out of their own pockets, and they willingly did so in this case.

Participation and Affordability: Maintenance and Repairs

As part of the argument on community participation and affordability, the ethnoengineering method claims that the cost of traditionalist constructions would be offset by their presumed longer durability, which in theory would be also a result of the process of community participation in the construction. The idea that the constructions in this project would last longer relied upon the assumption that villagers would be more inclined to perform maintenance and repairs, since they would feel the buildings belonged to them because they had partaken in the construction.

However, this assumption also turned out to be incorrect. As of the time of my fieldwork, in most cases no maintenance or repairs at all had been performed to the ethnoengineering project structures since the conclusion of the construction works, between one and two years earlier. The lack of repairs created a serious situation because many of the structures required not just routine maintenance but deep repairs from the very beginning. The reason was that they had been defectively built in the first place, for different reasons, including the villagers' lack of familiarity with traditionalist technologies, but also their rejection of the buildings, the high cost of the construction, and the fact that some of the structures were experimental. For instance, by the time the Chisulchi Chico construction was concluding, there were already deep fissures in some of the corners of its mud walling. In Tacole, some of the bamboo poles had cracks that already required them to be replaced. In Los Colorados, due to a budget that was, as mentioned, not even enough for the staircase, the structure was built without a necessary layer of insulation between the roofing and the bamboo framing. Holes that resulted from nailing down the zinc sheets created leaks that dripped to the poles, quickly deteriorating them.

In Michacalá, repairs were necessary even before the structure came into use. FISE delivered the building without fully repairing the construction problems, which resulted from the combination of a timber frame and a mud wall and from installing a steel door frame in that wall. Since mud dries at a different rate from wood, the wall was, naturally, separating from the timber frame that supported part of the structure, as well as from the metallic frame of a bathroom door. This door was originally supposed to be made of wood but, as in Apahua, villagers were already so infuriated with the ethnoengineering process that they defiantly told Bolívar Romero they were going to install a metal door regardless of his objections. As Romero self-critically described this episode to me, "They said: 'Leave us alone. We will put in the iron door, which is faster. We will go buy it and put it in, and the case is closed.'" The issue of mud walls splitting from the timber framing occurred after the villagers had already dealt with a good amount of rebuilding to correct other issues with the mud technology, including reerecting some portions of the walls that had collapsed while other issues with the timber structure were being addressed.

The issue of the lack of repairs was most concerning in the situations that called for immediate action because the buildings were structurally unsafe. There were instances in which, as a result of changes during the process of construction, the building had ultimately become a technologically risky structure. For example, in El Desquite, the construction had been roofed with a four-inch concrete slab, in a last-minute attempt by villagers to modernize this bamboo structure when the construction process was already ongoing.

However, the bamboo framing had not been calculated to support such heavy load. Because of that, the framing immediately bent, despite the addition of extra bamboo reinforcements during construction, as a carpenter who was part of the crew explained to me. This issue, the carpenter continued, made parents apprehensive about sending their children to school "because of the fear that the canes could break, and the thing could topple." In other cases, designers and other practitioners had intentionally used ethnoengineering for risky technological experimentation. In addition to the case of Azabí, mentioned earlier, in the case of Pilchipamba's cob experiment the design dispensed with iron reinforcements despite this being a place of great seismic activity. These are yet more examples of schoolchildren being exposed to serious risk in experimental social design projects, to add to the cases of Nueva Esperanza and Makoko described in the previous chapter.

Part of the reason the repairs to these constructions were not being carried out was their high cost. Performing the maintenance and repairs was a contractual commitment between the beneficiary comunidad and FISE, and villagers were in charge of funding this work by themselves. However, villagers regularly lacked these funds because these comunidades ranked as the poorest of the poor in the country. So, ultimately, not only was the construction of traditionalist buildings very expensive, but also maintenance and repair expenses posed an additional economic burden on villagers. The repairs were more expensive than usual because they were technologically complex and required specialized knowledge that was not always available in the comunidades. In the case of Michacalá, for instance, Bolívar Romero worried that the project had not yielded enough villagers trained in tapial technology to perform repairs. Because the construction process had taken too long, and because villagers often left in search of seasonal jobs, the community labor crew kept changing, making it impossible for any villager to learn the complete process. In Huasicashca, where villagers had decided to play it safe by strictly abiding by the traditionalist plans, they ended up implementing faulty design decisions, with the result that roof tiles fell off in the strong Andean winds. Solving that issue would be demanding because it would involve fully rebuilding the roof. In Domingo, defective bamboo poles urgently needed replacing, but due to the design's intricate structure, performing any such replacements was going to be very complicated. Villagers had not partaken in the construction process, and thus they had received no training for a task that would be difficult even for a specialized laborer. As mentioned, Miguel Camino's structures were not designed for easy replacement of broken bamboo pieces; changing one single piece required a major intervention that included disassembling the framing by removing several of the uncompromised poles, and also disman-

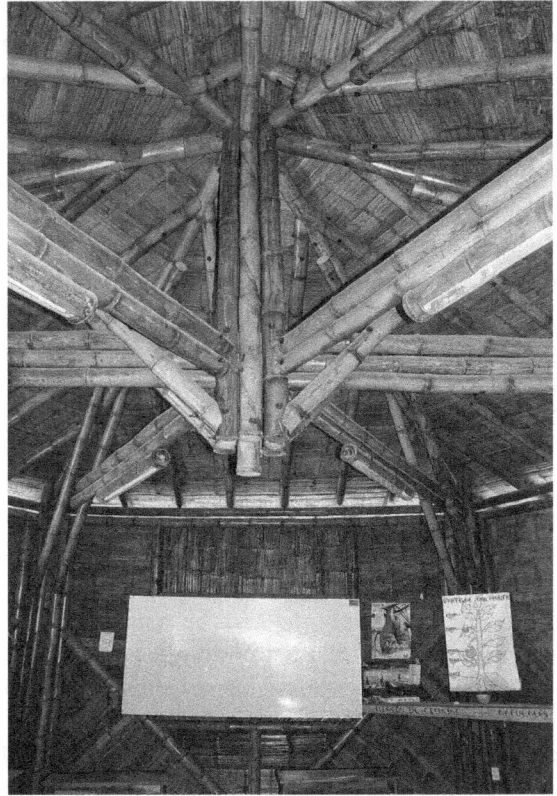

Fig. 68. The intricate bamboo structural system in the Domingo ethnoengineering construction.

tling the floor, which was made of customized wooden tiles of all different sizes (fig. 68).

In addition to the high cost, the fact that maintenance and repairs were not being done at all also bore witness to the villagers' silent but eloquent response to the project's imposition of traditionalism. One of the project's key premises was that maintenance and repairs depended on the appropriation of the project by users. However, since ethnoengineering had been largely imposed on rather than appropriated by the villagers, they had no apparent interest in carrying out these tasks. That is, villagers did not seem compelled to engage in the project of upkeeping traditionalist structures they had not wanted to build in the first place.

The most illustrative example is that of the two ethnoengineering prototype buildings, in Tacole and Michacalá. In both cases, villagers all but abandoned the buildings after the conclusion of the project. As of 2016, almost a decade after conclusion, the Tacole kitchen had never been used as intended.

A few years after not being used at all, it was made into a storage room. Still, it never received any maintenance and thus showed even more deterioration, especially in the bamboo framing. Similar was the case of the Michacalá day care structure, which, after a short period of use, was emptied, and it, too, was made into a storage space. The building also in this case became greatly deteriorated especially because of humidity. A few years later, the government sent a new school director to the village, and he decided to use the structure again. However, after seeing the consequences of the devastating Pedernales earthquake that hit Ecuador in 2016, he began to make plans to vacate the structure again and move the children to a modernist classroom constructed with reinforced concrete. This decision was motivated by his concerns about the safety of mud construction in an earthquake-prone area like Michacalá's.

SUSTAINABILITY AND PRIVILEGE

In sum, ethnoengineering's sustainability premises were ultimately based on myths and commonplaces emerging from a privileged view of environmentalism in connection to traditionalism. This privileged perspective inaccurately saw traditional life as being in harmony with nature, and traditional constructions as being more climate-efficient and more affordable than regular constructions. The last of these assumptions, affordability, relied heavily upon the notion of community participation in the project's construction and maintenance. However, this assumption ignored the villagers' high economic investment, most notably their labor.

Building on my study of the Ecuadorian ethnoengineering project and its outcomes, I will now return to the question of whether a deep embrace of participation makes any major difference in a social design project, compared to the cases in which participation is more limited, such as in those examined in chapter 2. As is evident from the ethnoengineering project, even when it is most comprehensively implemented, community participation in social design is still limited. I argue that this is due to the limitations inherent to the prevalent understanding of the notion of *community* in community participation. Those limitations were most evident in the ethnoengineering project because of a peculiar situation; that is, that FISE used the term "community" to mean two essentially different notions: one labeled a territorial division, and the other was the sociological notion. The local understanding of the territorial division, as I have explained, is "comunidad." The sociological meaning of "community," meanwhile, as defined by FISE, is a "group of people who maintain *common characteristics*" (FISE 2002, item 7.1.c, emphasis added). That is, the FISE office understood communities as being, by default, homogeneous: *the* community. Making this assumption explicit, the FISE III program's operating regulations state: "In this understanding [of participation], *the community* becomes the main actor" (2002, item 54.1, emphasis added). The regulations constantly invoke this notion in terms such as "community priorities," "community expectations," "community willingness," and "community acceptance" (2002).

Therefore, FISE regarded something as diverse and fragmented as a community as if it were a single body. This situation became more complicated because the ethnoengineering project took place in the territorial divisions called comunidades, and for the project execution FISE actually made both notions coalesce. That is, FISE often used the term "community" to mean simultaneously the territorial unit and the social group, implying that there exists a territorial division in Ecuador called "community" and that this territory is socially homogeneous. Consequently, throughout the project planning and execution, FISE worked under the assumption that, given that census data identified the selected comunidades as the poorest in the country, then all of the residents in a given comunidad were poor.

However, in these comunidades there did exist a clear social class divide, since there were residents who either self-identified or were identified by others as evidently distinct from the rest. First, in some comunidades there existed wealthy people from the city who had moved in and had established homesteads. This was the case of the Azabí del Mortiñal's project engineer and her husband. They were nature-loving people who had retired early to experience what they idealized as the paradisiacal life of a traditional village, and they had an economic interest in potentially developing a portion of their land as an ecotourism business. The villagers' interest in a modernist school design was obviously contrary to this couple's aesthetic taste and economic expectations. The couple's intervention was decisive in the deployment of the traditionalist project in that village. They owned a fruit plantation and were the sole major employers in the village; thus, their voice was clearly louder than that of their laborers. During the execution of the project, they remained the most involved people, to the point that the engineer became the technical director of this village's construction.

As for other instances of social division within the comunidades, among the native villagers there were also individuals who had developed a varied range of *capabilities* (Sen 1992, 1993), which placed them in a relative position of privilege with regard to the rest. This happened, for instance, because these villagers had a higher income, or because they had amassed more cultural capital (Bourdieu 1986) by virtue of, for example, being able to read and write, or simply having seen more of the world. This was the case of the young schooled Yanaturo community members who were pitted against the illiterate traditional leaders in the conflict about implementing ethnoengineering. Also in a different social class space were some villagers who had elevated themselves to the high political leadership roles in their villages and beyond. For example, in the conflict about the collapsed wall in Apahua, the rank-and-file villages accused the CEJA president of having single-handedly decided that the project for that village should be in mud. The CEJA president was also the president of the parish, which is a provincial administrative unit comprising different comunidades. Not only was he politically better positioned than most of the Apahua villagers, but he was also better ranked, socially speaking—unlike most villagers, he owned several properties and a vehicle, traveled often, and spoke very good Spanish, a sign of being more schooled.

These are examples of how, despite their being the poorest of the country per census averages, in the ethnoengineering beneficiary comunidades there still existed strong social class divisions. In these comunidades not everybody was poor, and also the levels of relative poverty varied in connection to people's different capabilities. The comunidades' subalterns, as in the members of the nonhegemonic social class, did perceive this class difference to such an extent that they had even coined a name for themselves as a social group: *comuneros*. Although in Spanish this term technically means the settlers of a comunidad, in our interviews they actually used it in the sense of the English "commoners."

Significantly, this pronounced class division within the comunidades was instrumental in the deployment of the ethnoengineering project because the villagers in privilege had either more power or more economic and other capital to overpower the majority in the decision of what approach to use for the project, whether ethnoengineering's traditionalist or a conventionally modernist approach. The village members in privilege tended to favor traditionalism because of aesthetic or economic considerations, as it was the case of the wealthier outside implants, or for political considerations as it was the case of the higher profile indigenous leaders.

In the latter case, ethnoengineering's traditionalism was in general seen favorably by some of the higher profile indigenous leadership because they considered it to be a political asset. As explained to me by the prominent indigenous leader Edwin Piedra, who consulted for FISE during the planning of the project in Quito, traditional building can be regarded as a form of cultural capital that yields concrete political gains. Thus, intensifying the narrative of traditionalism, including advocating for people's use and display of traditional material culture—arts, dress, architecture—is a strategic move for the Ecuadorian indigenous leadership in their goal of having the indigenous movement regain political space in the country. Building differently, just like dressing differently, is material proof that indigenous groups continue to exist as a special part of the Ecuadorian society, and as such they are entitled to fully participate in the country's political debate. This position was very sensible; however, still it reflected a social class disconnection, since the project's beneficiaries, who were generally more concerned with day-to-day issues connected to poverty (i.e., issues of pure and simple economic capital), instead preferred modernist functionalism as a more immediate solution to those issues.

As for the privilege of the outside promoters of ethnoengineering (i.e., FISE staff, designers, and UCAT members), following the descriptions provided to me by villagers, in general these promoters were perceived in the comunidades as people in a comparative position of privilege. Indeed, even in the cases in which the promoters came from modest backgrounds, such as in the case of some FISE staff members, they still arrived in the comunidades displaying fancy laptops and mobile phones; they traveled in official trucks and not on the bus, and in some cases they even landed by aircraft. Also, some of the promoters of the approach were objectively in great privilege as compared to most villagers. This was the case with the designers, who were all quite accomplished professionals, some of them even internationally recognized. It was also the case with the UCAT members, some of whom were in fact comparatively wealthy; some were well-connected politicians and activists, and some were well-respected university professors and researchers. Even those UCAT members with the lowest profiles were in a very different social space than most villagers; they came from the city, held university degrees, and used sophisticated jargon.

A class fraternity around the appreciation of traditionalism tacitly developed between the outside promoters of ethnoengineering, including the project designers, and community members in privilege. This means that, despite the designers' belief that they were working on behalf of "the community," their privileged view of traditionalism instead tended to align with that of the community members in comparative privilege. However, there was an exceptional case, that of Luis Gallegos, who decided to take a different approach upon seeing the village comuneros' rejection to the project. Gallegos decided to put the interests of these villagers above his own ideas of traditionalism. From Gallegos's approach, and its successful outcome, it is clear that the issues faced by the ethnoengineering project were not as much about privilege in and of itself as they were about how the designers used their privilege. Comparatively speaking, Gallegos was in a position of privilege just like the other designers and other project promoters; however, he decided to use this privilege in a different way by, for instance, advocating at FISE on behalf of villagers so they could modernize the predesigned traditionalist structure.

Therefore, considering both its positive and negative outcomes, the ethnoengineering project is a good example of the role and the effect of privilege in the advocacy of sustainability in social design. In this project, the majority of actors in privilege insistently advocated for traditionalism as a way toward sustainability, and in their advocacy they tended to disregard the burden that villagers in poverty experienced. However, the fact that the advocacy of traditionalism in this project was marked by privilege became an issue mostly when those actors in privilege stood by their own views, which was in most cases.

In chapter 2, I began to show how the connection between sustainability advocacy and social class privilege works in the field, by studying a number of high-profile social design projects. After having shown in this chapter how that connection might still remain even when community participation is embraced in a more comprehensive way, I will close my argument in the next chapter by reflecting upon the role that privilege plays in social design as a whole. I will do this as I revisit the two key localism premises of social design—those of using local designers and including community participation—in light of the findings from the detailed field exploration I have carried out.

CHAPTER 4

The Challenge of Social Design

In chapters 2 and 3, I offered a detailed field exploration of social design. I first explored a number of high-profile social design projects: Al Borde Architects' Nueva Esperanza School in El Cabuyal (Ecuador); Kunlé Adeyemi's Makoko Floating School in Lagos (Nigeria); Alfredo Brillembourg's coauthored research and design project on Torre David in Caracas (Venezuela); Giancarlo Mazzanti's Biblioteca España, a library in Medellín (Colombia); and Architecture for Humanity's Burrows Street Pocket Park in San Francisco (United States). The purpose of studying these projects was to assess the engagement of local designers (i.e., nationals or residents of the locations where they work) in local social design matters. I then turned to ethnoengineering, a large-scale social infrastructure project in Ecuador whose design guidelines and base models were developed by six (also local) designers, Grace Almeida, Edinson Benítez, Luis Gallegos, Jorge Morán, Bayardo Ramírez, and Bolívar Romero. I explored the outcome of the ethnoengineering venture through a field study of thirty construction projects in twenty villages, including Apahua, Azabí del Mortiñal, Chibuleo San Luis, Michacalá, and Yanaturo. The goal behind studying this project was to explore how community participation works in the field through direct inquiries among the people who partake in a deeply engaged participatory project.

Throughout this field exploration, I examined the two dimensions of *localism,* the solution widely proposed by both critics and supporters of social design to overcome the main challenge affecting this discipline, which has been in turn identified as *imperialism.* Testing this assumption, I first demonstrated that the premise that local designers should take charge of their own local matters might not make much difference in terms of the outcome of a given project and the burden to which people might be subjected; that is, the project can be just as limited as if it were run by a foreign designer. As I explored the second premise, regarding community participation, I focused on the question of whether implementing a deeply engaged participatory approach such as ethnoengineering actually improves the outcome of a social design project as compared to the limited material and/or social outcomes in cases like the high-profile projects studied earlier. With only a few remarkable exceptions (upon which I will reflect later), the physical and social outcomes of the ethnoengineering project suggest that the results of a more comprehensive use of community participation are not necessarily different from those of projects in which participation is by principle more restrictive.

Thus, in the vast majority of the cases I studied, the implementation of localism in both dimensions (i.e., local designers and community participation) basically offered no advantage either to the projects or their intended beneficiaries. Both the physical and social outcomes of these projects were in general very problematic and not different than if the projects had been in the hands of foreign designers. This was the case regardless of the fact that all of the designers of these projects were local or whether the community participation was constrained or more extensive. This finding then suggests that the widely upheld argument that localism is the solution to the challenge of social design is limited and should be reconsidered. As serious as the challenge of imperialism is in social design, the decision to involve local designers and community participation, no matter how extensively, might not make a major difference after all.

HOW SUSTAINABILITY REPRESENTS PRIVILEGE

The scale of my research sample suggests that the shortcomings of localism are in fact quite common in social design practice. Combining the five projects studied in chapter 2 with the thirty ethnoengineering projects yields a sample that is both large and diverse, comprising a total of thirty-five projects from different geographic areas. The projects included both high-profile and less publicized projects. They included both architectural and urban design projects (e.g., schools and parks). The projects' scale ranged from single buildings and small-scale projects (e.g., the school in Cabuyal and the pocket park in San Francisco) to urban-scale projects comprising dozens of megastructures (e.g., Medellín's social urbanism) to national-scale projects aiming to build hundreds of structures (e.g., ethnoengineering). The context also varied, from rural projects (e.g., the Nueva Esperanza School and the ethnoengineering structures) to periurban projects (e.g., Makoko and Medellín) to urban projects (e.g., the Caracas Torre David high-rise and the San Francisco pocket park). The budgets varied widely, from some projects claiming to have cost only US$200, to others that cost over US$6 million, up to US$45 million. My sample also included varying degrees of technical success, from projects that collapsed (e.g., Nueva Esperanza and Pilchipamba) to well-built projects (e.g., the pocket park in San Francisco and the school in Chibuleo San Luis). Lastly, the projects' design approach also varied, from visually striking buildings (e.g., those described in chapter 2) to more formally restrained ones (e.g., the ethnoengineering structures), and from geometric abstract designs (e.g., the Makoko Floating School) to neovernacular designs (e.g., the Michacalá day care center).

The size and diversity of this research sample allows for several generalizations with regard to the current state of the practice of social design. Even though the studied projects differed substantially in terms of location, recognition, scale, context, budget, outcome, and design, a number of common patterns existed. First and foremost, sustainability played a central role as the driving force of all of these projects. This confirms the assertion I made in chapter 1 that the notion of sustainability is fundamental to social design practice. Indeed, all of these projects embraced textbook principles of sustainable design, including striving for low cost and using local resources in the case of Nueva Esperanza; using sun and wind power, rainwater harvesting, and composting toilet technologies in Makoko; taking advantage of slum residents' day-to-day practices of recycling, adaptability, and resource saving in Torre David; preserving water sources and the natural environment in Medellín's social urbanism; greenifying the space and reactivating business in the San Francisco Portola district; and addressing issues of poverty, cultural change, and environmental degradation in the case of the ethnoengineering project.

Although all of the above ideas seem logical in theory, my field exploration of these projects revealed a hidden side of sustainability advocacy. In fact, these ideas made sense mostly from the standpoint of designers, who spoke from a position of comparative privilege with regard to the projects' beneficiaries. This was most evident in the case of the advocacy of traditionalism as a path toward sustainability. Such advocacy dictated that social infrastructure be provided in the form of, for example, traditionalist schools in palm thatch and mud, as opposed to modernist schools in steel and concrete. This was the case in the Nueva Esperanza school and to an even greater extent in the ethnoengineering project, since traditionalism was the key sustainability premise of this project. Generally speaking, the defense of traditionalism as a means to achieve sustainability reveals the comparative privilege of traditionalism advocates, because it relies upon popular narratives such as that of traditional life being in harmony with nature, and traditionalist buildings being more climate-efficient and more affordable than their modernist counterparts. These assumptions, although popular, are often based on the advocates' rather than the advocacy subjects' vision of traditional life, and often rely upon stereotypes and/or inconclusive or misinterpreted evidence.

In turn, this privilege-informed advocacy reveals the existence of a clear social class disconnection with regard to one of social design's fundamental questions—that is, how poverty should be addressed. For example, in the case of the Makoko Floating School, and contrasting with Adeyemi's description of this school as an idyllic tale of sustainability, there was instead a strong debate among Makoko residents about the real worth of that project, as some residents felt that their needs could have been better served with a much simpler and safer structure. In the case of Medellín, although the idea of overcoming poverty by the means of beautification made sense in the eyes of the designers who proposed it, residents countered that the first step in overcoming poverty should be to actually target the main markers of poverty: the serious issues of housing tenure and unemployment. In fact, if the millions of dollars invested in the artistic building had instead been invested in addressing the residents' main needs, this vast amount of funding indeed would have had a tremendously positive impact in those aspects. Instead, the result was quite the opposite: to make space for the architectural art piece, hundreds of residents were forcefully displaced from their homes. The social disconnection in the case of Architecture for Humanity's Burrows Street Pocket Park was also quite pronounced, since this project was directed only at the housed residents of the Portola, while homeless people were explicitly targeted as the demographic to be excluded from the proposed space. Lastly, this disconnection was also evident in the Ecuadorian ethnoengineering project's assumption that reembracing traditionalism was the best way to overcome poverty. This assumption was strongly protested by project beneficiaries, who argued that traditionalism posed a tremendous burden on them, mostly for economic reasons. Thus, in all of these cases, two radically contrasting views existed with regard to what should be done to overcome poverty: the view of designers and the view of the people actually experiencing poverty. The conflict between these views was a constant source of tension throughout most of these projects, since people often strongly disagreed with the proposals that were made on their behalf by the designers.

It is certainly reasonable to expect that different people will have different views of life and how to address its problems, and that these views are mostly based upon people's own unique experiences, whether privileged or not. However, the issue here is that, rather than aiming to bridge the divide between contrasting views, in most cases the designers, as well as their supporters, in fact pushed for, and ultimately imposed, their own ideas. Notably, they did this despite the fact that, in most cases, the projects used a community participation approach. Indeed, participation in these cases was largely used as a strategy to mask the impositions, even in the more deeply participatory projects studied. In Medellín, for example, a library project that had already been decided upon was presented by City facilitators to residents in a such a way that the project appeared to be requested by the latter. This was accomplished by constraining the subject on which the residents were allowed to participate. That is, participants were progressively led toward having only one option available for discussion: the library that the City and its designers had already envisioned. One of the comuna leaders described the outcome of this process using the metaphor of a popsicle. The facilitators basically put in the residents' mouths what they wanted them to say: it was as if the residents had been asked, "What do you want that comes on a little stick and you lick it?" The residents had to say the word "popsicle," that is, "library," so the facilitators could officially report that the library had been a residents' request. In another use of a constrained participation approach, in San Francisco the social disconnection was dealt with by making homeless people rhetorically invisible throughout a restricted understanding of the notion of community in the project's community participation premises, with "community" for this project referring to only housed residents. Restrictive participatory strategies were employed even in the ethnoengineering project, despite this project's comprehensive embrace of participation, which conferred upon participants a greater decision-making role than usual in social design. Despite the fact that the majority of villagers rejected traditionalism, this idea was largely imposed by the project promoters through the use of participatory strategies that involved "inducing" the idea (a village leader's term for the "popsicle trick" of progressively restricting the options); feeding villagers inaccurate information about the nature of the project (i.e., that the government mandated that it be a traditionalist project); threatening villagers that if they did not accept traditionalism then no project at all would be undertaken; and using the old tactic of dividing and conquering by capitalizing on internal divisions between those few villagers who favored traditionalism and the many who did not.

Another observable pattern from the studied cases is that, in the effort to materialize their own views on solving poverty, project designers and their supporters tended to side with local people in privilege—that is, individuals who held a hegemonic position with regard to the more vulnerable people in their communities. In San Francisco, designers ultimately sided with residents who, from the outset of the project, wanted to displace the homeless users of the park space. In the ethnoengineering construction of Azabí del Mortiñal, the fact that the local supporters of traditionalism were the village's main employers ensured that they faced no major opposition in their decisional support of the project. In other instances of the ethnoengineering project, supporters of traditionalism were at least endowed with basic markers of privilege, such as being better educated and speaking better Spanish, and they used these skills to overpower the comuneros or village subalterns with their arguments in favor of traditionalism. Even when some indigenous leaders advocated for traditionalism, such advocacy often revealed their newly raised status out of subalternity.

Another prominent indicator of a social class disconnection with regard to the question of addressing poverty was the high cost of the projects. For example, in the Makoko project, the budgeted cost of the school was about seven times that of the structure it was supposed to replace, while accommodating less than one-fourth the number of students that the original structure accommodated. Similarly, in the Medellín project, the library's cost was over US$6 million, and the structure still had to be demolished later. Even in the Nueva Esperanza project, the supposedly US$200 school ultimately cost at least twenty-five times that amount and was far more expensive than regular concrete block construction in the area. Similarly, in the ethnoengineering project, the traditionalist constructions were far more expensive than the regular modernist infrastructure that villagers favored. In Tacole, for instance, the cost of building with bamboo was three times as expensive as building with concrete. In Yanaturo, the cost of mud bricks was over two and a half times that of concrete blocks. In fact, the high cost of traditionalist construction was the reason many of the ethnoengineering constructions were left incomplete, as the budget was ultimately insufficient for this type of construction.

The projects' high cost often contrasted with the far lower cost of the beneficiaries' counterproposals, which were generally simple and practical solutions. These included building a regular one-story school in Makoko, supporting the existing network of community libraries that operated out of regular houses in the Medellín comunas, or building modernist gabled structures in the case of the ethnoengineering project. Importantly, however, these more-affordable alternatives were also less visually impressive, and this was partly the reason they were generally disregarded by some of the designers. This was also an instance of contrasting perspectives; while beneficiaries were focused on how to make the budget last, some of the designers were evidently looking for an opportunity to make artistic and other conceptual statements through their projects.

Despite the fact that the designers' proposed projects were far more costly than those counterproposed by the beneficiaries, the projects still appear usually described in media and books as affordable, due to the common practice in social design of ignoring the people's economic contributions in labor, materials, food, and/or transportation. These contributions were often excluded from project budgets on the grounds that people had provided them free of cost as part of their "participation" in the project. However, although those contributions were apparently "free" for the project, they were not actually free for the people, since they had to invest their own labor. Furthermore, in some cases, including ethnoengineering, people even had to pay for local materials and food from their own pockets. Given that these projects largely catered to economies of subsistence (i.e., the work that people did on a given day normally covered only their subsistence needs for the next day), the fact that people were mandated to make unpaid contributions to the projects created a tremendous economic burden for them, as it prevented them from working for their own sustenance. On the project side, however, given that labor costs are among the most expensive items in construction, excluding the people's unpaid labor from budgets drastically lowered (albeit artificially) the cost of some of the constructions. For example, it was by excluding labor (the most prominent omission amongst other expenses also excluded) that the Al Borde designers were able to make the spectacular claim that the Nueva Esperanza School had been built with a budget of only US$200. Similarly, in the ethnoengineering project, it was the community labor contribution that made the project's central premise of affordability possible, since the labor contribution sometimes accounted for as much as 50 percent of the total labor expenses of a given project. By contrast, the case of San Francisco's Burrows Street Pocket Park is indicative of just how expensive social design projects can be if the cost of labor is accounted for. Architecture for Humanity's own estimate of the cost of this tiny park was nearly half a million dollars. The organization arrived at that figure after factoring in the cost of the labor provided by its volunteers.

Additionally, most of these projects demanded a significant economic investment that sometimes had to continue even after construction. The reason for this was that beneficiaries were often left in charge of keeping the constructions standing, despite the fact that some of them had been designed or built defectively or were traditionalist structures that consequently demanded constant care. Furthermore, in the case of failing structures, the villagers had to duplicate their economic expense in labor and other items to avoid the loss of the whole effort, as ultimately occurred in the case of Pilchipamba. In the case of the ethnoengineering project as a whole, the villagers were contractually committed with the government to fund and perform on their own the structures' maintenance and repairs. However, due to the constant maintenance demands of the traditionalist structures and the high cost of repairing faulty constructions—which, in some cases, involved the rebuilding of entire portions—the villagers were often unable to fulfill this commitment, and nearly a decade after their construction most structures had undergone no maintenance or repairs at all. Leaving people with the responsibility to keep the designers' expensive work standing thus created an additional economic burden for them. Consequently, social design projects whose stated goal was to help overcome poverty either did not make any major impact on poverty or even contributed to making people even more economically strained.

One of the reasons the upkeep for some of these projects was so onerous was that they were formal and/or structural experiments. The clearest example of the burden that these experimental structures put on people is Kunlé Adeyemi's Makoko Floating School. In his report for the school's Aga Khan Award nomination, the architect Tomà Berlanda (2016a) observed the struggle of residents to procure funding for even the simplest maintenance tasks, such as replacing wooden pieces or light fixtures. This burden was quite visible in the case of the school teacher, who, in addition to taking care of more than 250 children, had been left in charge of ensuring the maintenance of the experimental structure. Considering the teacher's description of the events, his level of stress, and not only economic stress, must have been quite high. The structure was not properly moored, and children were expected to take classes there despite the fact that it bounced alarmingly. Parents were apprehensive about the structure and told the teacher that they would hold him responsible for any casualties if a collapse ever happened. Acting on these concerns, the teacher moved the children back to the old structure. However, after this move, the teacher was pressed by journalists inquiring why the artistic structure was not being used. The structure ultimately collapsed, just as the parents had feared. As experts on the subject argued, most likely the collapse was due to the defective mooring system, but Adeyemi still blamed the teacher for the supposed lack of maintenance. Despite all these struggles—pressure from all sides, fear, moving children back and forth, the structure's collapse, and the designer's accusations—the teacher ultimately found himself in exactly the same situation he had been in before the project: teaching in an overcrowded and crumbling old structure.

The case of Makoko also brings to light the problematic role of experimentation in social design. The notion of using sites of poverty to experiment with previously untested design and construction ideas has been lamentably advocated for by Alfredo Brillembourg, notably in his coauthored study of Caracas's Torre David. Moreover, the idea of intentionally taking design and technological risks with these experiments unfortunately has been not only promoted but also fully applied, and then proudly celebrated, by the designers of two additional projects studied here, Giancarlo Mazzanti and the Al Borde architects. Risky experiments were also sadly carried out in some of the ethnoengineering interventions, also with problematic results;

these included a failed mud technology transfer in a Pilchipamba school that collapsed during construction, and a risky self-supporting ceramic tile roof in an Azabí classroom, which a village builder described as a graveyard in the making. The fact that experimentation was taking place in so many of the studied cases attests to how widespread this practice is in social design.

Strikingly, in all these cases, these formal and technological experiments were carried out without observing human subject protection protocols, and without informing or gaining consent from the subjects upon whom the experiments were conducted. Another troubling fact is that most of these experiments were carried out in highly vulnerable areas, affected by strong winds, unstable land, and earthquakes. This was the case in the Makoko, Nueva Esperanza, and Pilchipamba school projects—as a technological experiment, the latter went so far as to dispense with steel reinforcements in an earthquake-prone area. Additionally, it is quite troubling that often the preferred building type to carry out these experiments was educational infrastructure—schools, classrooms, and libraries, which means that these experiments often involved putting children's lives at risk. For this reason, the structures resulting from these experiments were often a source of anxiety among parents and teachers. In fact, the fear of the Azabí teacher about the structural safety of the ethnoengineering classroom exactly mirrors that of the teacher in Adeyemi's Makoko school—a very striking similarity for projects on two different continents.

Despite people's concerns about safety, in addition to their many other concerns about these structures' cost, feasibility, practicality, and other issues, their perspectives were unfortunately ignored by some of the projects' designers. In general, despite the often-problematic results of these designers' attempts to implement their own vision of sustainability among communities in poverty, some of the designers still continued to present their projects as exemplary of sustainability. Additionally, in some cases, when the projects' negative outcomes became all too evident through the collapse of the structures, some of the designers reacted with complete denial. For example, the Al Borde designers downplayed the fact that the school had been structurally compromised during an earthquake, instead reporting that the structure was fine, and then proceeding to quietly rebuild from scratch an almost exact duplicate of the failed structure. Minimizing the serious structural failure, they continued to talk about the school as if nothing had happened, even at the Venice Biennale. Similarly, Adeyemi claimed at the Biennale that the collapse of the Makoko Floating School had been a preplanned "decommissioning." Then, when the evidence made it undeniable that the school had in fact abruptly collapsed, he shifted to blaming the teacher while continuing to disclaim any responsibility for the collapse. In yet another example, Grace Almeida, the designer of the collapsed Pilchipamba ethno-engineering structure, made the unfortunate decision to tell her country's own Congress the story of this project as if it had been a great success of sustainability. According to this story, the project had been completed and villagers were happily making profits from a sustainable clothing enterprise that the project had sparked. In reality, all that was left of the project was a large pile of mud and trash, and villagers who were greatly frustrated by their lost funding and efforts in a project that never materialized.

In conclusion, on the one hand, all of the studied projects were driven by a number of well-known and theoretically sound sustainability premises: using local resources, taking advantage of solar and wind power, implementing water-saving technologies as well as recycling and reusing practices, and applying naturalist and so-called culturally appropriate or traditionalist design principles, while striving for environmental protection and restoration as well as aiming for affordability and economic development. On the other hand, after the projects' materialization, the rationale that justified those premises was often proven inconclusive, unfeasible, inconvenient, contentious, or plainly incorrect. Thus, the application of these theoretically sensible sustainability premises paradoxically resulted in highly detrimental outcomes from both a material and a social standpoint. The structures were very costly, and people were burdened economically; furthermore, their economic contribution was often not even acknowledged. Additionally, the more economically realistic alternatives that people had counterproposed were often ignored. In some cases, the projects triggered gentrification and displacement of lower-income residents and homeless people. Also, people were often experimented upon through the deployment of risky structures. Consequently, they were often left in charge of projects that were defectively designed, poorly built, or left unfinished—in some cases, as we saw, the structures even collapsed. As a result, not only dissatisfaction and frustration but also fear often arose among people about the projects' structural safety. Some of these projects deepened internal social fissures and triggered conflicts between designers and project beneficiaries. In general, the beneficiaries' conditions following the projects were often left essentially unchanged or, in some cases, even worse than before. Nonetheless, despite all of these negative outcomes, some of the designers and their supporters not only disregarded the limitations of these proposals but actually intensified their efforts to materialize them. Thus, some of these supposedly participatory projects were instead imposed on people through the use of biased participatory techniques that involved manipulation, misinformation, threats, and divide-and-conquer tactics. Lastly, after the projects' failures became inescapably evident, some of the designers reacted with denial and continued to argue that their projects were sustainable. This denial is notable because it is the most powerful example that, regardless of being faced with strong evidence of the limitations of popular sustainability initiatives to address poverty, some advocates of these initiatives may still continue to believe they make sense, ignoring the extent of the users' predicament. This clearly reflects the degree to which sustainability advocacy is affected by social class privilege.

LOCALISM AND THE CHALLENGE OF SOCIAL DESIGN

Local Designers and Privilege

As shown above, detrimental outcomes can result from the implementation of a number of sustainability premises that make great sense in theory. I argue that this is partly where the problem lies: given that the notion of sustainability in principle makes so much sense, it can be easily deployed to justify *anything,* including impositions that might end up being highly detrimental to the people who should ostensibly be helped by the efforts. Thus, I argue that the projects studied here were problematic not *despite* their invocation of sustainability but, in fact, precisely *because* of their invocation of this notion. The main issue with sustainability advocacy in social design is that, when social design makes sustainability central to its agenda, it then—intentionally or not—aligns with a very popular but also very peculiar form of environmentalism. Sustainability is the environmentalism of privilege. This might not be an issue per se, since people in privilege are entitled to their own forms of environmentalism. Rather, the issue is that, as was the case with the projects studied here (which confirm the imperialism critique examined in chapter 1), at the same time that it embodies the environmentalism of privilege, sustainability often also embodies the environmentalism of the oppressor.

The fact that the sustainability paradigm might materialize in such detrimental ways among vulnerable populations gives credence to the arguments often raised that a form of green imperialism exists and that social design is imperialist. That is, taking into account the detrimental outcomes, it is clear that sustainability can easily become a tool for imperialism and that, since sustainability is also the focus of social design, social design practices can then become imperialist. Thus, considering these outcomes, it is possible to subscribe to the argument that one of the ways in which social design is imperialist is through its use of sustainability.

However, also considering that all of the projects studied here were projects by so-called local designers, it is clear that the challenge faced by social design practice in fact goes beyond imperialism. Thus, I am calling into question the solution widely proposed by the social design critique and promotion—that is, that the solution to the challenge of social design is localism, in the sense of deferring to local designers. I argue that a local practice is not necessarily the solution to the problems normally associated only with imperialism. Although local social designers' interventions can yield results that are largely positive, when it comes to their potentially negative impacts there is virtually no distinction between these and any foreign designers' interventions, as the cases studied here demonstrate. The reason for this is that local designers can also employ power strategies in seeking to materialize their own design ideas over the objections of beneficiaries. They are able to materialize these ideas by virtue of their own social class privilege, because it is this privilege that gives them a measure of inherent power over local subaltern populations.

Consequently, if local designers may engage in the same problematic practices as foreign designers, then the challenge of social design is not about sustainability and imperialism as much as it is about sustainability and privilege. Issues of privilege affect the practices of local and foreign designers alike. No designers are by default above, more enlightened, or better equipped than others in the process of working with people in conditions of subalternity.

That said, this argument is not meant to minimize the damaging role of imperialism in social design practices. Imperialism continues to be a serious challenge even in the field of humanitarian design—there is indeed such thing as *humanitarian imperialism* (see Bricmont 2006; De Waal 2007; Chomsky 2008; Fox 2008; Barnett 2013). However, to narrow the main charge against social design to imperialism means to rely upon an incomplete picture of the problem. Overfocusing on imperialism, as serious as it is, obfuscates the even more prevalent issue of social class privilege. The most conspicuous omission in social design's advocacy of localism has to do with the decisive role that social class privilege plays in local design practices. This privilege can enable the unjust abuse of power in the work with subaltern populations.

It is vital to also consider the question of why this abuse occurs. When we look at the high-profile projects described in chapter 2, from the designers' own descriptions of their projects it is clear that often the interlocutors in the conversation about social design projects are other designers, more than the project beneficiaries themselves, since the latter's voices tend to be muted. In fact, a prominent goal of high design–based social design practice (that is, the practice that uses iconic architecture as its means) is to use formal and conceptual explorations as a way to contribute to the dialogue on the scope of the architectural discipline as a whole. This focus on architectural discourse ultimately explains the eagerness among some project designers to experiment in sites of poverty. When Giancarlo Mazzanti or the Al Borde designers talk about taking risks (design risks that might lead to collapse), they are not addressing the beneficiaries of their projects. When Alfredo Brillembourg talks about "you" being able to do "whatever the hell you want" in a slum, the "you" he is referring to is not a slum resident. These designers' intended audience is different. In fact, it is noteworthy how central to high design–based social design practice is the premise of helping people, albeit through the implementation of innovative and daring designs. Thus, the first loyalty in this case is seemingly toward design, in the sense of high design, with comparatively much less consideration for the risks involved and the reasons people might instead favor much simpler designs.

Thus, the forces that propel some designers to engage in clearly abusive practices are broad forces derived from the great importance presently given to high design in the architectural discipline. Therefore, it is the high design approach, with its logic, narratives, goals, and paradigms, that must be taken to task when we set out to explore the challenge of social design. One of the most vexing patterns in cases such as those studied in chapter 2 is that people in conditions of poverty and vulnerability often become the advocacy targets of designers who (intentionally or otherwise) ultimately benefit from their own advocacy in terms of creating a name for themselves, receiving awards, and sometimes even getting important commissions afterward. By contrast, the subjects of this advocacy might not gain as much; instead, they might be subjected to risky experimentation without consent, forcefully displaced from their homes, or burdened with a high economic commitment, and thus their conditions overall might be left unchanged or even worse than before.

Despite the negative consequences on beneficiaries, problematic iconic interventions can in fact propel careers, offering the opportunity for young designers to jumpstart their practice on a promising path by gaining positive exposure through magazines, exhibits, and awards, and then receiving big commissions in only a few years. Consequently, sites of poverty have become, intentionally or not, the perfect career launching pad in architecture. This use of social design as a first step to carve a space in mainstream practice is progressively becoming a norm in the architectural design field. Because of that, social designers nowadays find themselves under considerable pressure to produce more and more daring artistic statements. It is paradoxical how architectural projects like some of those studied here—projects that were so defective from a structural standpoint that they even collapsed—still get published, exhibited, and awarded. The fact that this occurs demonstrates the extent to which present-day social design practice tends to privilege iconicity above all. Not uncommonly, accolades are written and awards are conferred not on the basis of a field exploration of a given project but, in fact, mostly on the basis of photographs.

Attesting to this fact, Al Borde's David Barragán has explained how his office's practice boomed following a single online post about the Nueva Esperanza School on *ArchDaily* (2010). That post attracted attention from other media, and soon after the project was being published in books and featured in exhibitions, eventually including the Venice Biennale. In Barragán's own words, such wide diffusion helped his office earn awards, because when they submitted the school to competitions the project was already well known: "Jurors, when they see a project that has been making the rounds on media, then they know where the project is going [i.e., the project's rationale], so they don't start from zero [in their assessment]" (Plataforma Arquitectura 2011, 2:42). Notably, although the *ArchDaily* post on the Nueva Esperanza School consisted of less than one page of text, it included almost fifty high-resolution images.

The power of images and their diffusion through media is essential to the Al Borde model of work, as Barragán himself acknowledged at his 2020 presentation at Columbia University. He clearly outlined his office's main business strategy in these terms: "To show the project as [much] as possible and [in] as many different types of media as possible" (2020, 1:26:46). The outcome of this strategy, he continued, is that eventually "someone shows any of our projects to the CEO of the social department of any company" (1:26:55). That, he explained, may result in a contract that the firm negotiates from a position of strength using a take-it-or-leave-it approach, given that they are the ones who have been contacted.

Barragán's statement illustrates, first, the powerful role of iconic imagery in the formation of a practice in social design today. Second, it makes evident the big role that social design presently plays in the formation of a successful architectural practice. With regard to the latter, in the case of Al Borde the Nueva Esperanza School, an iconic yet troublesome social design project that was constructed as a great success through the social media logic of likes and shares, jumpstarted a practice that only a few years later got to be named as one of the "world's best" (see Domus 2019).

One consequence of today's exaggerated focus on visual impact is that formally more modest, but perhaps socially more effective, social design initiatives such as Luis Gallegos's FunHabit might receive comparatively less attention in important publications or be less likely to be exhibited in galleries. Being featured in those venues has an impact not only on the formation of careers but also on the basic possibility for nonprofit social designers to do their work, because getting donations is closely linked to being well known.

Thus, nowadays in social design, the personal brand and the practice have become inextricably linked via an economic logic, and as a consequence social design has ended up inevitably been ruled by the conventional architectural hierarchies that put the designer's name above everything else. Just like architecture as a whole, social design practice has in the end come to be also ruled by the paradigmatic architectural star system; it is possible today to talk about *humanitarian starchitects.*

It is important to also consider the snowball effect of the star system on social design practice. As more and more iconic social design projects get published, exhibited, and awarded, more and more young architects decide to get into this field by designing projects that are even more iconic and thus even riskier and more daring, in search of an even higher degree of visual impact. This logic explains some of the projects studied here—projects that are highly striking from a visual standpoint but that turned out to be highly risky from a structural perspective. Thus, these problematic projects become, at best, a tremendous waste of resources and, at worst, a danger to the lives of the people they are supposed to serve. Not only this, but the risk and burdens imposed on people are apparently becoming greater over time.

However, despite the problematic outcomes of these projects, I do not believe there is inherently bad intention among iconic architecture-oriented social designers, including those whose work I have studied in this book. Their well-meaning initiatives and their great commitment to helping other people appear to be beyond any doubt. I believe, instead, that their involvement in these problematic practices has been fueled by forces that are not fully under their control. Clearly, projects like those examined in chapter 2 fully conform to the predominant ways in which ideas are nowadays being transmitted and careers are being formed in architecture via social design practice. Therefore, those problematic outcomes are as much the "fault" of the architects as they are the fault of *architecture* itself. Evidently, the challenge of social design cannot be appropriately addressed by using the conventional tools of architectural design based on the star-designer paradigms of iconicity and individual genius.

Thus, with regard to the first localism proposition widely upheld in social design critique and promotion—that of relying on local designers—I argue that the solution to the issues affecting this practice is not on the designers' side. That is, "local" is not necessarily better than "global," because the problem is not one of designers but instead one of *design.* Since the key to the problem actually lies in the great importance that social design practice presently confers to the act of high (iconic) design, the required change must be at the level of the practice, rather than just at the personal level. I will further elaborate upon this idea later.

The Mirage of Community Participation

Adopting community participation is the second localism proposition, also widely upheld by both critics and apologists of social design, to address the challenge of this practice. This call has been summarized with a well-known appeal: rather than designing *for* people, architects should design *with* people. This appeal became popular after the naming of two influential social design exhibits at New York's Cooper Hewitt Smithsonian Design Museum: *Design for the Other 90%* (see Smith 2007) and *Design with the Other 90%* (see Smith 2011). However—as the outcome of the projects studied here clearly demonstrates—just as in the case of the "local designers" premise, it is also necessary to consider more carefully the notion of community participation. An indication of why this is important is that, in the totality of these projects, community participation was in fact implemented in one way or another, and yet the outcomes were still tremendously problematic. This was the case even with the projects that used participation more comprehensively, like the Medellín and ethnoengineering projects.

The problematic outcomes of the studied projects offer powerful evidence that the notion of community participation has its limitations. This is partly due to the fact that it combines two separate notions, community and participation, which normally are taken for granted in social design but are each limited in their own way. The inherent limitations of these two notions explain the apparent paradox by which the outcomes of some social design projects can be so problematic notwithstanding these projects' implementation of community participatory approaches. I will elaborate on this idea in the next two sections.

ON "COMMUNITY"

The limitations of the notion of community participation begin with a popular assumption made in social design regarding the first notion, community. As shown by the many reactions to Bruce Nussbaum's piece discussed in chapter 1, in social design "community" tends to be understood as a compact and stable mass of consensus. According to the many calls for action that were made during the Nussbaum controversy, social designers should work with *the community,* they should consider the needs of *the community, the community* should be involved in the design process, and *the community* should decide. Thus, communities, according to this understanding, are seemingly homogeneous entities, with their members moving harmoniously in the same direction by default; they are *the* community. Further proof of the widespread nature of this assumption is how it was observed in all of the studied cases as well. For instance, speaking about the Makoko Floating School project, Kunlé

Adeyemi stated: "One of the first needs that *the community* expressed me was a school," and "We started by working with *the community*" (Esiebo 2016). Likewise, Al Borde stated, regarding the Nueva Esperanza project, "The agreement was that *the community* will built [*sic*] the platform" (ArchDaily 2010). Alfredo Brillembourg stated, regarding U-TT's work, "Generally, we engage *the community* profoundly in discussions and meetings" (Navarro-Sertich 2011). On Medellín's Biblioteca España, Giancarlo Mazzanti said: "The [project's] visual [part] is fundamental. It is what makes *the community* [want] to appropriate it" (Townsley 2013).[1] Regarding Burrows Street Pocket Park, Garrett Jacobs stated: "When *the community* decided what they wanted in the park, it decided a mural," and "Everyone believes in the importance of engaging *the community*" (Lincoln 2013c). Lastly, in FISE's understanding of participation, "*The community* becomes the main actor" (FISE 2002) (emphasis added in all the quotations above).

By contrast, however, in none of these projects did there seem to exist such a thing as "*the* community" as a solid, homogeneous, and harmonious body. Instead, these communities were quite fragmented, starting from the basic standpoint of social class fragmentation—the levels of relative poverty varied, and in some cases even quite wealthy residents partook in community decisions (e.g., the retirees in the Azabí del Mortiñal ethnoengineering project). However, this class heterogeneity extended to other markers of class beyond income, since it also included cultural capital (different educational levels) and sociopolitical capital (different degrees of influence and leadership among people).

All these factors of social heterogeneity combined often resulted in disagreements within the communities where the projects took place, disagreements that became evident in discrepancies and sometimes even conflict about the projects. For example, in the case of the Makoko Floating School, it is clear that the process was quite contentious from the very beginning, as it involved power struggles among leaders, and residents who were at odds with each other about the project both before and after the school's collapse. In Medellín, while some residents (e.g., the young woman interviewed for the *Maravillas de Colombia* documentary) were excited about the project, others were so upset that some died of "pena moral" (i.e., depression), according to the story often repeated in the barrio. In San Francisco's Burrows Street Pocket Park, despite the numerous narratives of a harmonious community in media and literature, the "community" these narratives referred to consisted in reality of a group of housed residents who had initiated the project in order to expel the homeless residents from that space. In Ecuador's ethnoengineering project, the fate of the project was sealed by the existence of a strong social class division within the communities; this was the case even in indigenous communities, despite the fact that they are often portrayed in the literature as a paradigm of social homogeneity.

Thus, despite the designers' belief that they were working with *the community,* for the most part they were really catering to the interests of subgroups within the communities where they were working; for example, the housed residents in the case of Burrows Street Pocket Park or the local elites in the case of the ethnoengineering project. The perspectives of those subgroups were sometimes mistakenly taken by designers to represent those of entire communities. Furthermore, in some cases *the community* was assumed to be that subgroup whose perspectives aligned with the designer's.

As a whole, such a limited understanding of community has a decisive impact on the outcome of a participatory process, bringing to light the importance of a fundamental question in participatory practice: *who participates?* Community participation is by default exclusive, as it tends to be restricted to subgroups within a given community. This might be inevitable, even when the target group is the relevant one in the sense of being the one to which the project caters—generally, in the case of social design, the social group in greater poverty. The issue, then, is not about working with a subgroup but rather failing to recognize when the perspectives of a given subgroup are being taken as a proxy for those of the community as a whole.

ON "PARTICIPATION"

A limited understanding of community in the sense of *the community* is only the first issue faced by the paradigm of implementing community participation in social design. This problem becomes even more complicated when we consider the second notion in this composite: participation. In the way it is commonly advocated for in social design, participation is also limited, because it easily lends itself to the abuse and oppression of subaltern groups in a given community, as the projects studied here also widely demonstrate. In fact, the problematic ways in which participation was used in these projects reveal a compendium of strategies commonly used in social design to control participation by limiting its impact and in some cases even manipulating participatory processes. Below, I will describe six of these strategies, which I label *participation as labor, participation as information provision, deceptive participation, manipulative participation, anodyne participation,* and *participation as everything.* These strategies are not mutually exclusive; in fact, they are often used simultaneously in participatory processes. The use of these strategies is so common that, arguably, these constrained forms of participation constitute the main way in which participation is currently used in social design, as the cases studied here attest. This is why the results of a participatory process might not really make a major difference as compared to a so-called top-down process, contrary to what observers might believe when proposing participation as the solution to this discipline's challenge.

Participation as Labor: One of the most common forms of participation in social design is that in which the participants' role is limited to execution; that is, people participate but only in the construction, building whatever the architects have designed. This was the case in the Nueva Esperanza School project, as described by the Al Borde designers themselves. This understanding of participation is problematic not only because it restricts people's ability to provide a meaningful and decisive intellectual contribution to the project in which they are participating but also because of the burden often imposed on people in cases in which they must provide unpaid labor, since having to make this contribution often hinders their ability to earn money for their own subsistence. This practice made the participation-as-labor premise of the ethnoengineering project tremendously problematic, as Funhabit's Vinicio Gallardo observed in our interview. The fact that men had to leave their villages in search of seasonal paid work meant that, in some cases, the project's "community participation" in labor had to be provided mostly by overworked women and their children.

Participation as labor becomes more problematic because, although people might make great efforts in providing their labor contribution, often this contribution is not even acknowledged in project budgets. A longstanding practice in social design is to exclude from budgets the beneficiaries' economic contribution in labor, in order to artificially lower the apparent cost of the project. This was largely the case in the ethnoengineering project, where removing the labor contributions from cost calculations was what made the project's sustainability premise of affordability possible. Most representative of this issue, however, was the case of Al Borde's Nueva Esperanza, where the beneficiaries' economic contribution (in the form of not only labor but also building materials) was completely erased in order to justify the famous and highly praised narrative that the project had been built with a budget of only US$200.

In addition to construction, a popular form of participation as labor is that of making people responsible for the maintenance and repairs of the delivered project. Advocates of this approach generally consider it to be a way to encourage people's "ownership" of the project. However, one of the main issues with this model is that people are often left with the burden of maintaining buildings that are defective due to formal experimentation, as in the cases of Makoko and the ethnoengineering project. Thus, while a designer might see maintenance and repair labor as necessary to generate ownership, people could experience this commitment differently. Ultimately, the frustration of the Makoko teacher and the many participants in the Ecuadorian ethnoengineering project was caused by the fact that they had been made "owners" of something they had not asked for, or at least not in the form in which it had been imposed upon them. Those projects were tremendously burdensome and expensive to maintain with the residents' limited income, and this burden had been placed on the residents despite the fact that, in some cases, they had indeed cautioned the designers against carrying out the projects in such problematic ways. Another illustrative example is that of Medellín, where Giancarlo Mazzanti affectionately spoke of how the library was his "child," which he was now giving to the residents (Townsley 2013, 39:24). By contrast, commenting on the serious disrepair of this building, comuna leader Jorge Corrales observed that the situation was not as simple as residents being given a child; as he put it, residents also needed help to raise that child (Bornacelly and Rocha 2014, 17:37).

Participation as Information Provision: Often, participation as labor is tied to another participatory practice that also regards people's assets as a resource that can be freely used. In this case, the assets are intellectual, consisting of people's knowledge. This notion has been epitomized by the work of Alfredo Brillembourg and his U-TT partner Hubert Klumpner. In *Torre David* as well as other publications, these authors usually regard slum residents as a valuable source of knowledge about successful dwelling strategies; notably, the authors then repackage this knowledge and offer it as a "kit" (see Brillembourg and Klumpner 2011). Another illustrative example of participation as information provision can be seen in the ethnoengineering project. Despite the fact that in this project participation was conceived as something very comprehensive, in terms of design the only way in which villagers were allowed to participate was by providing designers with information about their traditional architecture—the project designers were the ones in charge of designing the structures using this information as their raw intellectual material. Thus, unlike participation as labor, in this form of participation people are invited to intellectually participate in the project, but only as passive providers of knowledge. That is, they are not allowed to freely use their own knowledge to transform, or question, the nature of the project that is proposed to them. As a result, although the project is technically participatory, it still remains outside the participants' control.

Deceptive Participation: There exist other forms of participation in which, in contrast with the previous two, people are indeed given some decision power regarding the outcome of the project. However, those forms still might lend themselves to hidden impositions, in some cases quite deliberately hidden ones. Deceptive participation techniques were often employed during the ethnoengineering project, and we can distinguish five different ways they were used.

The first deceptive technique involved feeding participants misleading information about the project. Some of the UCAT technical advisors who advocated for traditionalism knowingly misled villagers into believing that the adoption of traditionalism was mandatory, that it was an order that the UCATs had to follow, that the project budget had been approved only for traditionalist construction, that the experimental nature of the project did not allow for any changes to the traditionalist designs, or that a modernist structure would be costlier than the available funding could cover. In reality, the opposite was true in all of these cases; however, on the basis of this incorrect information, villagers often ended up deciding in favor of a traditionalist project, thus betraying their own interests.

The second technique of deceptive participation used in the ethnoengineering project was that of overstating the advantages of the preselected option, while understating or completely denying the advantages of any user-proposed alternatives. In particular, UCAT advisors and other project promoters sought to overwhelm villagers with a long list of presumed advantages of traditionalist construction, while ignoring or downplaying the advantages that villagers saw in modernist construction.

The third deceptive technique was that of persuasion, with the goal of putting pressure on people to make them accept. Whenever the results of a participatory process contradicted the preplanned outcome, the project promoters repeatedly tried to persuade participants to nonetheless accept that outcome. For example, in the village of Tacole, in order to deal with the villagers' rejection of a traditionalist bamboo kitchen, the promoters persistently tried to convince villagers to accept the project by invoking many arguments that made their proposal sound compelling, thus making the villagers' refusal seem senseless.

The fourth deceptive technique appealed to the old tactic of dividing and conquering, capitalizing on normal social fragmentations in a community to empower the group that agreed with the designer while marginalizing those who opposed. This technique was employed in the village of Yanaturo.

The fifth such technique used in this project was intimidation, in the sense of triggering fears among participants with the goal of making them acquiesce to the project. Villagers were told that, if they opted for a modernist project, they would have to reapply for the program at the risk of not being selected. Other villagers were bluntly told that, if they did not agree to the proposed traditionalist project, then no project at all would be built, and their funding would be reassigned to another village. Out of fear of losing the project, villagers in these cases also ended up deciding against their own interests.

Manipulative Participation: There is also a "soft" strategy to control participation, whereby people are led in a subtler manner to choose a predetermined desired option. Due to its subtlety, this strategy has been called *teleguided* participation (see Rahnema 1992). The "popsicle" trick described by the Medellín comuna leader Corrales and the "inducing" trick described by the Tacole leader are examples of this strategy. In fact, these two cases are exemplary of one of the most common manipulative participation techniques: that of progressively restricting the options available to participants. Using this technique, facilitators of the participatory process in these two projects found powerful reasons why participants' proposed options could not be adopted, ultimately reaching a point at which participants were left with the project's preselected outcome as the only feasible option.

The case of the Azabí ethnoengineering construction exemplifies another common manipulative participation technique in which participants are restricted to choosing among a number of preselected alternatives. In Azabí, villagers were presented only with traditionalist options, which were further restricted to Andean traditionalist designs, excluding the Amazonian designs that villagers would end up finding more appealing. Another and more general example of the use of this technique is that of the waterless composting toilets proposed by Kunlé Adeyemi in the settlement of Makoko and Grace Almeida in the village of Pilchipamba. Although these toilets might make sense for sustainability advocates, traditional people often find them repugnant for cultural reasons. However, in alternative sanitation programs, participants are often given a portfolio of alternatives including only composting toilets. This then precludes any discussion of other types of toilets, and people who might object to composting toilets are left with no other option than to select one of them.

The case of the Michacalá ethnoengineering project is illustrative of one of the issues that make this pick-and-choose technique particularly problematic: although people are nominally participating, the fact that they are given preselected options prevents them from actually discussing the project's framework. In Michacalá, all of the options of materials with which villagers were presented were variations of mud construction. This choice restriction limited the project to traditionalism, thus eliminating the possibility that it could be modernist, as the villagers preferred. Another example of this problematic technique can be seen in Medellín's Biblioteca España, where the question that residents were asked about their preferred colors for the library walls immediately precluded the possibility for them to engage in the more decisive question of why this discussion was about a library rather than about housing, which was the priority they expected the project to address.

The instances of the ethnoengineering project in which villagers were given only the option of choosing between traditionalism or no project at all are representative of a very popular variation of this restrictive technique, which further constrains the options to only two: *yes* and *no.* Sometimes, the two options provided are *bad* and *worse:* in this case, one of the options presented was the preselected one (i.e., a traditionalist project), to which the participants objected, while the other was conspicuously detrimental to the participants' interests (i.e., no project at all). Thus, the participants presented with those options were left with no viable alternative to the preselected one.

Anodyne Participation: In yet another popular strategy to control participation, participants are given a measure of decision power, although on comparatively minor matters. Because of that, this form of participation has been called also *placatory* participation (see Till 2005), a term that nicely illustrates its essential spirit. An example is Medellín's Biblioteca España, in which the explanation provided by the youth student leader in the *Maravillas* documentary is indicative of what her focus group's participation in the project entailed. As she enthusiastically explained, in addition to being asked about the wall colors, participants were asked questions such as whether they wanted the library to have computers and books. She was proud of having made certain programmatic decisions that were later reflected in the building. However, it is obvious that the library would have included those services and spaces about which participants were consulted even if there had not been a participatory process.

Arguably, the majority of participation in social design is anodyne, since people are usually invited to participate mostly on minor aspects, when the key decisions about the project have already been made. The main objection to this approach is that, once the framework is defined (e.g., the library), the process of participation is already constrained and, as such, becomes relatively easy to control.

The fact that, in the cases of Medellín and ethnoengineering, the projects—which had already been conceptually developed—were introduced to participants mainly in order to get their approval is an example of another very common technique of anodyne participation, that of *participation as validation.* As can be seen in these two cases, this technique can be used in conjunction with some of the deceptive and manipulative participation techniques described above: in the case of these projects, whenever participants' stated objections, the other techniques were then deployed to overcome those objections.

Another very common technique of anodyne participation is that of *participation as consultation,* whereby the results of a participatory process are taken only as nonbinding suggestions or recommendations. This is the case with a popular participatory technique called *visioning,* where the participants' role is limited to declaring their general aspirations for the designers to consider in their sole-authorship design of the project. This was the technique used by Edinson Benítez in the Saparoan villages in which he carried out his fieldwork for the ethnoengineering project. Visioning is not a bad practice per se, but as a participatory approach it is limited, because it is ultimately just another way to develop an architectural brief (i.e., a list of elements for the designers to consider in their design).

Participation as Everything: The final constrained participation strategy on this list differs from all of the previous strategies, as, in this case, even the simplest form of people's engagement is deemed a form of participation. This includes the case of *participation as attendance,* by which, whenever people attend a meeting about the project (simply to become informed or out of curiosity), the project can be deemed as having been participatory. Another instance of participation as everything is that of *participation as paid work,* in which paid workers (e.g., carpenters) are hired for the project and their work is described as a form of community participation.

In participation as everything, the term *participation* is often used interchangeably with *partnership* and *collaboration,* terms that were also invoked in some of the projects studied here. Like 'participation," these are very open terms that can be used to mean ultimately anything and everything. Thus, participation as everything takes advantage of the fact that the notion of participation is naturally so broad that, in the end, anything can be technically regarded as participation. Even something as basic as *using a building* (i.e., going inside and walking around) can be called a form of participation (e.g., Stierli and Widrich 2016). An indicative example of the problem with participation as everything is that of the two Cooper Hewitt Museum exhibits mentioned earlier, *Design for the Other 90%* and *Design with the Other 90%.* By making a slight change in the terminology, from *for* to *with,* the museum intended to signify a powerful shift in the paradigm of social design with marginalized communities, from nonparticipatory to participatory. However, although the second exhibit featured a number of projects that had been carried out apparently using community participation, it included just as many projects that were clearly the result of a so-called top-down design process, just like the projects of the first exhibit, but now they were classified as participatory.

Participation and Surprise

In conclusion, participation can be easily controlled in order to ensure the materialization of a social design project regardless of any opposition. It is very easy to steer a participatory process so that it ends with the participants arriving, seemingly on their own, at the designers' own predetermined idea for a project. Indeed, a participatory process can be so easily manipulated that, as designers, we can do essentially whatever we want and still prove that our projects were participatory.

As seen from the examples presented in this study, such is the case for projects that use both "shallow" and "deep" forms of participation. However, there is a fundamental difference in the latter case, and it has to be considered if we are to rethink participation in social design. The more engaged forms of participation implemented in projects such as Medellín's Biblioteca España, San Francisco's Burrows Street Pocket Park, and Ecuador's ethnoengineering unveiled an essential aspect that usually goes unnoticed in participatory practice. Whenever people are allowed to participate in a stronger decision-making role, the process is prone to *surprises.* In Medellín, social urbanism planners and designers had the idea to build a library in a slum and were surprised to find that residents strongly objected to the construction of a library. In San Francisco, as it turned out, the intervention had been planned by the housed residents in order to oust the homeless users of the space.

In the case of ethnoengineering, the designers took for granted that the results of the participatory process would simply confirm, support, and validate what they assumed they already knew—that is, that villagers would be eager and enthusiastic about the project's endorsement of traditionalist buildings because they were traditional people. The results of the participatory process, in which the majority of villagers in fact rejected traditionalism, took the designers by surprise also in this case. As some of the designers described their experience to me, they were astonished when they traveled from village to village looking for a place to build their prototypes, and everybody refused. However, the designers continued to face surprises even after the project's imposition. For example, some villagers refused the designers' structures based on the villagers' own traditional housing language and instead adopted the traditional housing forms of different ethnocultural groups; others declined their mountain-adapted design and selected instead one for the lowlands; and others repeatedly refused a traditionalist design and instead embraced a Spanish colonial form. Designers were also surprised by the fact that, throughout the whole project, villagers constantly challenged popular paradigms of sustainability, subverting the logic of the environmental adequacy of the constructions by building in cold environments structures designed for hot and humid ones, as well as by showing a preference for materials such as concrete blocks and fiber-cement sheets and simple modernist designs, thus challenging the designers' assumption that environmental appropriateness was linked exclusively to traditionalist construction.

What then happens when we as social designers embrace participation in a more engaged way? As can be seen from these cases, the results of the participatory process can be surprising, even when the expected results initially seem very logical. Consider the case of the ethnoengineering project, which made a paradigmatic use of participation, covering all phases from planning to maintenance. This project endorsed a premise that is very popular in social design: that the advantages of a given project are greatly increased by integrating community participation:

"ethno" + engineering
traditional knowledge + professional knowledge
=
twice as good

According to this popular argument, through a community participatory approach, if the knowledge of traditional builders is added to that of construction professionals—or, in general, if the knowledge of end users is added to that of designers—the outcome would be twice as good as if only one of those perspectives were to be taken into account.

This notion of a sum of advantages is central to social design practice. However, one of the greatest lessons to be learned from the field exploration of Ecuador's ethnoengineering project is that the results of such addition might actually be unexpected and variable. In this project, sometimes the two advantages essentially neutralized each other because of a conflict of knowledges. In other cases, the addition made no difference since, for example, modernist structures performed similarly well to traditionalist structures with regard to temperature. Furthermore, in most cases, the result of the addition was in fact negative, since the projects were not concluded or were faulty from a technical and/or a social standpoint.

Thus, when it comes to community participation, one plus one does not necessarily equal two; rather, the result of this addition is unknowable beforehand. In a community participatory process, it is not possible to know the outcome ahead of time. The result of the equation is instead indefinite:

$$1 + 1 \neq 2$$
$$1 + 1 = ?$$

I use this numeric representation to illustrate the fact that any engaged process of community participation is prone to surprises. That is, a deeply participatory interaction between professionals and users is ruled by an essential principle of uncertainty.

In a larger sense, the existence of this surprise element means that, in a dialogue between social designers and end users, whatever we as designers ultimately hear will not necessarily coincide with what we *expected* to hear a priori. The issue of hearing is one of the central topics of subaltern studies, a field that offers a valuable perspective to explore alternatives in order to overcome the challenge of privilege in social design. Gayatri Spivak (2010) reflects upon this issue in "Can the Subaltern Speak?," perhaps the most influential piece of subaltern theory to date. Spivak initially asks this question in a historical context, referring to the British colonial authorities' prohibition of the *sati,* or widow suicide ritual, in India in the early 1800s. This ban came out of British humanitarian considerations, upon which Spivak poignantly comments, in a famous assertion, that "white men are saving brown women from brown men" (2010, 48). Spivak argues that, while the British authorities assumed these women were dying unwillingly, it is not possible to know this, since the women's voice does not appear recorded in the colonial narratives. Thus, one cannot possibly know whether they self-immolated willingly or not.

To some extent, the British colonial humanitarian concern is presently mirrored by that of social designers who set out on the project of saving traditional people from the ills of modernism. Often, we as designers simply discard modernism a priori, considering it to be solely the result of an imperialist imposition. For that reason, we tend to overlook the question of the extent to which some traditional people might in fact be willingly adopting that type of architecture, as was the case in the ethnoengineering project. This is just one example of how, despite the fact that the issues with modernism are real and the discussion on imperialism does make sense, our own *metropolitan anti-imperialism* (Spivak 1999) might paradoxically embody some of the issues that it critiques. That is, in our humanitarian, bona fide advocacy of measures on behalf of the well-being of the world's poor (measures such as reimplementing traditionalism), we as designers might be motivated by sensible anti-imperialist premises. However, in our attempt to materialize those proemancipatory ideas for other people, we might end up engaging in problematic impositions, sometimes through manipulating participation. Those impositions might then ultimately make our position not too different from that of the imperialists we critique, since they preclude the possibility for subaltern people to speak for themselves, even if they say things we would not like to hear, such as "The modern is good," which was the villagers' common counterargument during the ethnoengineering project.

Spivak argues that the answer to the question of whether the subaltern individual can speak lies in the issue of hearing: Can the subaltern be (possibly) heard? When it comes to social design, as designers in a position of relative privilege we often do not hear subaltern individuals' voices, as we make benevolent presumptions about what they think. From our standpoint, our presumptions might make so much sense that hearing these voices might seem irrelevant. However, even when we decide to hear, hearing is not an easy process. What if, after deciding to hear, the British authorities in Spivak's account found that the widows actually wanted to self-immolate? What if some of them did, while others did not? What if they were ambivalent? What if they were asked but decided not to speak? What if they spoke, but the questioner did not quite understand what they said? Considering that the process of hearing is subject to challenges like these, although in social design practice it is essential to proactively and deeply embrace the act of hearing, the issue is not as simple as setting out to hear by, for example, implementing deeper forms of community participation. The key issue to consider in participatory practice is that, once we as designers set out to hear, we cannot really tell beforehand what we *will* hear. The result of a participatory process cannot be predicted with certainty, unless of course the process is manipulated.

The inherent uncertainty about the outcome of a participatory process results from human agency. Agency is the variable that brings the indefinite results to the equation above because, ultimately, no one knows for certain what people participating in a community process might have in their minds. People bring to a participatory process not only their needs (which the practice of social design often fixates on) but also their ideals, their fears, their hopes, their doubts, their economic interests, their biases, their political agendas, and more, and the coming together of all these variables does affect their expectations of, and their position on, a given social design project.

In sum, the challenge of social design is neither as simple as relying solely upon local designers nor as simple as implementing community participation. As for the latter, I argue that, rather than assuming that participation is the panacea for social design's problems, it is imperative to implement an approach that allows for people to act upon a given project on the basis of their own agency. I will propose the terms for one such approach in the remainder of this chapter.

RETHINKING SOCIAL DESIGN

Throughout this book, I have been in conversation with the critique that links sustainability in general, and social design in particular, to imperialism. Although acknowledging the validity of this critique, I have made an argument that questions its premises: that the main challenge of social design is imperialism, and that the problems posed by imperialism are solved with localism (i.e., leaving matters to local social designers and involving community participation). On the basis of field evidence from an extensive and diverse set of cases, I have demonstrated the prevalence of the challenge of social class privilege in social design—a challenge that also impacts the work of local social designers, even when they, or any other designers, employ a community participation approach. This has led me to conclude that, although imperialism indeed remains a serious geopolitical issue that does affect the practice of social design, the most general and widespread challenge that this discipline presently faces is that of privilege. I have examined this challenge in connection to sustainability by explaining in detail how privilege affects the project of implementing, in sites of poverty, strategies of sustainability, which is the main focus of social design. This happens because sustainability, as an expression of the environmentalism of privilege, easily lends itself to the abuse and oppression of subaltern populations.

However, I am not claiming that every social design project is problematic because of its focus on sustainability. Rather than demonizing the notion of sustainability, my goal is to offer a word of caution regarding the fact that, because sustainability is such a powerful, hegemonic paradigm, its invocation makes it easy for designers to engage, intentionally or not, in strategies of oppression. Thus, I propose that we as social designers be cautious when embracing sustainability as our goal and that we view sustainability as a sociopolitical product, rather than as an unqualified and universal truth. The environmental problems of the planet are very real, as are the social problems connected to them. However, as designers concerned with social justice, we should consider that we might be contributing comparatively little to solving these issues by using sustainability as our preferred framework for social design practice.

In search of alternative forms of practice, it is necessary to reflect upon the limitations of the community participation approach that is so popular in both sustainability and social design advocacy. Those limitations can make participatory practice very problematic as I have explained. However, I am not advocating for doing away with participation. Rather, I am proposing to rethink the way we as designers use this approach. In the pages that follow,

I will propose a framework for *bottom-up* participation as an alternative to the mainstream, top-down, controlled participation strategies described earlier. Bottom-up participation is based on the visions that people have of their own future. There currently exist many sensitive participatory design practices that are also challenging the mainstream top-down participation framework. However, what I propose is different insofar as those practices tend to advocate for equality in the relationship between designers and users. I instead advocate for designers to position themselves at the bottom of the hierarchy in the design process.

The first consideration behind this positional shift pertains to privilege. I argue that the issue with privilege, more than privilege in and of itself, is about how designers use their privilege. Many social designers earnestly struggle with the idea of their inherited privilege when they arrive in places of endemic poverty. They become deeply troubled as they experience the contrast between the scarcity they are witnessing and what they have inherited by means of their origin, social class, or skin color. To deal with this contrast, some well-intended designers set out to do away with their own privilege by, for example, moving to a slum and living in poverty. However, even in such cases, these designers inevitably keep some of their capital, most notably their cultural capital (e.g., language or skin color). Also, they might not be perceived as poor by the slum residents, and, most importantly, they might also still retain their capabilities to end their condition of poverty at any time by leaving the slum and going back to their privileged social environment. Thus, dealing with the issue of privilege is not as simple as setting out to do away with one's own privilege. It is hard to remove privilege when one has it, and seeking to do so would be an unproductive effort.

Instead, the issue with privilege is about being aware of the fact that privilege exists and of how it is used. Although privilege can play a serious role in the detrimental effects of a social design intervention as I have shown, many practitioners of privileged backgrounds have, in both the past and the present, used their privilege to do very commendable work as well. Ultimately, privilege can be helpful in social design practice, if it is used in a way that aligns with the interests of the people to whom the designer intends to offer support. Privilege brings economic, social, and cultural capital that is quite valuable in social design advocacy. I have mentioned the case of Luis Gallegos, but there are numerous other cases of successful social design initiatives in which the designers have made their privilege work for the people's own needs, aspirations, and goals. Consequently, while privilege can be a liability, if sensibly used it can indeed become a valuable asset that the designer brings to the project. Privilege can be a tool for oppression, as it unintentionally became in the case of the projects presented in this book. However, it can also become a powerful tool to support internally driven processes of emancipation.

The second consideration is that the notion of participation belongs to the realm of professionals, rather than that of the subaltern populations who are regularly the targets of participatory processes. A powerful example in support of this observation comes from participatory design work I carried out earlier in my career among the Sieco_pai, an indigenous group in Ecuador's Upper Amazon. During the design workshop discussions, the Sieco_pai participants used to speak to each other in their own language, Pai coca. However, in their conversations, they conspicuously interspersed a few non–Pai coca words that apparently did not fully translate into their own language. Notably, these included a few architecture-related words, such as "project," "design," and "architect." They would say, for instance, "Je huë'e *architect* ne-si huë'e a-pi," or "That house was one made by the architect." "Participation" was another non–Pai coca word they invoked in their discussions. This suggests that, among populations like the Sieco_pai, certain notions that social designers might regard as self-evident might actually be perceived as foreign notions, to such an extent that these notions can be expressed only in the designers' own language. Thus, the way in which some people experience what we in the profession call participation might be radically different from our understanding. Some people might simply do community work because it is part of the day-to-day life of the group, as is the case with the Sieco_pai; it is routine. Some other people might engage in impromptu conversation or heated arguments, or somebody might start an independent initiative that is later embraced by the larger group. Thus, at a community level, a participatory process might be embedded into people's daily life in such a way that it is always ongoing, as an organic process that happens through its particular means, tools, language, and social conventions. Therefore, as social designers we should strive to go beyond participation by supporting organic community participatory processes, which are so intrinsic to community life that often they are not even called participation.

The third key consideration behind the positional shift I am proposing is that simply invoking "participation" or any of its surrogate terms, including "collaboration" and "partnership," is not enough to explain the people's involvement in a given project. It is necessary to also consider *what* exactly the project meant by participation and *how* the process of participation was carried out. Most importantly for the proposed change, it is necessary to consider *when* people started to participate in the project, whether before or after key decisions (e.g., on the type of project, goals, and design) have been made. This is a very important consideration because it brings up a number of questions that should be fundamental in participatory practice. The questions are: Did the participatory process allow for people to challenge the predefined framework, or was this process limited to a consultation about decisions that had already been made? Did the participatory process allow for people to participate in the intellectual aspects of the project (e.g., the design), or was it limited to people providing information or labor? Finally, if people did provide an intellectual contribution, to what extent did this contribution become part of the project? For instance, if they participated in the design, were they designing the project, or were they only allowed to make suggestions to the designers?

With these considerations in mind, within the proposed bottom-up participatory framework designers act as *supporters* of organic community decision-making processes. In this supporting position, they regard people as interlocutors with whom they have a dialogue that could lead to surprising outcomes, defying the designers' own expectations of the project. Methodologically speaking then, the notion of bottom-up participation relies on the fundamental principle that a participatory design process must be organic rather than controlled, and as such it must be able to accommodate serendipity, thus accepting uncertainty and surprises. This principle defies a key paradigm of architectural design practice—*predictability.* High architectural design projects often operate on the basis of a preplanned outcome that must be achieved as closely as possible to how the project was originally designed. Following this paradigm, ideally the designer should have fully thought out most of the project prior to commencing the construction work, and the construction should be carried out with as much loyalty to the original plans as possible. However, as many of the cases studied in this book demonstrate, when this principle is applied to social design practice, the designers' own insistence on materializing the original plans sometimes results in bitter conflicts with the project beneficiaries, with the ultimate result being projects that all but fail from a social or a construction standpoint, or both. Thus, a bottom-up participatory response to the architectural paradigm of predictability, which is limited for social design purposes, is the paradigm of *flexibility.* Given that it is not possible to know beforehand the final outcome of a project when users themselves take control of it, it is then not possible to, and in fact it is better not to, completely control the project's ultimate outcome.

Thus, from this flexibility standpoint the fact that a given project did not end as initially designed should not be considered a priori a failure if the project still contributed to solving the problem, even if did so through other means. For example, if the results of a participatory needs assessment indicate that a building is ultimately not what is required but, instead, a road is the main need, this finding might demand that designers defer to other professionals, such as engineers, and/or that designers contribute instead with the design of a system rather than a building. However, even when there is an actual need for a building, the proposed flexibility paradigm still accommodates surprises. For example, if the initial design premise of a given project is traditionalism, it is acceptable if the project ends up becoming a modernist project, as happened in some of the successful cases of ethnoengineering.

Consequently, a key difference between the proposed bottom-up participation and the conventional top-down participation approach pertains to the aspect of *control,* a central principle of high design practice. Often, architectural designers feel the necessity to exert a close control on the works in order to ensure that their authored project will be built as closely as possible to how they conceived it. A bottom-up participatory response to the architectural paradigm of control would be *messiness,* as in accepting that working with people is a complicated endeavor that often ends up yielding unexpected results. The strong emphasis that social design practice currently places on buildings often overlooks the human aspect, which is far more complex than that of static objects. A bottom-up participatory design practice would instead acknowledge that community processes are organic, not vertical; that they are complex, not unidimensional; and that relationships within a given community are not always harmonious. Thus, this proposed practice adopts the principle that there is no such thing as "*the* community," therefore rejecting generalizations and narratives of compactness that are often manifested in questionable claims of designers having worked with "the community." This practice also acknowledges that social class is one of the strongest elements of distinction even in traditional rural communities, and as such it has a decisive impact on the results of community participatory processes, especially when it comes to identifying needs and preferences. For example, the comparatively wealthier and better schooled leadership in a traditional community might favor traditionalist constructions, whereas the common villagers targeted by the project might instead favor simple modernist buildings. Consequently, a bottom-up participatory design practice would accept the existence of fissures within communities and the fact that upper and lower classes in a given community might have different and potentially incompatible visions of a given problem and its potential solutions. Thus, designers working within a bottom-up framework would be aware of the limitations of using the perspectives of community elites as the view of "the community" as a whole. However, they would be also aware of the problems associated with taking advantage of social class fissures in order to try to impose the designer's own agenda. In sum, designers using a bottom-up participatory framework would be keenly aware of privilege, both their own and the one within the communities where they work.

ETHNOARCHITECTURE AS AN ALTERNATIVE TO MAINSTREAM SOCIAL DESIGN PRACTICE

The notion of bottom-up participation thus aims to address the main issue posed by participation, which is that of social class privilege or *positionality*. We as designers can easily control participation to position ourselves above the people we work with and make decisions for them—just as in the type of regular top-down design approach that participation is supposed to contest. This issue of positionality extends even to the most sensitive approaches to community participation, including the classic ethnographic approach, which inspired ethnoengineering. Ethnography is generally regarded as the gold standard for community-based work. However, from the troubling outcomes of the ethnoengineering project it is clear that a given approach will not automatically work just because it is guided by ethnography.

Indeed, the main issue with the classic ethnographic method is the positionality issue. Positionality has been in the DNA of classic ethnographic work from the very development of ethnography's key methodological tool, namely, *participant observation.* The term for this approach is very illustrative: while researchers participate in the life of a group, they also observe. The logic behind this key ethnographic premise is that only by experiencing everyday life in a given group can researchers obtain insight into fundamental existential questions among the members of that group. In its most ideal sense, and following the classic formulation of the ethnographic method by Bronisław Malinowski (1922), only after the researchers have stayed for a long time as members of a given group does that "magic" (1922, 6) occur. The practices of this group become so embodied in the researchers' own lives that they suddenly understand why these people engage in certain actions, such as killing other people, marrying their own kin, or performing eerie rituals to build a house. In these ideal terms, participant observation is like a culturally mediumistic experience. Participant observers are "possessed" by the other people's culture, and then, after a year or two in that condition, they emerge to describe their experience. In ethnography's early days, the results of such experiences were announced with definitive and jubilant titles, such as those in Lucien Lévy-Bruhl's encyclopedic (and highly biased) compilations of proto-ethnographic knowledge, *Primitive Mentality* (1923), *How Natives Think* (1926), and *The "Soul" of the Primitive* (1928).

Despite its being highly revered as a methodological approach, participant observation is deeply problematic in many respects, as has been acknowledged since the early 1970s (see, e.g., Geertz 1973). The most obvious issue with this approach is that individuals in relative privilege—that is, the researchers—might end up inviting themselves to form part of the life of a group whose interactions may be disrupted by the researchers' own presence. In consequence, as has been discussed in critical anthropological literature, in some cases it is possible that events of social conflict narrated by famous anthropologists were at least partly triggered by their own presence. However, even if this is not the case, the whole spirit of participant observation embodies privilege. For example, the participant observers are supposed not to affect the interactions that take place during mealtimes with their "true" presence—that is, their presence as ethnographers, as opposed to their adopted role as tribespeople. However, they are still not fully present in their tribal persona because they inevitably have to be analyzing the scene, scrutinizing everything that happens (e.g., where people sit, who eats first, who eats what, etc.). Figuratively speaking, then, in participant observation the researchers might position themselves almost at the level of a god who can see and understand everything that happens as if from above. Ethnography's participant observation, then, actually epitomizes the issues of privilege.

Attempts to correct this asymmetrical relationship between researchers and subjects are currently being made in the anthropological field, where the subject of social design has become one of great interest (see Rabinow et al. 2008; Tunstall 2013; Marcus 2016). This is part of anthropology's rising interest in the general subject of design (see Rabinow 2011; Clarke 2011, 2018; Redfield 2012a, 2012b, 2016, 2018; Gunn, Otto, and Smith 2013; Buchli 2013; Redfield and Robins 2016; Smith et al. 2016; Escobar 2018). One such attempt to level the researcher/subject relationship has been proposed by Caroline Gatt and Tim Ingold (2013); it is based on the notion of *correspondence* as an alternative to participant observation. Correspondence entails shifting the top-down relationship between researchers and subjects to a level relationship in which, rather than being passive providers of knowledge, subjects become part of a research partnership, in which both they and the researchers equally benefit from the research project. For example, as the outcome of one such correspondence relationship, researchers could obtain data while subjects obtain a product that has been created in order to fully or partially generate the data. As they carry out fieldwork, for instance, the researchers could offer expertise in the production of something materially useful to the research subjects, such as a development plan or a bridge. It would be through the collaborative process of producing such an artifact that researchers would learn about, for example, power relationships or the role of knowledge within the researched group.

Thus, this approach, which the authors call "anthropology by means of design," proposes that, in material terms, something is left to the research subjects as a product—or, at least, a byproduct—of the research. This is a significant proposition, which could in fact result in a revolution in the way ethnographic research is carried out. However, I argue that, for the purposes of social design practice, the centrality of the research (i.e., the importance still placed on the researcher's agenda) continues to represent a limitation. It is a positive thing that, under the correspondence and other leveling models, the researchers' and subjects' interests are now proposed to be on an equal level. However, for the case of social design practice, I argue that practitioners should instead give more importance to the subjects' agenda. This is the rationale behind the bottom-up participatory approach I am proposing—to engage on a radical change in positionality, from the classical top-down participant observation or even a leveled relationship to a bottom-up relationship between practitioners and subjects.

Although leveling the playing field between researchers and subjects is a promising gesture in the field of anthropology, in social design the real change will happen when we as designers radically shift our understanding of the ethnographic approach for the purposes of architectural practice. From ethnography in the sense of orientalism (e.g., ethnoengineering) and even in the sense of correspondence, we should instead strive to (re-)embrace the most essential principle of ethnography, that of viewing things *from the other side's perspective*. That is, the agenda, means, and materialization of a social design project should be based upon the perspective of those who are intended to be the primary users of the project. This is what I mean by bottom-up participation from a methodological standpoint.

I call this approach to participation *ethnoarchitecture*. The prefix *ethno-* here emphasizes the fundamentally relativistic spirit of the ethnographic approach, indicating that this is an approach to architecture that dwells upon ethnography's strengths while also seeking to overcome its limitations. The term "ethnoarchitecture" has been used before in academic literature to describe a number of different notions, including the name for an approach to study the relationship between people and environment (Rapoport 1976), a synonym for vernacular architecture (Egenter 1992), the name for an approach to study rural, preindustrial housing and settlement (Toffin 1994), and the study of the knowledge systems of aboriginal builders (Memmott 2007).

In contrast to these uses of the term, I propose to use "ethnoarchitecture" to describe a disciplinary hybrid, bottom-up participatory approach to carrying out social design work among people from sociocultural backgrounds that are different from the practitioner's. Under this approach, the work is carried out in the people's own terms, thus honoring their right to become agents of their own future.

By defining ethnoarchitecture as a hybrid approach, I mean that, although it includes elements of both the architectural and ethnographic methods, it is not either of these methods. Methodologically speaking, ethnoarchitecture is a "third space" (Bhabha 1988) or a *thirdspace* (Soja 1996).

$$\text{ethnoarchitecture} \neq \text{ethnography} + \text{architecture}$$
$$\text{ethnoarchitecture} = \text{thirdspace}$$

Thus, as an approach to social design, ethnoarchitecture (or even *ethnotecture,* to signify its third-spatial or hybrid nature) goes beyond simply proposing a sum of advantages. Rather than being a form of addition, ethnoarchitecture is instead a form of synergy. Consequently, the result of an ethnoarchitectural design process (as in the construction itself) can be numerically represented by the following equation:

$$1 + 1 = 3$$

This means that if, as mentioned earlier, in the 1 + 1 collaboration between practitioners and subjects the result in terms of the process is indefinite (1 + 1 = ?; that is, one cannot tell a priori what will be the outcome), when it comes to the material outcome the result is more than simply a building (that is, 1 + 1 = 3). This is the case because the process also yields a plethora of non-building-related advantages that include the fostering of ownership, leadership, and organizational capabilities. However, the building itself is also a different entity. Take for example the discussion about the best alternative for poverty alleviation in traditional environments, whether traditionalism or modernism. The result of an ethnoarchitectural bottom-up intervention would be a hybrid building in the sense that it can be identified at once as traditionalist, modernist, or both. As for how this hybrid building would look, elsewhere I have described a project in Guyana in which I implemented this ethnoarchitectural approach in participatory work with indigenous villagers of the Macushi and other ethnicities (see Arboleda 2014, 2020). The villagers designed hybrid homes that combined industrial materials (like metal and cement) with traditional spaces (such as verandas). Their homes also included two kitchens, an interior modernist one to cook with a gas stove, and an exterior traditional one for the making of cassava bread in a wood stove.

Thus, ethnoarchitecture as a bottom-up approach to participation endeavors to challenge both shallow and deep forms of participation. That is, it challenges the mainstream, top-down participatory approach that can easily become yet another tool for social oppression. However, it also challenges ethnography's participant observation notion that practitioners can become members of a group without affecting the social processes within that group.

In doing so, this approach aims to challenge the notion of transparency, as this term is understood in subaltern theory. That is, not transparency in the sense of stating one's intentions and their limitations but, instead, in the sense of practitioners pretending to be invisible and claiming that they are providing a value-judgment-free description of subjects. A common assumption of participant observation is that practitioners can provide a transparent window into the minds of other people (i.e., it is not the practitioner speaking but the villager speaking through the practitioner's mouth). By questioning the participant observer's authoritativeness in such descriptions about how others think, as a bottom-up approach to participation ethnoarchitecture thus defies the paradigm of the practitioner's intrinsic superiority.

In conclusion, then, as a form of practice the ethnoarchitectural approach here proposed endeavors to challenge the default high positionality of designers, by embracing a positionality shift where designers become the *supporters,* as opposed to the *drivers,* of the design process. In this approach, designers metaphorically move downward, no longer being the ones in control of the design. However, this downward move does not stop at the level of project beneficiaries, since this approach also challenges the premise of designers being equals with beneficiaries, which the discourses of participation, both shallow and deep, often endorse. Here, instead, designers move further downward, striving to metaphorically position themselves at the bottom of the design hierarchy, becoming neither the project authors (designers) nor the partners (co-designers) but instead the supporters of a design process (fig. 69). As such, the designers' role would consist of offering professional assistance (e.g., planning, technical, and organizational advice) to make the people's ideas feasible technologically, spatially, and economically speaking. Thus, this supporting role would be directed to assisting people so they are able to materialize their own design ideas, rather than those of the designer.

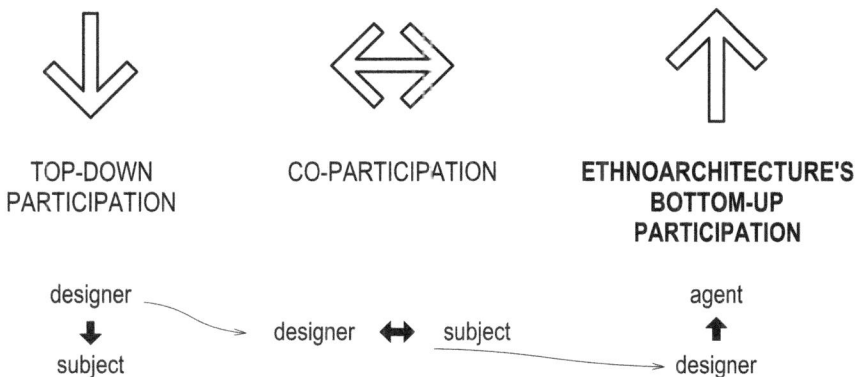

TOP-DOWN PARTICIPATION

CO-PARTICIPATION

ETHNOARCHITECTURE'S BOTTOM-UP PARTICIPATION

designer
↓
subject

designer ↔ subject

agent
↑
designer

Fig. 69. A proposed positionality shift for the practice of social design.

Just as the designers would strive to position themselves at the bottom of the process, in this approach to social design beneficiaries would rise to assuming a decisional role in the project. Their role would include participating first and foremost in defining the framework (i.e., what is the project about?), and then designing the project. Thus, in this approach people are no longer regarded as passive beneficiaries but instead they become *agents*. As an approach to social design practice, ethnoarchitecture endeavors to make this practice more about the service and less about the designers. Under this approach, designers would still offer help, but in the people's own terms. Rather than saying "I am proposing this design to you," or the often tokenistic "Let's design together," ethnoarchitectural designers would instead ask, "What can I help with, if my help is even needed?"

NOTES

1. Social Design, Sustainability, and Imperialism

1. "Model of Architecture Serving Society."
2. The Brundtland Report is named after Gro Harlem Brundtland, the WCED committee chairperson who oversaw its writing. Brundtland served as prime minister of Norway for three terms and has been head of several international organizations.
3. For a history of the process of writing the Brundtland Report, and the complex negotiations that took place in that process, see Borowy 2014.
4. Overall, these arguments constitute the dependency, postdevelopment, and intermediate technology critiques to development.
5. To clarify, I am not debating the accuracy of the connection between indigenous people and environmentalism. Instead my concern is how some people are represented by others as living examples of how life was in the past, causing the aspirations that some of them might have of enjoying, like everyone else, the possibilities of modern life to be deemed an abnormality.
6. From the Spanish, *Coordinadora de las Organizaciones Indígenas de la Cuenca Amazónica* (Coordinator of Indigenous Organizations of the Amazon Basin).
7. Nongovernmental organizations.
8. It is worth mentioning that Sinclair was not speaking as a pro bono designer himself. His six-figure salary actually made him the highest paid member of Architecture for Humanity, and along with Stohr the only paid director, as the organization's tax returns show.

2. Is Localism the Solution?

1. "Me di cuenta que el futuro de la arquitectura moderna, de la experimentación, pudiera ser en los barrios, porque los barrios eran zonas blancas de la ciudad. Eran zonas que no tenían registro, catastro; eran zonas que no tenían zonificación. O sea que, si lograbas intervenir en un barrio, podías hacer lo que te diera la gana" (Arquine 2013, 02:20).
2. Raúl Fajardo, designer of the Coltejer building, which is Medellín's most iconic high-rise structure.
3. I will be capitalizing the term *City* when it refers to the mayor's office, or its dependencies in charge of the social urbanism project.
4. The issue of whether this was a design or a construction problem has been the

source of a years-long dispute between the architect and the construction company. In 2017 the City of Medellín decided to sue both.

5. Community action committee.

6. This is the estimate by the Santo Domingo Junta de Acción Comunal about the total number of residents who were displaced for the construction of the Biblioteca España.

7. For instance, *Mesa Inter-Barrial de Desconectados* (Interbarrio board of residents whose access to public utilities has been cut off [because of late payments]), *Mesa de Vivienda y Servicios Públicos Domiciliarios Comuna 8* (Comuna 8 board of housing and public utilities), and *Movimiento de Pobladores por la Construcción y Defensa de Nuestros Territorios* (Settlers' movement for the construction and defense of our territories). There are also a few nonprofit organizations whose work has a strong land rights component. These organizations are usually formed by professionals (often professionals from the own comunas) and regular community members. They include *Corporación Con-vivamos, Corporación El Megáfono, Fundación Sumapaz,* and *Corporación Ecológica y Cultural Penca de Sábila.*

8. This number is according to a list prepared by URBAM, Alejandro Echeverri's research center at Universidad EAFIT, for the 2014 World Urban Forum (see EAFIT 2014).

9. Considering 2004 and 2006 housing density data from the two comunas collected by the City of Medellín's Planning Department, and analyzed by Dapena and Peláez (2009).

10. Incidentally, *Architectural Digest*'s marketing department was one of the project's main sponsors.

11. Lincoln also had a say in the final design approval process (Tittmann 2014a, 42).

3. Localism

1. Now called *Practical Action,* this is a UK-based organization established in 1966 by economist Ernst Friedrich "Fritz" Schumacher, author of the classic *Small Is Beautiful* (1973).

2. FISE (phonetically *fee-seh*) is the Spanish acronym for Fondo de Inversión Social de Emergencia (Emergency Social Investment Fund), the now-defunct government infrastructure office that ran this program. The Roman numeral III was meant to indicate the third (and eventually last) phase in this office's program of infrastructural investment. I use "program" when referring to the FISE III ethnoengineering umbrella program, and "project" when referring to the project of implementing ethnoengineering.

3. By "amateurism" I refer to the practice of social design carried out in marginalized communities by architecture students or young professionals with little or no prior field experience in construction and/or poverty action.

4. The budget allocation was made in US dollars, which is Ecuador's official currency.

5. Comités de Ejecución y Administración de Proyectos.

6. Unidades de Capacitación y Asistencia Técnica.

7. This was the number of comunidades in which the FISE III participatory program ended up constructing buildings and not, for example, roads or water and sanitation infrastructure. The FISE III program covered 940 comunidades in total.

8. No prototypes were built in the Amazon.

9. In this and other quotes from my interviews with villagers, I use a code composed of letters identifying the village and numbers for the person. My own interventions are marked as GA.

10. In these dialogues, the phrases in quote marks are quotations that villagers themselves are making of things that were said in their meetings with the project's representatives.

11. Wherever there exist verb tense disagreements, such as in this case, I am translating these literally from the original interview.

12. The Azabí villagers also changed the supporting structure of their ethnoengineering bridge from wood to metal, following the example of pedestrian bridges some of them had seen in the city of Quito. A similar case of modernization of the project's wooden bridges happened in the villages of Pilancón and Sarahuasi.

13. Dirección Provincial de Educación Tungurahua.

4. The Challenge of Social Design

1. Granted, the leaders of Medellín's Barrio Santo Domingo also invoked the notion of "the community" as homogeneous when they protested how residents had been manipulated into selecting a library. Their use of this notion was a strategic essentialist self-representation, useful in their struggle over housing rights.

REFERENCES

Abu-Lughod, Janet. 1992. "Disappearing Dichotomies: First World–Third World; Traditional–Modern." *Traditional Dwellings and Settlements Review* 3, no. 2: 7–12.

AFH (Architecture for Humanity), ed. 2006. *Design Like You Give a Damn: Architectural Responses to Humanitarian Crises.* New York: Metropolis Books.

———, ed. 2012a. *Design Like You Give a Damn [2]: Building Change from the Ground Up.* New York: Abrams Books.

———. 2012b. "SF Mayor Launches Development Initiative Off Chapter Pocket Park." AFH website. March 7, 2012. https://web.archive.org/web/20140403104834 /http://architectureforhumanity.org/updates/2012-03-07-sf-mayor-launches -development-initiative-off-chapter-pocket-.

———. 2013a. *5 Year Strategic Plan.* San Francisco: AFH.

———. 2013b. "2013 Year in Review." AFH website. December 30, 2013. https://web .archive.org/web/20150123024139/http://www.architectureforhumanity.org/blog /12-30-2013/2013-year-review.

———. 2013c. "Reimagining community spaces takes the entire community." Facebook, October 15, 2013. https://web.archive.org/web/20180918111358/https://www .facebook.com/ArchForHumanity/posts/10151718411351409.

———. 2013d. "SF Pocket Park to Cut Ribbon, Launch Phase 2." AFH website. July 15, 2013. https://web.archive.org/web/20140403105433/http://architecturefor humanity.org:80/updates/2013-07-15-sf-pocket-park-to-cut-ribbon-launch -phase-2.

———. 2013e. "When a neighborhood association posts construction photos, you know you're on the right track!" Facebook, March 28, 2013. https://web.archive.org /web/20180918111521/https://www.facebook.com/ArchForHumanity/posts /569379113095608.

———. 2014a. "Our Services." AFH website. 2014. https://web.archive.org/web /20140220124713/http://architectureforhumanity.org:80/services.

———. 2014b. "The One Burrows Pocket Park in San Francisco is Now Open!" AFH website. August 8, 2014. https://web.archive.org/web/20141228160947/http:// architectureforhumanity.org/blog/08-8-2014/one-burrows-pocket-park-san -francisco-now-open.

———. n.d. "1 Burrows." Plan drawing. https://web.archive.org/web/20181028054701 /http://3.bp.blogspot.com/-Tw7jBCfR7lQ/TlgWPjvMGVI/AAAAAAAAAu8 /pd51Wf6HMWg/s1600/burrows1.jpg.

Aga Khan Award [The Aga Khan Award for Architecture]. 1980. *Courtyard Houses: Agadir, Morocco.* Geneva: Aga Khan Award for Architecture.

Agyeman, Julian. 2005. *Sustainable Communities and the Challenge of Environmental Justice.* New York: New York University Press.

———. 2013. *Introducing Just Sustainabilities: Policy, Planning and Practice.* London: Zed Books.

Agyeman, Julian, Robert Bullard, and Bob Evans. 2002. "Exploring the Nexus: Bringing Together Sustainability, Environmental Justice and Equity." *Space and Polity* 6, no. 1: 77–90.

———. 2003. *Just Sustainabilities: Development in an Unequal World.* First edition. London: Earthscan.

Al Borde. 2016. "Gracias a todos los que nos han preguntado por la Comunidad de Puerto Cabuyal" [Thanks to all of you who have asked us about the Puerto Cabuyal community]. Facebook, April 21, 2016. https://web.archive.org/web /20190814143953/https://www.facebook.com/albordearquitectos/photos /a.806672736069748/1017810024956017/?type=3&__xts__%5B0%5D=68.AR AgN036x40u5QNUlwwn6NzzRHmb1E6ujJ_TeL88Yi7TtQMgXFXezg2ElYmet 3VJo45Y2gyrMCmraLj7O1qJ198vx_YuRxfeb2PH.

———. n.d.a. "Nueva Esperanza—New Hope School." Al Borde website. https://web .archive.org/web/20170307014208/http://www.albordearq.com/escuela-nueva -esperanza-nueva-esperanza-school.

———. n.d.b. "Quiénes Somos—Who We Are." Al Borde website. https://web.archive .org/web/20170626190855/http://www.albordearq.com/quienes-somos_who-we -are/.

Alcaldía (Alcaldía de Medellín). 2004. Resolución no. 115 de 2004. Gaceta Oficial no. 2268.

———. 2007. *Encuesta Calidad de Vida Medellín 2006* [Quality of life survey Medellín 2006]. Medellín, Colombia: Alcaldía de Medellín.

———. 2011a. *BIO 2030: Plan Director Medellín, Valle de Aburrá* [BIO 2030: Master plan Medellín, Aburrá Valley]. Medellín, Colombia: Mesa Editores.

———. 2011b. *Laboratorio Medellín: Catálogo de Diez Prácticas Vivas* [Medellín laboratory: Catalog of ten living practices]. Medellín, Colombia: Mesa Editores.

———. 2016. *Plan de Desarrollo: Medellín Cuenta con Vos* [Development plan: Medellín counts on you]. Medellín, Colombia: Alcaldía de Medellín.

———. 2021. "Con la Rehabilitación de Su Biblioteca, Renace la Esperanza en la Zona Nororiental de Medellín" [With the rehabilitation of its library, hope is reborn in Medellín's Northeastern Zone]. City of Medellín website, March 29, 2021. https:// web.archive.org/web/20210417092745/https://www.medellin.gov.co/irj/portal /medellin?NavigationTarget=contenido%2F9459-Con-la-rehabilitacion-de-su -biblioteca-renace-la-esperanza-en-la-zona-nororiental-de-Medellin.

Allen, Patricia, and Carolyn Sachs. 1991. "The Social Side of Sustainability: Class, Gender and Race." *Science as Culture* 2, no. 4: 569–90.

———. 1992. "The Poverty of Sustainability: An Analysis of Current Positions." *Agriculture and Human Values* 9, no. 4: 29–35.

AlSayyad, Nezar, and Gabriel Arboleda. 2011. "The Sustainable Indigenous Vernacular: Interrogating a Myth." In *Aesthetics of Sustainable Architecture,* edited by Sang Lee. Rotterdam: 010 Publishers.

Ambole, Amollo. 2020. "Rethinking Design Making and Design Thinking in Africa." *Design and Culture* 12, no. 3: 331–50.

Anastasopoulos, Nicholas. 2016. "Interview with Al Borde—Events in the Greek Pavilion, Venice Biennale." *Archisearch.gr,* July 24, 2016. https://web.archive.org /web/20190815124644/https://www.archisearch.gr/press/interview-with-al -borde-events-in-the-greek-pavilion-venice-biennale/.

Anaya, James. 2010. *Report of the Special Rapporteur on the Situation of Human Rights and Fundamental Freedoms of Indigenous People. Addendum: The Situation of Indigenous Peoples in Botswana.* Geneva: United Nations Human Rights Council.

Andreou, Alex. 2015. "Anti-Homeless Spikes: 'Sleeping Rough Opened My Eyes to the City's Barbed Cruelty.'" *Guardian,* February 18, 2015. https://web.archive.org/web /20150218215955/https://www.theguardian.com/society/2015/feb/18/defensive -architecture-keeps-poverty-undeen-and-makes-us-more-hostile.

Anguelovski, Isabelle, James Connolly, Melissa Garcia-Lamarca, Helen Cole, and Hamil Pearsall. 2019. "New Scholarly Pathways on Green Gentrification: What Does the Urban 'Green Turn' Mean and Where Is It Going?" *Progress in Human Geography* 43, no. 6 (December): 1064–86.

Antonelli, Paola. 2012. "States of Design 10: Social Design." *Domus* 955 (February). https://web.archive.org/web/20130416231807/http://www.domusweb.it/en/design /2012/02/22/states-of-design-10-social-design.html.

Aquilino, Marie, ed. 2011. *Beyond Shelter: Architecture and Human Dignity.* New York: Metropolis Books.

Arboleda, Gabriel. 2012. "Ethnoengineering: Negotiating the Modern in a 'Culturally Appropriate' Government Program in Ecuador." PhD diss. University of California, Berkeley. ProQuest (1666449202).

———. 2014. "Participation Practice and Its Criticism: Can They Be Bridged? A Field Report from the Guyana Hinterland." *Housing and Society* 41, no. 2: 195–227.

———. 2020. "Beyond Participation: Rethinking Social Design." *JAE: Journal of Architectural Education* 74, no. 1 (March): 16–26.

ArchDaily. 2010. "Nueva Esperanza School/al bordE." *ArchDaily,* January 7, 2010. https://web.archive.org/web/20181203114551/http://www.archdaily.com/45942 /nueva-esperanza-school-al-borde.

Architizer. n.d. "Nueva Esperanza School." *Architizer.* https://web.archive.org/web /20190814115225/https://architizer.com/projects/nueva-esperanza-school/.

Arquine. 2013. "Alfredo Brillembourg | Congreso Arquine No. 14." Published April 25, 2013. Video, 10:38. https://youtu.be/HITANh27avU. Permalink: https://archive .org/details/alfredobrillembourg-congrescarquine.

Article 25. n.d.a. "About." Article 25 Facebook page. https://web.archive.org/web 20190804114141/http://www.facebook.com/pg/Article25/about/.

———. n.d.b. "Vision, Mission and Values." Article 25 website. https://web.archive .org/web/20160315223525/http://www.article-25.org:80/about-article-25/vision -mission-and-values/.

Asamblea (Asamblea Nacional del Ecuador). 2009. "Sesión 12 Intervención de Asambleísta Grace Almeida" [Session 12, address by assemblyperson Grace Almeida]. October 28, 2009. Video, 7:53. http://www.youtube.com/watch?v=2UCXq0EpC_8. Permalink: https://archive.org/details/asamblea_sesion12.

———. 2010. "Sesión 53 Intervención de Asambleísta Grace Almeida" [Session 53, address by assemblyperson Grace Almeida]. September 1, 2010. Video, 7:14. http://www.youtube.com/watch?v=2CHk4MElIu0. Permalink: https://archive.org/details/asamblea_sesion53.

Asar, Rodolfo (@rodolfoasar). 2016. "En Puerto Cabuyal, comunidad a la que sólo se llega 4x4" [In Puerto Cabuyal, community that can only be reached by 4x4]. Twitter, April 24, 2016, 3:45 p.m. https://web.archive.org/web/20190815090902/https:/twitter.com/rodolfoasar/status/724323432062660608.

ASF (Architecture Sans Frontières). 2017a. "Become a Sponsor." ASF website. https://web.archive.org/web/20190804132528/https://www.asfint.org/become-a-sponsor/.

———. 2017b "Mission Statement." ASF website. https://web.archive.org/web/20190804115432/https://www.asfint.org/asf-document/mission-statement/.

Atkinson, Rowland, and Aidan While. 2015. "Defensive Architecture: Designing the Homeless Out of Cities." *Conversation,* December 30, 2015. https://web.archive.org/web/20160322014037/http://theconversation.com/defensive-architecture-designing-the-homeless-out-of-cities-52399.

Baeten, Guy. 2000. "The Tragedy of the Highway: Empowerment, Disempowerment and the Politics of Sustainability Discourses and Practices." *European Planning Studies* 8, no. 1: 69–86.

Barnett, Michael. 2013. *Empire of Humanity: A History of Humanitarianism.* Ithaca, NY: Cornell University Press, 2013.

Barragán, David. 2020. "Al Borde." Lecture delivered at Columbia University, October 12, 2020. https://www.arch.columbia.edu/events/1996-al-borde. Permalink: https://archive.org/details/al-borde-columbia.

Behling, Stefan, and Sophia Behling. 1996. *Sol Power: The Evolution of Solar Architecture.* Munich: Prestel.

Bell, Bryan, ed. 2004. *Good Deeds, Good Design: Community Service through Architecture.* New York: Princeton Architectural Press.

Ben-Eli, Michael. 2005. "Sustainability: The Five Core Principles, A New Framework." Sustainability Laboratories. https://web.archive.org/web/20130629132104/https://sustainabilitylabs.org/files/Sustainability%20-%20The%20Five%20Core%20Principles_0.pdf.

Benítez, Edinson. n.d. "Taller de Etnoingeniería" [Ethnoengineering workshop]. PowerPoint presentation, n.p.

Bergdoll, Barry. 2015. "El Porvenir Social Kindergarten." In *Designed for the Future: 80 Practical Ideas for a Sustainable World,* edited by Jared Green. New York: Princeton Architectural Press.

Berlanda, Tomà. 2015. "Shade of Meaning: Clinic in Turkana, Kenya, by Selgas Cano, Ignacio Peydro and MIT students." *Architectural Review,* no. 1417 (March).

———. 2016a. *Makoko Floating School.* Geneva: Aga Khan Foundation. https://web.archive.org/web/20190817085713/https://s3.amazonaws.com/media.archnet.org/system/publications/contents/10740/original/DTP103125.pdf?1475749432.

———. 2016b. "Media Attention Overload: The Collapse of Makoko's Floating School." *Architectural Review,* June 10, 2016. https://web.archive.org/web/20170212092310/https://www.architectural-review.com/rethink/media-attention-overload-the-collapse-of-makokos-floating-school/10007451.article.

Bhabha, Homi. 1988. "The Commitment to Theory." *New Formations* 5 (1988): 5–23.

Bhan, Niti. 2010. "Post-Colonial Design Blowback: The Challenge Facing the Global

Design Industry." *Perspective* (blog), July 16, 2010. https://web.archive.org/web
/20190813101201/http://nitibhan.com/2013/09/22/post-colonial-design-blow
back-the-challenge-facing-the-global-design-industry/.

Birch, Thomas. 1990. "The Incarceration of Wildness: Wilderness Areas as Prisons."
Environmental Ethics 12, no. 1: 3–26.

Bornacelly, Jaime, prod., and Jorge Luis Rocha, dir. 2014. Biblioteca España Sí, pero
No Así [Biblioteca España, yes, but not like that]. Documentary based on the thesis
"Análisis Territorial y Discursivo de los Parque Biblioteca de Medellín, Colombia"
[Territorial and discursive analysis of Medellín, Colombia's library parks], by Jaime
Bornacelly, Universidad de Antioquia. Produced 2014. Video, 24:54. https://www
.youtube.com/watch?v=6XzctMxDIUo. Permalink: https://archive.org/details
/biblioteca_espana_si...pero_no_asi.

Borowy, Iris. 2014. *Defining Sustainable Development for Our Common Future:
A History of the World Commission on Environment and Development (Brundtland
Commission)*. New York: Routledge.

Bourdieu, Pierre. 1984. *Distinction: A Social Critique of the Judgement of Taste*. Cambridge, MA: Harvard University Press.

———. 1986. "*The Forms of Capital*." In *Handbook of Theory and Research for the Sociology of Education,* edited by John Richardson. New York: Greenwood.

———. 1987. "What Makes a Social Class? On the Theoretical and Practical Existence
of Groups." *Berkeley Journal of Sociology* 32: 1–17.

———. 1993. *The Field of Cultural Production: Essays on Art and Literature*. New York:
Columbia University Press.

———. 1996. *The Rules of Art: Genesis and Structure of the Literary Field*. Stanford, CA:
Stanford University Press.

Bourke, Simon, and Tony Meppem. 2000. "Privileged Narratives and Fictions of Consent in Environmental Discourse." *Local Environment* 5, no. 3: 299–310.

Bricmont, Jean. 2006. *Humanitarian Imperialism: Using Human Rights to Sell War*.
Translated by Diana Johnstone. New York: Monthly Review Press, 2006.

Brillembourg, Alfredo, and Hubert Klumpner, eds. 2013. *Torre David: Informal Vertical
Communities*. Zürich: Lars Müller.

———. 2010. "Rules of Engagement: Caracas and the Informal City." In *Rethinking the
Informal City: Critical Perspectives from Latin America,* edited by Felipe Hernán-
dez, Peter Kellett, and Lea Allen. New York: Berghahn Books.

———. 2011. "Slumlifting: An Informal Toolbox for a New Architecture." In *Beyond
Shelter: Architecture and Human Dignity,* edited by Marie Aquilino. New York:
Metropolis Books.

Brillembourg, Alfredo, Kristin Feireiss, and Hubert Klumpner. 2005. *Informal City:
Caracas Case*. Munich: Prestel.

Bruckner, Pascal. 2013. *The Fanaticism of the Apocalypse: Save the Earth, Punish
Human Beings*. Cambridge, UK: Polity Press.

Bryant, Bunyan. 1995. "Introduction." In *Environmental Justice: Issues, Policies, and
Solutions*. Washington, DC: Island Press.

Buchanan, Peter. 2012. "The Big Rethink Taking Stock." *Architectural Review* 231, no.
1379 (January): 68–77.

Buchli, Victor. 2013. *An Anthropology of Architecture*. London: Bloomsbury.

Bullard, Robert. 1990. *Dumping in Dixie: Race, Class, and Environmental Quality*.
Boulder, CO: Westview Press.

———. 1994. "The Legacy of American Apartheid and Environmental Racism." *Journal of Civil Rights and Economic Development* 9, no. 2: 445–74.

———. 2001. "Environmental Justice in the 21st Century: Race Still Matters." *Phylon* 49, no. 3/4: 151–71.

Bullard, Robert, Paul Mohai, Robin Saha, and Beverly Wright. 2008. "Toxic Wastes and Race at Twenty: Why Race Still Matters after All of These Years." *Environmental Law* 38, no. 2 (Spring): 371–411.

Cabrera, Juan Daniel, Sebastián Coral, and Wilson Moya. 2017. *Propuesta de Refuncionalización de la Ex-escuela "Gonzalo Díaz de Pineda" en la Comunidad San Luis de Chibuleo* [Repurposing proposal for the former 'Gonzalo Díaz de Pineda' school in the San Luis de Chibuleo comunidad]. Report. Ambato, Ecuador: Universidad Técnica de Ambato.

Cardoso, Fernando, and Enzo Faletto. 1979. *Dependency and Development in Latin America.* Berkeley: University of California Press.

Carson, Rachel. 1962. *Silent Spring.* Boston: Houghton Mifflin.

Cary, John. 2010. *The Power of Pro Bono: 40 Stories about Design for the Public Good by Architects and Their Clients.* New York: Metropolis Books.

Chang, Jiat-Hwee. 2012. "Tropical Variants of Sustainable Architecture: A Postcolonial Perspective." In *The SAGE Handbook of Architectural Theory,* edited by Greig Crysler, Stephen Cairns, and Hilde Heynen. London: Sage Publications.

Charlesworth, Esther, and Iftekhar Ahmed. 2015. *Sustainable Housing Reconstruction: Designing Resilient Housing after Natural Disasters.* New York, NY: Routledge.

Chavis, Benjamin, and Charles Lee. 1987. *Toxic Wastes and Race in the United States.* New York: United Church of Christ Commission for Racial Justice.

Checker, Melissa. 2011. "Wiped Out by the 'Greenwave:' Environmental Gentrification and the Paradoxical Politics of Urban Sustainability." *City & Society* 23, no. 2: 210–29.

———. 2019. Environmental Gentrification: Sustainability and the Just City." In *The Routledge Handbook of Anthropology and the City,* edited by Setha Low. New York: Routledge.

Chino, Mike. 2014. "San Francisco's Burrows Street Pocket Park Opens to the Public!" *Inhabitat,* August 15, 2014. https://web.archive.org/web/20140816094358/https://inhabitat.com/san-franciscos-burrows-street-pocket-park-opens-to-the-public/.

Chomsky, Noam. 2008. "Humanitarian Imperialism: The New Doctrine of Imperial Right." *Monthly Review* 60, no. 4, September 2008.

Cifuentes, Fabian. 2012. "Cassia Coop Training Centre/TYIN Tegnestue Architects." *ArchDaily,* September 24, 2012. https://web.archive.org/web/20190804145749 /https://www.archdaily.com/274835/casia-coop-training-centre-tyin-tegnestue -architects.

Clarke, Alison, ed. 2011. *Design Anthropology: Object Culture in the 21st Century.* New York: Springer.

———, ed. 2018. *Design Anthropology: Object Cultures in Transition.* London: Bloomsbury.

Cole, Luke, and Sheila Foster. 2000. *From the Ground Up: Environmental Racism and the Rise of the Environmental Justice Movement.* New York: New York University Press.

Cook, Sara, and Bryn Golton. 1994. "Sustainable Development: Concepts and Practice in the Built Environment—A UK Perspective." *CIB TG* 16 (November): 677–85.

Connelly, Steve. 2007. "Mapping Sustainable Development as a Contested Concept." *Local Environment* 12, no 3: 259–78.

Corporación Con-vivamos. 2005. *Plan de Desarrollo Local Comuna Uno Popular* [Local development plan, Comuna Uno Popular]. Medellín, Colombia: Corporación Con-vivamos.

Correa, Maryluz, Adriana Franco, John Garcés, Diana González, Erika Palacio, Juan Peláez, Alejandra Ramírez, Laura Sánchez, and Valentina Venegas. 2013. "Programa Urbano Integral—PUI-NOR. Experiencia de Construcción de Ciudad desde la Planeación, la Gestión del Desarrollo y la Vivienda" [PUI-NOR Integral Urban Program: Experience of city-making from planning, development, and housing]. Bachelor's thesis, Universidad de Anticquia

Coulombel, Patrick. 2011. "Open Letter to Architects, Engineers, and Urbanists." In *Beyond Shelter: Architecture and Human Dignity,* edited by Marie Aquilino. New York: Metropolis Books.

———. 2019. Arrêtons L'amateurisme au Nom de L'urgence: De Haïti à Notre-Dame, la Reconstruction en Question [Let's stop amateurism in the name of emergency: Questioning reconstruction, from Haiti to Notre-Dame]. Paris: NBE.

Cronon, William, ed. 1996. *Uncommon Ground: Rethinking the Human Place in Nature.* London: W. W. Norton.

Cross, Jamie. 2013. "The 100th Object: Solar Lighting Technology and Humanitarian Goods." *Journal of Material Culture* 18, no. 4: 367–87.

Crysler, Greig. 2015. "The Paradoxes of Design Activism: Expertise, Scale and Exchange." *Field,* no. 2 (Fall): 77–124.

Crysler, Greig, Stephen Cairns, and Hilde Heynen. 2012. *The SAGE Handbook of Architectural Theory.* London: Sage Publications

Cunningham, David. 2016. "Architecture, the Built and the Idea of Socialism." In *Can Architecture Be an Emancipatory Project?: Dialogues on Architecture and the Left,* edited by Nadir Lahiji. Alresford, UK: Zero Books.

Curran, Winifred, and Trina Hamilton, eds. 2017. *Just Green Enough: Urban Development and Environmental Gentrification.* New York: Routledge.

Dapena, Luis Fernando, and Pedro Pablo Peláez. 2009. *Densidades y Hábitat: Una Aproximación al Análisis de las Densidades y su Confrontación con las Morfologías Urbanas en la Ciudad de Medellín* [Densities and habitat: An introduction to the analysis of densities vis-à-vis urban morphologies in the city of Medellín]. Project report. Medellín, Colombia: Universidad Nacional.

Dasmann, Raymond. 1985. "Achieving the Sustainable Use of Species and Ecosystems." *Landscape Planning* 12, no. 3 (November): 211–19.

Dauvergne, Peter. 2016. *Environmentalism of the Rich.* Cambridge, MA: MIT Press.

Dauvergne, Peter, and Jane Lister. 2013. *Eco-Business: A Big-Brand Takeover of Sustainability.* Cambridge, MA: MIT Press.

Davis, Howard. 1999. *The Culture of Building.* Oxford: Oxford University Press.

De Puy Kamp, Majlie. 2021. "How Marginalized Communities in the South Are Paying the Price for 'Green Energy' in Europe." CNN, July 9, 2021. https://web.archive.org/web/20210709123715/https://edition.cnn.com/interactive/2021/07/us/american-south-biomass-energy-invs/.

De Waal, Alex. 2007. "No Such Thing as Humanitarian Intervention." *Harvard International Review,* March 21, 2007. https://web.archive.org/web/20110719211323/http://hir.harvard.edu/no-such-thing-as-humanitarian-intervention/.

Desmond, Matthew. 2016. *Evicted: Poverty and Profit in the American City.* New York: Crown Publishers.

Dineen, J. K. 2017. "City's $300,000 Restores Facade of Historic Site in Portola District." *San Francisco Chronicle,* September 16, 2017. https://web.archive.org /web/20170916164100/https://www.sfchronicle.com/politics/article/City-s-300 -000-restores-facade-of-historic-12201917.php.

Domus. 2019. "Al Borde: An Ecuadorin [sic] Architecture Collective." In "100+ Best Architecture Firms 2019." Special issue, Domus. March 5, 2019. https://web .archive.org/web/20210420142351/https://www.domusweb.it/en/speciali/best -architecture-firms/2019/al-borde.html.

Dooling, Sarah. 2009. "Ecological Gentrification: A Research Agenda Exploring Justice in the City." *International Journal of Urban and Regional Research* 33, no. 3: 621–39.

Douglas, Gordon. 2014. "Do-It-Yourself Urban Design: The Social Practice of Informal 'Improvement' Through Unauthorized Alteration." *City & Community* 13: 5–25.

———. 2019. "Privilege and Participation: On the Democratic Implications and Social Contradictions of Bottom-Up Urbanisms." In *The Palgrave Handbook of Bottom-Up Urbanism,* edited by Mahyar Arefi and Conrad Kickert. New York: Palgrave Macmillan.

Dowie, Mark. 2009. *Conservation Refugees: The Hundred-Year Conflict between Global Conservation and Native Peoples.* Cambridge, MA: MIT Press.

Drenthen, Martin, Jozef Keulartz, and James Proctor. 2007. "Nature in Motion." In *New Visions of Nature: Complexity and Authenticity.* New York: Springer.

Droege, Peter. 2012. "Beyond Sustainability: Architecture in the Renewable City." In *The SAGE Handbook of Architectural Theory,* edited by Greig Crysler, Stephen Cairns, and Hilde Heynen. London: Sage Publications.

Duffield, Mark. 2019. *Post-Humanitarianism: Governing Precarity in the Digital World.* Cambridge, UK: Polity Press.

Duque, Mary Luz. 2015. "Significados del Reasentamiento Involuntario para los Pobladores Trasladados en los Proyectos de Desarrollo Urbano: Metroplús y Conexión Vial Aburrá—Río Cauca. Estudio de Caso 2005–2015" [Meanings of the involuntary resettlement for resettled people in the urban development projects Metroplús and Aburrá—Río Cauca road connection. Case study 2005–2015]. Master's thesis, Universidad Pontificia Bolivariana.

EAFIT. 2014. "Guía Medellín. Proyecto Urbano Integral PUI Comuna Nororiental" [Medellín guide. Integral urban project, PUI Northeastern Commune]. https:// web.archive.org/web/20140806080903/http://www.eafit.edu.co/wuf/guia -medellin/Paginas/pui-nororiental.aspx.

Echeverri, Alejandro, and Francesco Orsini. 2010. "Informalidad y Urbanismo Social en Medellín" [Informality and social urbanism in Medellín]. In *Medellín: Medio-Ambiente, Urbanismo, Sociedad* [Medellín: environment, urbanism, society], edited by Michel Hermelin, Alejandro Echeverri, and Jorge Giraldo. Medellín, Colombia: Universidad EAFIT.

EDU (Empresa de Desarrollo Urbano). 2012. Video Cinturón Verde Metropolitano [Metropolitan green belt video]. Produced 2012. Video, 1:53. https://www.youtube .com/watch?v=oNzK6Tm_yyc. Permalink: https://archive.org/details/cinturon verde.

———. 2013. "Cinturón Verde Metropolitano—Jardín Circunvalar de Medellín" [Metropolitan green belt—Medellín's roundabout garden]. Published July 15, 2013. Video, 3:51. https://www.youtube.com/watch?v=8DuxfdkPIkQ. Permalink: https://archive.org/details/jardincircunvalar.

Egenter, Nold. 1992. *Architectural Anthropology: The Present Relevance of the Primitive in Architecture.* Lausanne: Structura Mundi.

Ehrenfeld, John. 2008. *Sustainability by Design.* New Haven: Yale University Press.

El Diario. 2012. "La Tierra se Abre en la Costa Norte" [The earth cracks open in the North Coast]. *El Diario,* November 18, 2012. https://web.archive.org/web/20190911145750/http://www.eldiario.ec/noticias-manabi-ecuador/248124-la-tierra-se-abre-en-la-costa-norte/.

Enzensberger, Hans Magnus. 1974. "A Critique of Political Ecology," *New Left Review* 1, no. 84: 3–31.

Escobar, Arturo. 1995. *Encountering Development: The Making and Unmaking of the Third World.* Princeton, NJ: Princeton University Press.

———. 2018. *Designs for the Pluriverse: Radical Interdependence, Autonomy, and the Making of Worlds.* Durham, NC: Duke University Press.

Escobar, David, ed. 2008. *Del Miedo a la Esperanza: Enero de 2004, Diciembre de 2007* [From fear to hope: January 2004, December 2007]. Medellín, Colombia: Alcaldía de Medellín.

Esiebo, Andrew, prod. 2016. Makoko: The Water World of Lagos. Published February 23, 2016. Video, 3:46. https://web.archive.org/web/20160303185624im_/https://cdn.theguardian.tv/mainwebsite/2016/02/23/160223MakokoWaterworld_desk.mp4.

Esteva, Gustavo. [1992] 2007. "Development." In *The Development Dictionary: A Guide to Knowledge as Power,* edited by Wolfgang Sachs. New York: Zed Books.

Esteva, Gustavo, and Madhu Suri Prakash. 1992. "Grassroots Resistance and Sustainable Development: Lessons from the Banks of the Narmada." *Ecologist* 22, no. 2 (March–April): 45–51.

Esteva, Gustavo, Salvatore Babones, and Philipp Babcicky. 2013. *The Future of Development: A Radical Manifesto.* Bristol, UK: Policy Press.

Evernden, Neil. 1992. *The Social Creation of Nature.* Baltimore, MD: Johns Hopkins University Press.

Fairs, Marcus. 2016. "Kunlé Adeyemi's Floating School Posed 'Danger to the Kids,' Headmaster Claims." *Dezeen,* June 11, 2016. https://web.archive.org/web/20160612121458/https://www.dezeen.com/2016/06/11/kunle-adeyemis-floating-school-posed-danger-to-the-kids-headmaster-claims/.

Falkeis, Anton, and Lukas Feireiss. 2015. *Social Design, Public Action: Arts as Urban Innovation.* Basel: Birkhäuser.

Farley, Heather, and Zachary Smith. 2020. *Sustainability: If It's Everything, Is It Nothing?* Second edition. Abingdon, UK: Routledge.

Farmer, Graham, and Simon Guy. 2005. "Hybrid Environments: The Spaces of Sustainable Design." In *Sustainable Architectures: Cultures and Natures in Europe and North America,* edited by Simon Guy and Steven Moore. New York: Taylor and Francis.

Fathy, Hassan. 1973. *Architecture for the Poor: An Experiment in Rural Egypt.* Chicago: University of Chicago Press.

FAU (Fondation Architectes de l'Urgence). n.d. "Qui Sommes Nous." [Who we are].
FAU website. https://web.archive.org/web/20190804134317/https://www.archi
-urgent.com/qui-sommes-nous/.

Feireiss, Kristin, and Lukas Feireiss, eds. 2008. *Architecture of Change: Sustainability
and Humanity in the Built Environment. 1.* Berlin: Gestalten.

Feireiss, Kristin, Lukas Feireiss, and Peter Sloterdijk, eds. 2009. *Architecture of
Change: Sustainability and Humanity in the Built Environment. 2: [Includes]
Interviews with Peter Sloterdijk and Chris Luebkeman.* Berlin: Gestalten.

FISE (Fondo de Inversión Social de Emergencia). 2002. *Reglamento Operativo para
el Programa FISE Tercera Etapa* [Operating regulations for the FISE phase three
program]. Quito: FISE.

———. 2009. "Análisis de Cumplimiento del Plan de Trabajo Aprobado y Nueva Propuesta para la Liquidación del FISE" [Compliance analysis of the approved work
plan, and new proposal for FISE's liquidation]. March 1, 2009.

Fixsen, Anna. 2015. "Back to Basics: An Ecuadorian Firm Builds Both Structures and
Community." *Architectural Record* 203, no. 8 (August): 49.

Foucault, Michel. 1991. "Governmentality." In *The Foucault Effect: Studies in Governmentality,* edited by Graham Burchell, Colin Gordon, and Peter Miller. Chicago:
University of Chicago Press.

Fox, Gregory. 2008. *Humanitarian Occupation.* Cambridge: Cambridge University
Press, 2008.

Fox, Mindy. 2000. "Building Dreams: An Interview with Samuel Mockbee." In *Sustainable Architecture White Papers.* New York: Earth Pledge Foundation.

Frangie Mawad, Tony. 2021. "Designing for the Next Wave of Urban Poverty."
Bloomberg, July 20, 2021. https://web.archive.org/web/20210805100309/https://
www.bloomberg.com/news/articles/2021-07-20/the-best-design-ideas-from-the
-world-s-poorest-neighborhoods.

Frankfurt, John. 2005. "Beyond the Barrio." *Dwell* (September): 110–12.

Fredriksen, Aurora. 2014. "Emergency Shelter Topologies: Locating Humanitarian
Space in Mobile and Material Practice." *Environment and Planning D: Society and
Space* 31: 147–62.

Fry, Tony. 2009. *Design Futuring: Sustainability, Ethics and New Practice.* Oxford:
Berg.

———. 2011. *Design as Politics.* New York: Berg.

———. 2017. "Design for/by 'The Global South.'" *Design Philosophy Papers* 15, no. 1:
3–37.

Fuad-Luke, Alastair. 2009. *Design Activism: Beautiful Strangeness for a Sustainable
World.* London: Earthscan.

Fukuyama, Francis. 1992. *The End of History and the Last Man.* New York: Free Press.

Gaestel, Allyn. 2018. "Things Fall Apart." *Atavist,* no. 76 (February). https://web
.archive.org/web/20180307190141/https://magazine.atavist.com/things-fall
-apart-makoko-floating-school.

———. 2019. "The Center of the World Is Everywhere: On Humanitarian Architecture
and the Western Gaze." *Very Vary Veri* 4: 74–80.

Gatt, Caroline, and Tim Ingold. 2013. "From Description to Correspondence: Anthropology in Real Time." In *Design Anthropology: Theory and Practice,* edited
by Wendy Gunn, Ton Otto, and Rachel Smith. London: Bloomsbury Academic.

Geertz, Clifford. 1973. *The Interpretation of Cultures.* New York: Basic Books.

Giddens, Anthony. 1979. *Central Problems in Social Theory: Action, Structure, and Contradiction in Social Analysis.* Berkeley: University of California Press.

———. 1987. *Social Theory and Modern Sociology.* Stanford, CA: Stanford University Press.

———. 1993. *New Rules of Sociological Method: A Positive Critique of Interpretative Sociologies.* Stanford, CA: Stanford University Press.

Glassner, Barry. 2018. *The Culture of Fear: Why Americans Are Afraid of the Wrong Things.* Updated edition. New York: Basic Books.

Golden, Elizabeth. 2014. "Challenging the Standard: Girls' Schools as Agents for Change in Afghanistan." In *Globalizing Architecture: Flows and Disruptions.* 102nd ACSA Annual Meeting Proceedings. Vol. 2. Washington, DC: ACSA Press.

———. 2018. *Building from Tradition: Local Materials and Methods in Contemporary Architecture.* Abingdon, UK: Routledge.

Goldman, Michael. 2001a. "The Birth of a Discipline: Producing Authoritative Green Knowledge, World Bank-Style." *Ethnography* 2, no. 2: 191–217.

———. 2001b. "Constructing an Environmental State: Eco-Governmentality and Other Transnational Practices of a 'Green' World Bank." *Social Problems* 48, no. 4: 499–523.

———. 2005. *Imperial Nature: The World Bank and Struggles for Social Justice.* New Haven, CT: Yale University Press.

Goodell, Jeff. 2017. "The Climate Apartheid: How Global Warming Affects the Rich and Poor." *Rolling Stone,* October 24, 2017. https://web.archive.org/web/20171024214629/https://www.rollingstone.com/politics/news/the-climate-apartheid-how-global-warming-affects-the-rich-and-poor-w509956.

Gould, Kenneth, and Tammy Lewis. 2012. "The Environmental Injustice of Green Gentrification: The Case of Brooklyn's Prospect Park." In *The World in Brooklyn: Gentrification, Immigration, and Ethnic Politics in a Global City,* edited by Judith DeSena et al. Lanham, MD: Lexington Books.

Gould, Kira. 2008. "The Social Art of Architecture: Good Design for All." In *Architecture: Celebrating the Past, Designing the Future,* edited by Nancy Solomon and the American Institute of Architects. New York: Visual Reference Publications.

Gramsci, Antonio. 1971. "State and Civil Society." In *Selections From the Prison Notebooks of Antonio Gramsci,* edited and translated by Quentin Hoare and Geoffrey Nowell Smith. London: Lawrence & Wishart.

———. 1994. *Letters from Prison.* Vol 2. Translated by Raymond Rosenthal. New York: Columbia University Press.

Greenberg, Miriam. 2013. "What on Earth Is Sustainable? Toward Critical Sustainability Studies." *Boom: A Journal of California* 3, no. 4 (Winter): 54–66.

Greer, Jed, and Kenny Bruno. 1996. *Greenwash: The Reality behind Corporate Environmentalism.* Penang, Malaysia: Third World Network.

Griborio, Andrea, ed. 2020. *Al Borde: Less Is All.* Mexico City: Arquine.

Guerra, Mónica. 2014. "Regulating Neglect: Territory, Planning, and Social Transformation in Medellín, Colombia." PhD diss. University of California, Berkeley.

Guldberg, Helene, and Peter Sammonds. 2001. "Design Tokenism and Global Warming." In *Sustaining Architecture in the Anti-Machine Age,* edited by Ian Abley and James Heartfield. Chichester, UK: Wiley-Academy.

Gunder, Michael. 2006. "Sustainability: Planning's Saving Grace or Road to Perdition?" *Journal of Planning Education and Research* 26: 208–21.

Gunn, Wendy, Ton Otto, and Rachel Smith, eds. 2013. *Design Anthropology: Theory and Practice.* London: Bloomsbury Academic.

Guy, Simon. 2012. "Introduction: Whither 'Earthly' Architectures: Constructing Sustainability." In *The SAGE Handbook of Architectural Theory,* edited by Greig Crysler, Stephen Cairns, and Hilde Heynen. London: Sage Publications.

Guy, Simon, and Graham Farmer. 2001. "Reinterpreting Sustainable Architecture: The Place of Technology." *Journal of Architectural Education* 54, no. 3 (February): 140–48.

Haar, Sharon. 2014. "Other Localisms: Reframing 'Social Architecture' within Globalism, the Case of the Butaro Hospital." In *Globalizing Architecture: Flows and Disruptions.* 102nd ACSA Annual Meeting Proceedings. Vol. 1. Washington, DC: ACSA Press.

Hadley, Alexander. 2020. "Bjarke Ingels and the Art of Greenwashing." *Failed Architecture,* January 28, 2020. https://web.archive.org/web/20201125220319/https://failedarchitecture.com/bjarke-ingels-and-the-art-of-greenwashing/.

Hagerman, Chris. 2007. "Shaping Neighborhoods and Nature: Urban Political Ecologies of Urban Waterfront Transformations in Portland, Oregon." *Cities* 24: 285–97.

Hall, Gillette, and Harry Anthony Patrinos, eds. 2006. *Indigenous Peoples, Poverty and Human Development in Latin America: 1994–2004.* New York: Palgrave MacMillan.

———. 2012. *Indigenous Peoples, Poverty, and Development.* Cambridge, UK: Cambridge University Press.

Hancox, Dan. 2014. "Enough Slum Porn: The Global North's Fetishisation of Poverty Architecture Must End." *Architectural Review* 236, no. 1411 (September): 22, 25.

Haque, Reaz. n.d. "Projects." LinkedIn page. https://web.archive.org/web/20181001090321/https://www.linkedin.com/in/reaz-haque-0b212114/?locale=de_DE.

Haraway, Donna. 1989. *Primate Visions: Gender, Race and Nature in the World of Modern Science.* New York: Routledge.

Harris, Victoria. 2011. "The Architecture of Risk." In *Beyond Shelter: Architecture and Human Dignity,* edited by Marie Aquilino. New York: Metropolis Books.

Harris-Brandts, Suzanne. 2015. "The Humanitarian Architect: Notes on Ethical Engagement." *The Expanding Periphery and the Migrating Center.* 103rd ACSA Annual Meeting Proceedings. Washington, DC: ACSA Press.

Harvey, David. 2014. "The Crisis of Planetary Urbanization." In *Uneven Growth: Tactical Urbanisms for Expanding Megacities,* edited by Pedro Gadanho. New York: Museum of Modern Art.

Hawthorne, Christopher. 2011. "Altruism, Architecture and Disaster." *Architect* (September): 150–53.

Hazen, Don. 2002. "Grappling with the Politics of Fear." *AlterNet,* November 25, 2002. https://web.archive.org/web/20201008111356/https://www.alternet.org/2002/11/grappling_with_the_politics_of_fear/.

Henn, Rebecca, and Andrew Hoffman, eds. 2013. *Constructing Green: The Social Structures of Sustainability.* Urban and Industrial Environments. Cambridge, MA: MIT Press.

Hill, Glen. 2008. *Design, Heidegger, and the Earth: The Unsustainability of Sustainable Design.* Saarbrücken: VRM Verlag Dr. Müller.

Hobbs, Alex. 2018. "Community Organizes to Solve the RV Issue." *Portola Planet* (blog), October 18, 2018. https://web.archive.org/web/20181031113131/http://portolaplanet.com/2018/10/community-organizes-to-solve-the-rv-issue/.

Hoggett, Paul, ed. 1997. *Contested Communities: Experiences, Struggles, Policies.* Bristol, UK: Policy Press.

Hohenadel, Kristin. 2014. "Are Anti-Homeless Sidewalk Spikes Immoral?" *Slate,* June 12, 2014. https://web.archive.org/web/20190404181720/https://slate.com /human-interest/2014/06/artist-nils-norman-documents-anti-homeless-spikes -and-other-defensive-architecture-in-cities-around-the-world.html.

Holifield, Ryan. 2001. "Defining Environmental Justice and Environmental Racism." *Urban Geography* 22, no. 1: 78–90.

Hope, Alison, and Julian Agyeman. 2011. *Cultivating Food Justice: Race, Class, and Sustainability.* Cambridge, MA: MIT Press.

Hubbard, Phil. 2016. "Hipsters on Our High Streets: Consuming the Gentrification Frontier." *Sociological Research Online* 21, no. 3: 1–6.

IGEPN (Instituto Geofísico Escuela Politécnica Nacional). 2016. "Informe Sísmico Especial N. 13–2016" [Special seismic report no. 13–2016]. April 17. https://web .archive.org/web/20160419172905/https://www.igepn.edu.ec/servicios/noticias /1317-informe-sismico-especial-n-13-2016.

ILFI (International Living Future Institute). 2016. *Living Building Challenge 3.1: A Visionary Path to a Regenerative Future.* Seattle: International Living Future Institute.

ILO (International Labour Organization). 1989. *C169—Indigenous and Tribal Peoples Convention.* Geneva: ILO.

Jackson, Dough, ed. 2017. *SOUPERgreen!: Souped-up Green Architecture.* New York: Actar Publishers.

Jacobs, Garrett. 2017. Alternative Architectural Practice. Presentation, Architecture Department, California College of the Arts, San Francisco, CA, September 11, 2017. Part 2. Video, 20:26. https://www.youtube.com/watch?v=cPfFRmcJtkc. Permalink: https://archive.org/details/alternative_architectural_practice_2.

Jacobs, Michael. 1999. "Sustainable Development: A Contested Concept." In *Fairness and Futurity: Essays on Environmental Sustainability and Social Justice,* edited by Andrew Dobson. Oxford: Oxford University Press.

Jarzombek, Mark. 1999. "Molecules, Money and Design: The Question of Sustainability's Role in the Architectural Academe." *Thresholds* 18: 32–38.

———. 2006. "Sustainability: Fuzzy Systems and Wicked Problems." *Log,* no. 8 (Summer): 7–12.

Jiménez, Daniela. 2019. "Biblioteca España, Otros Cuatro Años en Blanco" [Biblioteca España, another four blank years]. *El Colombiano,* June 8, 2019. https://web.archive .org/web/20190609135932/https://www.elcolombiano.com/antioquia/biblioteca -espana-otros-cuatro-anos-en-blanco-CI10933375.

Johnson, Cedric. 2011. "The Urban Precariat, Neoliberalization, and the Soft Power of Humanitarian Design." *Journal of Developing Societies* 27, nos. 3–4: 445–75.

Jones, Paul, and Kenton Card. 2011. "Constructing 'Social' Architecture: The Politics of Representing Practice." *Architectural Theory Review* 16, no. 3: 228–44.

Keil, Roger. 2007. "Sustaining Modernity, Modernizing Nature: The Environmental Crisis and the Survival of Capitalism." In *The Sustainable Development Paradox: Urban Political Economy in the United States and Europe,* edited by Rob Krueger and David Gibbs. New York: Guilford Press.

Kennedy, Joseph, ed. 2004. *Building without Borders: Sustainable Construction for the Global Village.* Gabriola Island, BC, Canada: New Society.

Keshavarz, Mahmoud. 2020. "Violent Compassions: Humanitarian Design and the Politics of Borders." Design Issues 36, no. 4: 20–32.

Keskeys, Paul. 2018. "Can Participatory Design Save the World?" *Architectural Digest,* July 25, 2018. https://web.archive.org/web/20180726015959/https://www.archi tecturaldigest.com/story/participatory-design-open-architecture-collaborative.

Klein, Naomi. 2014. *This Changes Everything: Capitalism vs. The Climate.* New York: Simon and Schuster.

Kliwadenko, Katerina, and Mario Novas, dirs. 2017. *Do More with Less.* Quito: Ministerio de Cultura y Patrimonio.

Kloppenburg, Joanna. n.d. "Al Borde Arquitectos on Practicing Life through Architecture." *Architizer.* https://web.archive.org/web/20190814131953/https://architizer .com/blog/practice/tools/al-borde-life-through-architecture/.

Knight, Danielle. 1998. "'An Enemy of Indigenous Peoples': The Case of Loren Miller, COICA, the Inter-American Foundation and the Ayahuasca Plant." *Multinational Monitor* 19, no. 6: 24–26.

Krähmer, Karl. 2021. "Are Green Cities Sustainable? A Degrowth Critique of Sustainable Urban Development in Copenhagen." European Planning Studies 29, no. 7: 1272–89.

Krech, Shepard. 1999. *The Ecological Indian: Myth and History.* New York: W. W. Norton.

Krier, Leon. 2006. "Classicus and Vernaculus." *Log,* no. 8: 25–30.

Krückeberg, Lars, Wolfram Putz, and Thomas Willemeit, eds. 2016. *Architecture Activism.* Basel: Birkhäuser.

Krupar, Shiloh, and Stefan Al. 2012. "Notes on the Society of the Brand." In *The SAGE Handbook of Architectural Theory,* edited by Greig Crysler, Stephen Cairns, and Hilde Heynen. London: Sage Publications.

Lahiji, Nadir, ed. 2016. *Can Architecture Be an Emancipatory Project?: Dialogues on the Left.* Alresford, UK: Zero Books.

Lal, Deepak. 1995. "Eco-Fundamentalism." *International Affairs* 71, no. 3: 515–28.

Lara, Juan Felipe, Juan Pablo Caicedo, Nátaly Urrea, Juan David Nieves, and Vanessa López, prods. [2011?]. Parque Biblioteca España un Monumento a las Malas Construcciones de la Ciudad [Parque Biblioteca España a monument to the city's poor constructions]. Published November 10, 2014. Video, 12:37. https://www.youtube .com/watch?v=0TINEURgSXU. Permalink: https://archive.org/details/parque _biblioteca_espana_un_monumento_a_las_malas_construcciones_de_la_ciudad.

Latour, Bruno. 1993. *We Have Never Been Modern.* Translated by Catherine Porter. Cambridge, MA: Harvard University Press.

———. 2004. *Politics of Nature: How to Bring the Sciences into Democracy.* Cambridge, MA: Harvard University Press.

———. 2008. "'It's development, stupid!' or How to Modernize Modernization?" EspacesTemps.net. May 29, 2008. https://web.archive.org/web/20180420143845 /http://www.espacestemps.net/en/articles/how-to-modernize-modernization/.

Leguía, Mariana. 2011. "Introduction: Latin America at the Crossroads." *Architectural Design* 81, no. 3 (May–June): 8–15.

LeonVest, Sandy. 2011. "The Greening of Disaster Capitalism." *Solar Times,* fourth quarter.

Lepik, Andres, ed. 2013. *Think Global, Build Social! Architectures for a Better World.* Published as *Arch +* nos. 211/212, in conjunction with an exhibition of the same title, presented at the German Architecture Museum, Frankfurt, June 8–September 1, 2013.

Lévy-Bruhl, Lucien. 1923. *Primitive Mentality.* Translated by Lilian A. Clare. New York: Macmillan.

———. 1926. *How Natives Think.* Translated by Lilian A. Clare. New York: Alfred Knopf.

———. 1928. *The 'Soul' of the Primitive.* Translated by Lilian A. Clare. New York: Macmillan.

Li, Tania. 2007. *The Will to Improve: Governmentality, Development, and the Practice of Politics.* Durham, NC: Duke University Press.

———. 2011. "Rendering Society Technical Government through Community and the Ethnographic Turn at the World Bank in Indonesia." In *Adventures in Aidland: The Anthropology of Professionals in International Development,* edited by David Mosse. New York: Berghahn Books.

Lincoln (Lincoln Motor Company). 2013a. "Lincoln, with Architectural Leaders, Says 'Hello, Again' to Inspired Urban Design." *Ford Motor Company Media Center,* October 15, 2013. https://web.archive.org/web/20131111172726/https://media.lincoln.com/content/lincolnmedia/lna/us/en/news/2013/10/15/lincoln—with-architectural-leaders—says-hello—again-to-inspir.html.

———. 2013b. "Reimagining a Community Space." Lincoln website. October 15, 2013. https://web.archive.org/web/20131022053216/http://now.lincoln.com:80/2013/10/reimagining-a-community-space/.

———. 2013c. "Seamless Design in the Burrows Street Park." Published December 23, 2013. Video, 3:07. https://archive.org/details/seamless_design_burrows.

———. 2014. "Celebrating the Opening of Burrows Street Park with Architecture for Humanity | Lincoln." Published October 15, 2014. Video, 2:44. https://archive.org/details/celebrating_the_opening_of_burrows_st.

———. 2015. "The Lincoln Reimagine Project." Published on April 30, 2015. Video, 3:25. https://web.archive.org/web/20180929120133/https://video.architecturaldigest.com/watch/the-lincoln-reimagine-project.

Linsell, Nikki. 2014. "Designing Like You Give a Damn: About What Exactly? Exploring the Ethics of 'Humanitarian' Architecture." *Architecture Otherwhere.* Proceedings, 25th World Congress of Architecture. Durban, South Africa: UIA.

———. 2015. "To Hell with Good Intentions." The Architect's Journal. February 7, 2015. https://web.archive.org/web/20201008112951/https://www.architectsjournal.co.uk/practice/culture/to-hell-with-good-intentions-2.

Lizarralde, Manuel. 2003. "Green Imperialism: Indigenous People and Conservation of Natural Environments." In *Our Backyard: A Quest for Environmental Justice,* edited by Gerald Visgilio and Diana Whitelaw. Oxford: Rowman and Littlefield.

Logan, Katharine. 2020. "Environmental Inequity." *Architectural Record* 208, no. 10 (October): 114–18.

Lohmann, Larry. 1993. "Green Orientalism." *Ecologist* 23, no. 6: 202–4.

Lucente, Roberta, and Nicoletta Trasi, eds. 2019. *Disasters Otherwhere: New Forms of Complexity for Architecture.* Macerata, It.: Quodlibet.

Malinowski, Bronisław. 1922. *Argonauts of the Western Pacific: An Account of Native Enterprise and Adventure in the Archipelagoes of Melanesian New Guinea.* London: Routledge.

Marcus, George. 2016. "Jostling Ethnography between Design and Participatory Art Practices, and the Collaborative Relations It Engenders." In *Design Anthropological*

Futures, edited by Rachel Smith, Kasper Tang Vangkilde, Mette Gislev Kjaersgaard, Ton Otto, Joachim Halse, and Thomas Binder. London: Bloomsbury.

Marcuse, Peter. 1998. "Sustainability Is Not Enough." *Environment and Urbanization* 10, no. 2: 103–11.

MASS (Mass Design Group). 2017a. *Purpose Built Case Study: Presidio Trails, Bikeways, and Overlooks Project.* Boston: MASS. https://archive.org/details/purpose-built-presidio-trails-bikeways-and-overlooks-project.

——. 2017b. *Purpose Built Toolkit 1.0. Planning for Impact: A Guide to Impact-Driven Design.* Boston: MASS. https://archive.org/details/purpose-built-planning-for-impact.

——. n.d. "Method." MASS website. https://web.archive.org/web/20190803105006/https://massdesigngroup.org/method.

May, Shannon. 2011. "Ecological Modernism and the Making of a New Working Class." In *New Directions in Sustainable Design,* edited by Adrian Parr and Michael Zaretsky. New York: Routledge.

May, Todd. 2004. "Religion, the Election and the Politics of Fear." *CounterPunch,* November 20, 2004. https://web.archive.org/web/20190824152304/https://www.counterpunch.org/2004/11/20/religion-the-election-and-the-politics-of-fear/.

Mazzanti, Giancarlo. 2009. "Dos Bibliotecas en Medellín" [Two libraries in Medellín]. *ARQ,* no. 71 (April): 21–31.

McDonough, William, and Michael Braungart. 2002. *Cradle to Cradle: Remaking the Way We Make Things.* New York: North Point Press.

——. 2013. *The Upcycle: Beyond Sustainability—Designing for Abundance.* New York: North Point Press.

McGranahan, Gordon, Jacob Songsore, and Marianne Kjellen. 1996. "Sustainability, Poverty and Urban Environmental Transitions." In *Sustainability, the Environment and Urbanization,* edited by Cedric Pugh. London: Earthscan.

McGuirk, Justin. 2014a. "'It's Knee-Jerk Political Correctness of a Simple-Minded Kind.'" *Architectural Review,* September 24, 2014. https://web.archive.org/web/20190815023933/https://www.architectural-review.com/your-views-its-knee-jerk-political-correctness-of-a-simple-minded-kind/8670135.article.

——. 2014b. *Radical Cities: Across Latin America in Search of a New Architecture.* London: Verso.

McLennan, Jason. 2004. *The Philosophy of Sustainable Design: The Future of Architecture.* Bainbridge Island, WA: Ecotone.

Meinhold, Bridgette. 2013. *Urgent Architecture: 40 Sustainable Housing Solutions for a Changing World.* New York: W. W. Norton.

Mejía, Mónica. 2009. "Reasentamiento de Población Vulnerable en Vivienda en Altura" [Resettlement of vulnerable population in high-rise housing]. Paper presented at the Eight ACIUR conference, Bogotá, Colombia, September 2009.

——. 2012. "Habitabilidad en la Vivienda Social en Edificios para Población Reasentada: El Caso de Medellín, Colombia" [Livability in social housing buildings for a resettled population: The Medellín, Colombia case]. *EURE* 38, no. 114 (May): 203–27.

Melosi, Martin. 1995. "Equity, Eco-Racism and Environmental History." *Environmental History Review* 19, no. 3: 1–16.

Memmott, Paul. 2007. *Gunyah, Goondie + Wurley: The Aboriginal Architecture of Australia.* Brisbane: University of Queensland Press.

Mena, Elvia. 2011. "Habitabilidad de la Vivienda de Interés Social Prioritaria en el Marco de la Cultura: Reasentamiento de Comunidades Negras de Vallejuelos a Mirador de Calasanz en Medellín, Colombia" [Livability of priority social housing within the culture framework: Resettlement of black communities from Vallejuelos to Mirador de Calasanz in Medellín, Colombia]. *Cuadernos de Vivienda y Urbanismo* 4, no. 8 (July–December): 296–314.

Merker, Blaine. 2010. "Taking Place: Rebar's Absurd Tactics in Generous Urbanism." In *Insurgent Public Space: Guerrilla Urbanism and the Remaking of Contemporary Cities,* edited by Jeffrey Hou. London: Routledge.

Merriam-Webster. 2019. s.v. "sustainable." https://web.archive.org/web/201908111 34817/https://www.merriam-webster.com/thesaurus/sustainable.

Miller, Michelle. 2014. "Classic Architecture with a Social Agenda (1960–Today)." *ArchDaily,* May 23, 2014. https://web.archive.org/web/20140524060833/http://www .archdaily.com/508534/classic-architecture-with-a-social-agenda-1960-today/.

Mitcham, Carl. 1997. "The Sustainability Question." In *The Ecological Community,* edited by Roger Gottlieb. New York: Routledge.

Mitchell, Don. 1995. "There's No Such Thing as Culture: Towards a Reconceptualization of the Idea of Culture in Geography." *Transactions of the Institute of British Geographers, New Series* 20, no. 1: 102–16.

Monk, Daniel Bertrand, and Andrew Herscher. 2021. *The Global Shelter Imaginary: IKEA Humanitarianism and Rightless Relief.* Minneapolis: University of Minnesota Press.

Moore, Steven, and Andrew Karvonen. 2008. "Sustainable Architecture in Context: STS and Design Thinking." *Science Studies* 21, no. 1: 29–46.

Moore, Steven, and Barbara Wilson. 2014. *Questioning Architectural Judgement: The Problem of Codes in the United States.* New York: Taylor & Francis.

Morán, Jorge. 2004. Letter to Aníbal Borbúa (FISE manager). December 21.

MoreLab. 2014. "Burrows Street Pocket Park." MoreLab website. October 15, 2014. https://web.archive.org/web/20151125035211/http://morelab.com/portfolio/ burrows-street-pocket-park/.

———. n.d. "Help Us Find a Home for the Groove Grove!" MoreLab website. https://web .archive.org/web/20170720000344/http://morelab.com/help-us-find-a-home-for -the-groove-grove/.

Mosse, David. 2011. "Social Analysis as Corporate Product: Non-Economists/Anthropologists at Work at the World Bank in Washington, D.C." In *Adventures in Aidland: The Anthropology of Professionals in International Development,* edited by David Mosse. New York: Berghahn Books.

Navarro-Sertich, Adriana. 2011. "From Product to Process: Building on Urban-Think Tank's Approach to the Informal City." *Architectural Design* 81, no. 3 (May–June 2011): 104–9.

NLÉ. 2012. *Makoko Floating School: Research Report.* Amsterdam: NLÉ. https://web .archive.org/web/20190816111313/https://ng.boell.org/sites/default/files/uploads /2014/06/introduction.pdf.

———. 2016a. *Makoko Floating School: Project Description.* Amsterdam: NLÉ. https:// www.dropbox.com/sh/07b9ne8iz6fzqmu/AAB1gvfk6nn2ok6155pWHxoja/ NL%C3%89_Makoko%20Floating%20School%20Project%20Description%20Jan%20 2016.pdf?dl=0. Permalink: https://archive.org/details/nle-makoko-floating -school-project-description-jan-2016.

———. 2016b. *Makoko Floating School FAQs—On Collapse & Regeneration Plans*. Amsterdam: NLÉ. https://web.archive.org/web/20190816121148/https://gallery .mailchimp.com/75e591db8b22aa2c51b6c7278/files/161130_Makoko_Floating _School_FAQs_and_appendices.02.01.pdf?utm_source=NL%C3%89+December +Newsletter+2016&utm_campaign=4f74efd607-EMAIL_CAMPAIGN_2016_1.

Norgaard, Richard. 1994. *Development Betrayed: The End of Progress and a Co-Evolutionary Revisioning of the Future*. London: Routledge.

Nussbaum, Bruce. 2010. "Is Humanitarian Design the New Imperialism?" *Fast Company Design*, July 6, 2010. https://web.archive.org/web/20190813105250/https:// www.fastcompany.com/1661859/is-humanitarian-design-the-new-imperialism.

O'Connor, James. 1988. "Capitalism, Nature, Socialism: A Theoretical Introduction." *Capitalism, Nature, Socialism* 1, no. 1: 11–38.

OAC (Open Architecture Collaborative). 2017. "Burrows Pocket Park." OAC website. 2017. https://web.archive.org/web/20180213045509/http://openarchcollab.org /429/burrows-pocket-park/.

OAN (Open Architecture Network). n.d. "1 Burrows Pocket Park." OAN database. https://web.archive.org/web/20150123045109/http://openarchitecturenetwork .org/projects/1_burrows.

Oelschlaeger, Max. 1991. *The Idea of Wilderness: From Prehistory to the Age of Ecology*. New Haven: Yale University Press.

Ogunlesi, Tolu. 2016. "Inside Makoko: Danger and Ingenuity in the World's Biggest Floating Slum." *Guardian*, February 23, 2016. https://web.archive.org/web /20160223144905/https://www.theguardian.com/cities/2016/feb/23/makoko -lagos-danger-ingenuity-floating-slum.

Okoroafor, Cynthia. 2016. "Does Makoko Floating School's Collapse Threaten the Whole Slum's Future?" *Guardian*, June 10, 2016. https://web.archive.org/web /20160610121548/https://www.theguardian.com/cities/2016/jun/10/makoko -floating-school-collapse-lagos-nigeria-slum-water.

Oliver, Paul, ed. 1997. *Encyclopedia of Vernacular Architecture of the World*. 3 vols. Cambridge, UK: Cambridge University Press.

———. 2006. *Built to Meet Needs: Cultural Issues in Vernacular Architecture*. Oxford: Architectural Press.

Orkidstudio. 2015. *Join Our Team: Committee Applications*. Glasgow: Orkidstudio. https://web.archive.org/web/20190803103416/https://s3-eu-west-1.amazonaws .com/orkidstudio/pdf/Committee_Application2015.pdf.

———. n.d.a. "Africa Solo." Orkidstudio website. https://web.archive.org/web /20190803095430/https://orkidstudio.org/africa-solo/.

———. n.d.b. "Our Approach." Orkidstudio website. https://web.archive.org/web /20190804130524/https://orkidstudio.org/approach/.

Ovink, Henk, and Elien Wierenga, eds. 2009. *Design and Politics*. Volume 1. Rotterdam: 010 Publishers.

Oyewole, Nurudeen. 2016. "How Makoko Floating School's Dreams Got Set Adrift." *Daily Trust*, July 9, 2016. https://web.archive.org/web/20160710151741/https:// www.dailytrust.com.ng/news/around-and-about/how-makoko-floating-school-s -dreams-got-set-adrift/154523.html.

Papanek, Victor. 1995. *The Green Imperative: Natural Design for the Real World*. New York: Thames and Hudson.

Parr, Adrian. 2009. *Hijacking Sustainability*. Cambridge, MA: MIT Press.

Passmore, Matthew. 2014. "Mode by Alta Public Art Component: Matthew Passmore Resume/Work Samples." Official website of the city of San Mateo, CA. February 6, 2014. https://web.archive.org/web/20181120102316/https://www.cityofsanmateo.org/DocumentCenter/View/40579/February-10-2014-CAC–2090-Delaware-Application.

Pawley, Martin. 2000. "Keynote Speech." Presented at the Building Audacity Conference, The Building Centre, London, July 10, 2000.

Peláez, Luz Amparo. 2013. "Realizaciones y Sofismas del Restablecimiento del Hábitat en Procesos de Reasentamiento por Alto Riesgo: Experiencias en Medellín: 1990–2010" [Realities and sophisms in habitat resettlement in high-risk resettlement processes: Experiences in Medellín: 1990–2010]. Master's thesis, Universidad Nacional.

Perafán, Carlos. 2001. *Etnoingeniería, Marco Conceptual* [Ethnoengineering: A conceptual framework]. Washington, DC: Inter-American Development Bank.

Perafán, Carlos, Steven Geiger, Diego Belmonte, Vianney García, Bayardo Ramírez, and Francisco Santacruz. 2005. *Guías de Etnoingeniería* [Ethnoengineering handbook]. Washington, DC: Inter-American Development Bank.

Pereira, Helder, and Coral Gillett. 2014. "Africa: Designing as Existence." In *Design in the Borderlands,* edited by Eleni Kalantidou and Tony Fry. Abingdon, UK: Routledge.

Pérez, Elkin. 2015. Presentation, Con-vivamos, Medellín, Colombia, June 6, 2015.

Petrucci, Mario. 2002. "Sustainability—Long View Or Long Word?" *Social Justice* 29, no. 1: 103–15.

Pieris, Anoma. 2006. "Is Sustainability Sustainable?" In *Tropical Sustainable Architecture: Social and Environmental Dimensions,* edited by Joo Hwa Bay and Boon Lay Ong. Oxford: Architectural Press.

Pilloton, Emily. 2010. "Are Humanitarian Designers Imperialists? Project H Responds." *Fast Company Design,* July 11, 2010. https://web.archive.org/web/20190813105638/https://www.fastcompany.com/1661885/are-humanitarian-designers-imperialists-project-h-responds.

Plataforma Arquitectura. 2011. "Testimonial, Al Borde." Published July 28, 2011. Video, 3:01. https://www.youtube.com/watch?v=ySiL5TVZE5s. Permalink: https://archive.org/details/testimonialalborde.

Popova, Maria. 2010. "The Language of Design Imperialism." *Design Observer,* July 29, 2010. https://web.archive.org/web/20190813102049/https://designobserver.com/feature/the-language-of-design-imperialism/14718/.

Pratt, Larry, and Wendy Montgomery. 1997. "Green Imperialism: Pollution, Penitence, Profits." *Socialist Register* 33: 75–95.

Purdy, Jedediah. 2015. "Environmentalism's Racist History." *New Yorker,* August 13, 2015. https://web.archive.org/web/20150813222542/https://www.newyorker.com/news/news-desk/environmentalisms-racist-history.

Pyla, Panayiota. 2008. "Counter-histories of Sustainability." *Volume* 18: 14–17.

———. 2012. "Beyond Smooth Talk: Oxymorons, Ambivalences, and Other Current Realities of Sustainability." *Design and Culture* 4, no. 3: 273–78.

Quintal, Becky. 2014. "Critics and Peers Comment on Shigeru Ban's Pritzker Prize." *ArchDaily,* March 25, 2014. https://web.archive.org/web/20140327024337/https://www.archdaily.com/489809/critics-and-peers-comment-on-shigeru-ban-s-pritzker-prize/.

Rabinow, Paul. 2011. *The Accompaniment: Assembling the Contemporary.* Chicago: University of Chicago Press.

Rabinow, Paul, George Marcus, James Faubion, and Tobias Rees. 2008. *Designs for an Anthropology of the Contemporary.* Durham, NC: Duke University Press.

Raco, Mike. 2014. "The Post-Politics of Sustainability Planning: Privatisation and the Demise of Democratic Government." In *The Post-Political and Its Discontents: Spaces of Depoliticization, Spectres of Radical Politics,* edited by Japhy Wilson and Erik Swyngedouw. Edinburgh: Edinburgh University Press.

Rahnema, Majid. 1992. "Participation." In *The Development Dictionary: A Guide to Knowledge as Power,* edited by Wolfgang Sachs. New York: Zed Books.

Ramírez, Bayardo. 2009. "Registro Proyectos Etnoingeniería" [Record (of) ethnoengineering projects]. Excel datasheet. February 9.

Rapoport, Amos. 1976. "Introduction" and "Conclusion." In *The Mutual Interaction of People and Their Built Environment.* The Hague: Mouton.

———. 1994. "Sustainability, Meaning and Traditional Environments." *Traditional Dwellings and Settlements Working Paper Series* 75: 1–64.

———. 2005. *Culture, Architecture, and Design.* Chicago: Locke Science Publishing Company.

Redclift, Michael. 1987. *Sustainable Development: Exploring the Contradictions.* London: Methuen.

Redfield, Peter. 2012a. "Bioexpectations: Life Technologies as Humanitarian Goods." *Public Culture* 24, no. 1: 157–84.

———. 2012b. "The Unbearable Lightness of Expats: Double Binds of Humanitarian Mobility." *Cultural Anthropology* 27, no. 2: 358–82.

———. 2016. "Fluid Technologies: The Bush Pump, the LifeStraw® and Microworlds of Humanitarian Design." *Social Studies of Science* 46, no. 2: 159–83.

———. 2018. "On Band-Aids and Magic Bullets." *Limn,* no. 9: 10–16.

Redfield, Peter, and Steven Robins. 2016. "An Index of Waste: Humanitarian Design, 'Dignified Living' and the Politics of Infrastructure in Cape Town." *Anthropology of Southern Africa* 39, no. 2: 145–62.

Redford, Kent. 1990. "The Ecologically Noble Savage." *Orion Nature Quarterly* 9, no. 3: 29.

Riis, Jacob. 1890. *How the Other Half Lives: Studies among the Tenements of New York.* New York: Charles Scribner's Sons.

———. 1902. *The Battle with the Slum.* New York: Macmillan.

Robledo, Jorge. 1996. "Un Siglo de Bahareque en el Antiguo Caldas" [A century of rammed earth in Old Caldas]. Paper, Guadua, Vivienda y Construcción [Guadua, housing and building] conference, Armenia (Colombia), June 27, 1996.

Romero, Bolívar. 2004. "Consultoría de Estudios y Diseños Aplicando el Concepto de Etnoingeniería en la Zona Sierra del Ecuador. Memoria Técnica del Proyecto: Criterios de Diseño, Materiales y Técnicas Constructivas" [Studies and design consultancy applying the ethnoengineering concept in the Sierra region of Ecuador. Project technical report: design criteria, materials, and building techniques]. Report to FISE.

Røstivk, Harald. 2011. "The Vernacular, the Iconic and the Fake." In *Aesthetics of Sustainable Architecture,* edited by Sang Lee. Rotterdam: 010 Publishers.

Roy, Ananya. 2001. "Traditions of the Modern: A Corrupt View." *Traditional Dwellings and Settlements Review* 12, no. 2: 7–19.

Rudofsky, Bernard. 1964. *Architecture without Architects: A Short Introduction to Non-Pedigreed Architecture.* Garden City, NY: Doubleday.

———. 1979. *The Prodigious Builders: Notes toward a Natural History of Architecture.* New York: Harcourt Brace Jovanovich.

Rule, Alix. 2008. "The Revolution Will Not Be Designed." *In These Times,* January 11, 2008. https://web.archive.org/web/20080113060822/http://inthesetimes.com/article/3464/the_revolution_will_not_be_designed/.

Sachs, Wolfgang. 1993. "Global Ecology and the Shadow of 'Development.'" In *Global Ecology: A New Arena of Political Conflict.* London: Zed Books.

Sachs, Wolfgang, Reinhard Loske, and Manfred Linz. 1998. *Greening the North: A Post-Industrial Blueprint for Ecology and Equity.* London: Zed Books.

Saha, Robin. 2010. *Encyclopedia of Geography,* s.v. "Environmental Racism." London: Sage Publications.

Said, Edward. 1978. *Orientalism.* New York: Pantheon Books.

———. 1993. *Culture and Imperialism.* New York: Vintage Books.

Sassen, Saskia. 2014. "Complex and Incomplete: Spaces for Tactical Urbanism." In *Uneven Growth: Tactical Urbanisms for Expanding Megacities,* edited by Pedro Gadanho. New York: Museum of Modern Art.

Savić, Selena. 2015. "Architects Are Purposely Designing Uncomfortable Park Benches." *Quartz,* March 26, 2015. https://web.archive.org/web/20150327143715/https://qz.com/370163/architects-are-purposefully-designing-uncomfortable-park-benches/.

Schmink, Marianne, Kent Redford, and Christine Padoch. 1992. "Traditional Peoples and the Biosphere: Framing the Issues and Defining the Terms." In *Conservation of Neotropical Forests: Working from Traditional Resource Use,* edited by Kent Redford and Christine Padoch. New York: Columbia University Press.

Schultz, Tristan, Danah Abdulla, Ahmed Ansari, Ece Canlı, Mahmoud Keshavarz, Matthew Kiem, Luiza Prado de O. Martins, and Pedro J.S. Vieira de Oliveira. 2018. "What Is at Stake with Decolonizing Design? A Roundtable." *Design and Culture* 10, no. 1: 81–101.

Schumacher, Ernst Friedrich. 1973. *Small Is Beautiful: Economics As If People Mattered.* New York: Harper and Row.

Schwittay, Anke. 2014. "Designing Development: Humanitarian Design in the Financial Inclusion Assemblage." *PoLAR: Political and Legal Anthropology Review* 37, no. 1: 29–47.

Scott-Smith, Tom. 2013. "The Fetishism of Humanitarian Objects and the Management of Malnutrition in Emergencies." *Third World Quarterly* 34, no. 5: 913–28.

———. 2018. "A Slightly Better Shelter?" *Limn,* no. 9: 67–73.

Scott, Kathryn, Julie Park, and Chris Cocklin. 2000. "From 'Sustainable Rural Communities' to 'Social Sustainability': Giving Voice to Diversity in Mangakahia Valley, New Zealand." *Journal of Rural Studies* 16: 433–46.

Semana. 2017. "La Premiada Megabiblioteca que se Cae a Pedazos" [The award-winning megalibrary that is falling to pieces]. *Semana,* January 7, 2017. https://web.archive.org/web/20170108064609/https://www.semana.com/nacion/articulo/biblioteca-espana-de-medellin-permanece-cerrada/511559.

Sen, Amartya. 1992. *Inequality Reexamined.* Oxford: Oxford University Press.

———. 1993. "Capability and Well Being." In *The Quality of Life,* edited by Martha Nussbaum and Amartya Sen. Oxford: Oxford University Press.

Shioiri-Clark, Marika. 2013. "Building a Rwandan Wall: Design to Balance Local

Traditions and New Solutions." *Good,* March 7, 2013. https://web.archive.org/web
/20170716201014/https://www.good.is/articles/building-a-rwandan-wall-design
-to-balance-local-traditions-and-new-solutions.

Shiva, Vandana. 1993. "The Greening of Global Reach." In *Global Ecology: A New
Arena of Political Conflict,* edited by Wolfgang Sachs. Halifax, Canada: Fernwood
Books.

Sinclair, Cameron. 2007. "Design Like You Give a Damn." Lecture delivered at the
University of California, Berkeley, October 17, 2007. DVD. 110 min.

———. 2010. "Admiral Ackbar, It's a Trap!—How Over-Simplification Creates a
Distorted Vision of Humanitarian Design." *Cameron's Blog,* July 8, 2010. https://
web.archive.org/web/20120103193802/http://www.cameronsinclair.com/index
.php?q=node/74.

———. 2019. "Housing the Next Billion. Lecture of Cameron Sinclair." In *Disasters
Otherwhere: New Forms of Complexity for Architecture,* edited by Roberta Lucente
and Nicoletta Trasi. Macerata, Italy: Quodlibet.

Sinha, Sumita. 1994. "A House from Bankura District, India." *Traditional Dwellings
and Settlements Working Paper Series* 70: 89–102.

———. 2012. *Architecture for Rapid Change and Scarce Resources.* Abingdon, UK:
Earthscan.

Skene Catling, Charlotte. 2014. "Damned If You Do, Damned If You Don't: What Is the
Moral Duty of the Architect?" *Architectural Review,* September 22, 2014. https://
web.archive.org/web/20190818162955/https://www.architectural-review.com
/archive/viewpoints/damned-if-you-do-damned-if-you-dont-what-is-the-moral
-duty-of-the-architect/8669956.article.

Smith, Cynthia, ed. 2016. *By the People: Designing a Better America.* New York: Cooper
Hewitt.

———. 2007. *Design for the Other 90%.* New York: Assouline Publishing.

———. 2011. *Design with the Other 90%: Cities.* New York: Cooper Hewitt.

Smith, Jeffrey, and Alex Gladstein. 2018. "How the UN's Sustainable Development
Goals Undermine Democracy." *Quartz,* June 7, 2018. https://web.archive.org
/web/20201126113931/https://qz.com/africa/1299149/how-the-uns-sustainable
-development-goals-undermine-democracy/.

Smith, Rachel, Kasper Tang Vangkilde, Mette Gislev Kjaersgaard, Ton Otto, Joachim
Halse, and Thomas Binder, eds. 2016. *Design Anthropological Futures.* London:
Bloomsbury.

Soja, Edward. 1996. *Thirdspace.* Malden, MA: Blackwell.

Sparling, Nina. 2018. "Enraged Portola Residents Blast Supervisor Ronen and Other
Officials over RVs on their Streets." *Mission Local,* October 10, 2018. https://web
.archive.org/web/20181011023817/https://missionlocal.org/2018/10/enraged
-portola-residents-blast-ronen-and-other-officials-over-rvs-off-their-streets/.

Spivak, Gayatri Chakravorty. 1990. "The Problem of Cultural Self-representation."
Interview with Walter Adamson. In *The Post-colonial Critic: Interviews, Strategies,
Dialogues,* edited by Sarah Harasym. New York: Routledge.

———. 1999. *A Critique of Postcolonial Reason: Toward a History of the Vanishing
Present.* Cambridge, MA: Harvard University Press.

———. 2010. "'Can the Subaltern Speak?' Revised Edition, from the 'History' Chapter
of Critique of Postcolonial Reason." In *Can the Subaltern Speak?: Reflections on the*

History of an Idea, edited by Rosalind C. Morris. New York: Columbia University Press.

Staff and Agencies. 2014. "Anti-Homeless Studs at London Residential Block Prompt Uproar." *The Guardian,* June 7, 2014. https://web.archive.org/web/20140607224630/https://www.theguardian.com/society/2014/jun/07/anti-homeless-studs-london-block-uproar.

Stairs, David. 2007. "Why Design Won't Save the World." *Design Observer,* August 20, 2007. https://web.archive.org/web/20190813111947/https://designobserver.com/feature/why-design-wont-save-the-world/5777/.

———. 2009. "Arguing with Success." *Design Altruism Project,* September 14, 2009. https://web.archive.org/web/20190813112318/http://design-altruism-project.org/2009/09/14/arguing-with-success/.

———. 2010. "An Open Letter to Bruce Nussbaum." *Design Altruism Project,* August 30, 2010. https://web.archive.org/web/20190813112921/http://design-altruism-project.org/2010/08/30/an-open-letter-to-bruce-nussbaum/.

———. 2015. "Social Entrepreneurism with a Swiss Army Knife." *Design Altruism Project,* January 1, 2015. https://web.archive.org/web/20150302075154/http://design-altruism-project.org/2015/01/01/social-entrepreneurism-with-a-swiss-army-knife/.

Stang, Alanna, and Christopher Hawthorne. 2005. *The Green House: New Directions in Sustainable Architecture.* New York: Princeton Architectural Press.

Sterli, Martino, and Mechtild Widrich, eds. 2016. *Participation in Art and Architecture: Spaces of Interaction and Occupation.* London: I. B. Tauris.

Swan, Rachel. 2018. "Southeast Neighborhoods Grapple with RVs—Next Phase of the Homeless Crisis." *San Francisco Chronicle,* October 11, 2018. https://web.archive.org/web/20181011163036/https://www.sfchronicle.com/bayarea/article/Southeast-neighborhoods-grapple-with-RVs-next-13297778.php.

Swyngedouw, Erik. 2007. "Impossible/Undesirable Sustainability and the Post-Political Condition." In *The Sustainable Development Paradox: Urban Political Economy in the United States and Europe,* edited by David Gibbs and Rob Krueger. New York: Guilford Press.

———. 2009. "The Antinomies of the Postpolitical City: In Search of a Democratic Politics of Environmental Production." *International Journal of Urban and Regional Research* 33, no. 3: 601–20.

———. 2010a. "Apocalypse Forever? Post-political Populism and the Spectre of Climate Change." *Theory Culture & Society* 27, nos. 2–3: 213–32.

———. 2010b. "Trouble with Nature: 'Ecology as the New Opium for the Masses.'" In *The Ashgate Research Companion to Planning Theory: Conceptual Challenges for Spatial Planning,* edited by Jean Hillier and Patsy Healey. Farnham, UK: Ashgate.

———. 2016. "On The Impossibility of an Emancipatory Architecture: The Deadlock of Critical Theory, Insurgent Architects, and the Beginning of Politics." In *Can Architecture Be an Emancipatory Project? Dialogues on Architecture and the Left,* edited by Nadir Lahiji. Alresford, UK: Zero Books.

Syrkett, Asad. 2012. "Nueva Esperanza School." *Architectural Record,* March 16, 2012. https://web.archive.org/web/20190814104743/https://www.architecturalrecord.com/articles/6479-nueva-esperanza-school.

Tatarella, Francesca, ed. 2014. *Natural Architecture Now: New Projects from Outside the Boundaries of Design.* New York: Princeton Architectural Press.

TEDx Vienna. 2011. "Cameron Sinclair—Architecture for Humanity." November 12, 2011. Video, 18:43. https://youtu.be/HZexxM0XmGc. Permalink: https://archive .org/details/tedx_vienna_cameron_sinclair_architecture_for_humanity.

The Spectator. 2015. "Defensive Architecture, a Hostile Form of Alienating the Already Marginalized." *Edinboro Now,* November 4, 2015. https://web.archive.org/web /20190824112644/http://www.edinboronow.com/article/defensive-architecture -a-hostile-form-of-alienating-the-already-marginalized-.

Thomas, Mary Adam. 2016. *The Living Building Challenge: Roots and Rise of the World's Greenest Standard.* Portland, OR: Ecotone.

Thyssen, Ole. 2009. "Nature Is Silent." In *Green Architecture for the Future,* edited by Michael Holm and Kjeld Kjeldsen. Humlebæk, Denmark: Louisiana Museum of Modern Art.

Till, Jeremy. 2005. "The Negotiation of Hope." In *Architecture and Participation,* edited by Peter Blundell Jones, Doina Petrescu, and Jeremy Till. Abingdon, UK: Taylor and Francis.

Tittmann, Hester. 2014a. "Who Is Welcome Here?: An Ethnographic Analysis of Small-Scale Urban Design in Oakland & San Francisco." Bachelor's thesis. Hampshire College.

———. 2014b. "Who Is Welcome Here?" Submission to the ACSA Conference. Unpublished manuscript, last modified December 11, 2014. PDF file.

———. 2015. "New Frontiers of Gentrification." Lecture, Amherst College, Amherst, MA, April 28, 2015.

Toffin, Gérard. 1994. "The Intersecting Fields of Ethno-Architecture: From the Indo-Himalayan World to Occidental Europe." *Diogenes* 42, no. 2: 23–48.

Torres, Lars Hasselblad. 2010. "Bruce Nussbaum: The New Imperialism." *MIT Ideas Global Challenge Notebook* (blog), July 8, 2010. https://web.archive.org/web /20190813102624/http://mitpsc.mit.edu/globalchallenge/?p=417.

Townsley, Graham, dir. 2013. *Maravillas de Colombia* [Wonders of Colombia]. Episode 4, "Biblioteca España." Aired July 28, 2013, on Discovery Channel. 43:23. https:// www.youtube.com/watch?v=pft1So0oVls. Permalink: https://archive.org/details /maravillasdecolombia.

Trujillo, Camilo. 2017. "Se Enredó la Reparación del Parque Biblioteca España" [The repairing of the Parque Biblioteca España has become messy]. *El Colombiano,* January 20, 2017. https://web.archive.org/web/20170120071148/http://www .elcolombiano.com/antioquia/obras/se-enredo-la-reparacion-del-parque -biblioteca-espana-BM5781355.

Tunstall, Elizabeth. 2013. "Decolonizing Design Innovation: Design Anthropology, Critical Anthropology, and Indigenous Knowledge." In *Design Anthropology: Theory and Practice,* edited by Wendy Gunn, Ton Otto, and Rachel Smith. London: Bloomsbury Academic.

TYIN (TYIN Tegnestue). n.d.a. "Klong Toey Community Lantern." TYIN website. https://web.archive.org/web/20190804142238/http://www.tyinarchitects.com /works/klong-toey-community-lantern/.

———. n.d.b. "Soe Ker Tie House." TYIN website. https://web.archive.org/web /20190804143243/http://www.tyinarchitects.com/works/soe-ker-tie-house/.

U-TT (Urban-Think Tank). 2012. "Torre David." https://web.archive.org/web/20121027000112/http://torredavid.com:80/.

UNHSP (United Nations Human Settlements Programme). 2003. *The Challenge of Slums: Global Report on Human Settlements 2003.* London: Earthscan.

UNPFII (United Nations Permanent Forum on Indigenous Issues). 2006. "About UNPFII/History." UNPFII. https://web.archive.org/web/20060219170158/http://www.un.org/esa/socdev/unpfii/en/history.html.

UNPFII Secretariat (United Nations Secretariat of the Permanent Forum on Indigenous Issues). 2004. *The Concept of Indigenous Peoples.* Background paper prepared by the Secretariat of the Permanent Forum on Indigenous Issues. New York: United Nations.

Vale, Lawrence. 2002. "Introduction: Reclaiming Public Housing." In *Reclaiming Public Housing: A Half Century of Struggle in Three Public Neighborhoods.* Cambridge, MA: Harvard University Press.

Van der Ryn, Sim, and Stuart Cowan. 1996. "Sustainability and Design." In *Ecological Design.* Washington, DC: Island Press.

Van Zeijl, Femke. 2016. "The Rise and Fall of the Floating School." *Zam,* July 11, 2016. https://web.archive.org/web/20161226005726/https://www.zammagazine.com/chronicle/chronicle-26/436-the-rise-and-fall-of-the-floating-school.

Varley, Ann. 2013. "Postcolonialising Informality?" *Environment and Planning D: Society and Space* 31, no. 1: 4–22.

Velásquez, Carlos. 2014. "Diagnóstico y Propuestas Comunitarias para el Mejoramiento Integral del Barrio El Faro, Comuna 8, Medellín" [Diagnosis and community proposals for the integral improvement of Barrio El Faro, Comuna 8, Medellín]. *El Ágora* 14, no. 2 (June-December): 601–36.

Vellinga, Marcel. 2013. "The Noble Vernacular." *Journal of Architecture* 18, no. 4: 570–90.

———. 2014. "Vernacular Architecture and Sustainability: Two or Three Lessons. . . . " In *Vernacular Architecture: Towards a Sustainable Future,* edited by Camilla Mileto, Fernando Vegas, Lidia García Soriano, and Valentina Cristini. Leiden, The Netherlands: CRC Press.

Viollet-Le-Duc, Eugène-Emmanuel. 1876. *The Habitations of Man in All Ages.* Translated by Benjamin Bucknall. London: Simpson Low, Marston, Searle and Rivington.

Waddling, Chris. 2011. "Portola Pocket Park." *D10 Watch* (blog), August 26, 2011. https://web.archive.org/web/20181029124252/http://d10watch.blogspot.com/2011/08/portola-pocket-park.html.

———. 2013. "Portola Neighborhood Association Unveils Burrows Pocket Park." *D10 Watch* (blog), July 8, 2013. https://web.archive.org/web/20181028051449/http://d10watch.blogspot.com/2013/07/portola-neighborhood-association.html.

Wallace, Elizabeth. 2018. "What's Behind the Uptick in Hostile Architecture?" *Architectural Digest,* March 21, 2018. https://web.archive.org/web/20180322024827/https://www.architecturaldigest.com/story/hostile-architecture.

Wallace, Ruth. 2012. "The Portola's Newest Park Takes Shape at Burrows and San Bruno Avenue." *Portola Planet* (blog), February 7, 2012. https://web.archive.org/web/20120317124542/http://portolaplanet.com/2012/02/the-portolas-newest-park-takes-shape-at-burrows-and-san-bruno-avenue/.

Watson, Joseph. 2012. "Aid, Capital, and the Humanitarian Trap." *Thresholds,* no. 40: 237–44.

WCED (World Commission on Environment and Development). 1987. *Our Common Future.* Oxford: Oxford University Press.

Welford, Richard. 1997. "From Green to Golden: The Hijacking of Environmentalism." In *Hijacking Environmentalism: Corporate Responses to Sustainable Development.* London: Earthscan.

Welt. 2016. "The Bitter Fight for Nigeria's Water Slum." *Welt,* 2016. https://web.archive .org/web/20171006203928/http://www.welt.de/reportage/water/habitat/article 158122289/the-bitter-fight-for-nigeria's-water-slum.html.

Wigley, Mark. 1999. "Recycling Recycling." In *Eco-Tec: Architecture of the In-Between,* edited by Amerigo Marras. New York: Princeton Architectural Press.

Williams, Austin. 2001. "Zen and the Art of Life-Cycle Maintenance." In *Sustaining Architecture in the Anti-Machine Age,* edited by Ian Abley and James Heartfield. Chichester, UK: Wiley-Academy.

———. 2008. *The Enemies of Progress: The Dangers of Sustainability.* Exeter, UK: Imprint Academic.

Williams, Richard. 2009. "The Politics of Liberation." In *Brazil: Modern Architectures in History.* London: Reaktion Books.

Wilmes, Adam. 2015. *Altruism by Design: How to Affect Social Change as an Architect.* New York: Routledge.

Wilson, Barbara Brown. 2018. "San Francisco: Reconsidering Parklets in Ciencia Pública: Agua." In *Resilience for All: Striving for Equity through Community-Driven Design.* Washington, DC: Island Press.

Winter, Catherine. 2015. "What Happened to Architecture For Humanity?" *Inhabitat,* February 27, 2015. https://web.archive.org/web/20150228234531/http://inhabitat .com/what-happened-to-architecture-for-humanity/.

Wolch, Jennifer, Jason Byrne, and Joshua Newell. 2014. "Urban Green Space, Public Health, and Environmental Justice: The Challenge of Making Cities 'Just Green Enough.'" *Landscape and Urban Planning* 125: 234–44.

World Bank. 2005. *Operational Policy 4.10 Indigenous Peoples.* Washington, DC: World Bank.

Worster, Donald. 1993. "The Shaky Ground of Sustainability." In *Global Ecology. A New Arena for Political Conflict,* edited by Wolfgang Sachs. London: Zed Books.

Young, Kenneth. 2020. "The Climate Framework in Sustainability Research: A Geo-graphic Critique from the Global South." In *The Elgar Companion to Geography, Transdisciplinarity, and Sustainability,* edited by Fausto Sarmiento and Larry Frolich. Cheltenham, UK: Edward Elgar Publishing.

Zapata, Jaime. 2017. "Así Fue 'la Película' de la Biblioteca España" [This is what the Biblioteca España 'movie' was about]. *El Mundo,* February 26, 2017. https://web .archive.org/web/20170310192402/http://www.elmundo.com/noticia/Asi-fuela -peliculade-la-Biblioteca-Espana/47193.

Zapata, Juan Fernando. 2014. *Impactos del POT [Plan de Ordenamiento Territorial] en la [Zona] Nororiental* [Impacts of POT (Land Management Plan) on the Northeast-ern (Zone)]. Report no. 3. Medellín: Observatorio Derecho a la Ciudad.

Zaretsky, Michael. 2011. "Design From the Ground Up: Risks and Opportunities in Humanitarian Design." In *New Directions in Sustainable Design,* edited by Adrian Parr and Michael Zaretsky. New York: Routledge.

——. 2016. "Unintended Consequences." In *Shaping New Knowledges*. 104th ACSA Annual Meeting Proceedings. Washington, DC: ACSA Press.

Žižek, Slavoj. 2007. "Censorship Today: Violence, or Ecology as a New Opium for the Masses." Lecture. Tilton Gallery, New York. November 28, 2007. https://web.archive .org/web/20141012173917/https://www.youtube.com/watch?v=fi57r_JByNE.

——. 2010. "First as Tragedy, Then as Farce." Lecture. RSA (Royal Society for the Encouragement of Arts, Manufactures and Commerce). *YouTube.* March 10, 2010. https://web.archive.org/web/20201003121125if_/https://www.youtube.com /watch?v=cvakA-DF6Hc<cstyle>.

INDEX

Italicized page numbers refer to illustrations.

sures, 127, 234n11; anything and everything counted as, 217; and Biblioteca España project, 104–5; bottom-up approach to, 223–27, 229–32; circumvented and ignored entirely, 156–58; defining, 105; as different for designers than for beneficiaries, 224; divide-and-conquer approach, 159–62, 198, 214; in ethnoengineering project in Ecuador, 137, 144–46, 198–99; and human agency, 221; and International Style of modernism, 44; intimidation used, 214–15; labor as strategy of, 212–13; in Makoko Floating School, 84, 87, 210; misleading information in, 154–56, 214; negotiations of projects' implementations, 173–79, *174, 176, 178, 179;* and options given, 153–54, 215–16; outcome of, versus FISE goal, 152–53; and privilege, 8, 133; residents' movements in low-income areas of Medellín, 106, 234n7 (ch. 2); teleguided approach, 105, 197–98, 215; "top-down" versus "bottom-up," 15, 223–27, 229–32; types of, 14; and unexpected outcomes, 218–20, 221; use of local knowledge as strategy of, 213; in U-TT projects, 88; when initiated, 224–25

computer-aided design (CAD) software, 10

comunidad (territorial division in Ecuador): defined, 19, 145; social class divisions within, 189–90

concrete (building material), *3, 47, 90, 91, 140, 147, 148, 149, 160, 165, 174, 178;* combined with traditional elements, 140, 186–87; and community preferences, 7, 28, 145, 146, 149, 152–53, 154, 155, 159–60, 161, 175, 219; cost, 29, 80, 147, 182, 184, 199; and environment, 138, 139; as iconic modern material, 21; local knowledge of building with, 151; maintenance, 174; problems with poor quality, 163–64

conservation refugees, 56

construction: costs of traditionalist versus modernist approaches, 80, 138, 150–51, 184–85, 199; demands of traditionalist versus modernist, 182; of Ecuadorian ethnoengineering project, 138, 145; green building standards, 39; training required for building using traditional methods, 29, 150–51

construction materials: affordability of modern versus traditional, 154–56, 181; combining modern with traditional, 174; descriptions of modern and traditional, 21; economic impact of use of traditional, 7; Ecuadorian ethnoengineering project, 145; fossil fuels used, 45; functionalism of, 178; as imposed upon traditional people,

48; opposition to using traditional, 145, 146; preferred in Ecuadorian ethnoengineering project, 145, 146–49, *147, 148, 149,* 159, *160;* subaltern priorities versus project leaders' preferences, 152–54; traditional, 80, 138, 140, 150–51, 184–85, 199. *See also* bamboo construction; concrete (building material); earth construction; thatch construction; zinc (corrugated metal roofing)

Cooper Hewitt, Smithsonian Design Museum, 4, 209, 217

Corbusian modernism, 21, 146. *See also* International Style; modernism

Corrales, Jorge, 104, 105

correspondence relationships in anthropology, 228–29

costs: Biblioteca España, 99, 213; Burrows Street Pocket Park, 200; as computed by designers, 8; displacement of residents, 7, 57, 104, 106, 109, 111; Ecuadorian ethnoengineering project, 137, 138; of labor of beneficiaries, 8, 29–30, 138, 181–85, 199–200, 212; of maintenance and repairs, 8–9, 185–89, 200–201, 212–13; Makoko Floating School, 87; Nueva Esperanza School, 75, 79–80, 200, 212; people's economic contributions of labor, materials, food, and/or transportation ignored by designers, 199–200; of traditional construction, 28–29, 79–80, 138, 150–51, 181, 182–85, 199. *See also* affordability

Cotopaxi, Ecuador. *See* ethnoengineering project in Ecuador

Coulombel, Patrick, 35

Cradle to Cradle (McDonough and Braungart), 53

cultural capital: defined, 16; of designers, 223; and social class, 190; and traditionalism, 191; use of traditional material culture as political asset, 191–92

culturally appropriate building, 45

Curry Stone Foundation. *See* Nueva Esperanza School (Puerto Cabuyal, Ecuador)

Curry Stone Foundation's Design Prize, 100

"Damned If You Do, Damned If You Don't: What Is the Moral Duty of the Architect?" (Skene Catling), 95–96

Davis, Howard, 45

decolonialization and Eurocentric mind frame, 64

defensive design, 119–25

design activism, 1. *See also* social design

designers: assumptions about traditional people's lives, 196–97; as benefiting more

144; experimentation in, 169–73, *170, 171;* as paradigm of social design, 136–37; repairs, 185–87; safety issues, 186–87; strong social class divisions within communities, 210–11; successful projects, 173–79, *174, 176, 178, 179;* surprises for designers during, 218–19; sustainability's connection to traditionalism, 137–38, 196; traditionalist approach by Romero, 45, *46*

ethnographic method, 227–28

ethnotecture, 230. *See also* ethnoarchitecture

Etomi, Isi, 86

Evicted (Desmond), 128

exclusivity and community, 18

experimentation: by designers, 8–9, 81, 87–89, 90–93, 98, 103, 169–73, *170, 171,* 201–2; in Ecuador's ethnoengineering project, 169–73, *170, 171;* Medellín as laboratory for, 98–99; slums as zones of, 89, 90–93, 98, 103; sustainability as justification for, 93

Fajardo, Raúl, 233n2 (ch. 2)

Fajardo, Sergio, 97, 99–100, 105, 108. *See also* Biblioteca España (barrio of Santo Domingo in Medellín, Colombia); Northeastern Zone Project

Fathy, Hassan, 31–32, 45; mosque at New Gourna, Egypt, *32*

favelas. *See* slums/favelas

fear component in environmental advocacy, 54–55, 59

FISE (Fondo de Inversión Social de Emergencia, Emergency Social Investment Fund) III, 136, 189–90, 234n2, 234n7 (ch. 3). *See also* ethnoengineering project in Ecuador

formal beauty as ruling principle in social design, 11. *See also* iconicity

Foucault, Michael, 23, 55–56, 60. *See also* governmentality

Fukuyama, Francis, 39

Funhabit, 151, 182

Gaestel, Allyn, 88

Gallardo, Vinicio, 182, 212

Gallegos, Luis, 137, 151, 174–75, 182, 192, 207. *See also* ethnoengineering project in Ecuador

Gangotena, Pascual, 74

Gatt, Caroline, 28

Giddens, Anthony, 17

Global North/Global South dichotomy, 24

Golden, Elizabeth, 74

governmentality, 23, 61, 62

Gramsci, Antonio, 16

Green Belt (Medellín, Colombia), 111–13, *112*

green building standards, 39

green economy, 59, 61–62

green gentrification: commercial changes resulting from, 120, 121, 129–30, *131,* 132; and displacement from housing, 57–58, 111–14; and homelessness, 128; and pocket parks, 120, 129; rising costs in physically improved neighborhoods, 111; and sustainability, 132

Green Imperative, The (Papanek), 32

green imperialism: green orientalism as basis for, 22, 49; traditional people in narrative of, 59–60; transition from imperialism to, 50

Green Infrastructure: Generation, Conservation, and Upkeeping of Green Spaces program (Medellín), 113

green neoliberalism, 43

green orientalism, 22, 49, 50

Griborio, Andrea, 74

Groove Grove, 125, 126

Guerra, Mónica, 98

Hancox, Dan, 93, 95

Haque, Reaz, 126

Haraway, Donna, 49

Harris, Victoria, 34

Harvard University Green Prize in Urban Design, 100

Hawthorne, Christopher, 1

hegemony, 55–56, 60

high design: and control of outcomes, 226; described, 2, *2;* and ethnoarchitecture, 15; importance of, in discipline of architecture, 206; as model for social design, 10, 205–6; and poverty alleviation, 12; and predictability, 225; problematic practices and paradigm of, 27–28; and social improvement in slums, 97

Hippo-Roller, 66, *67,* 68

homelessness: and Burrows Street Pocket Park, *120,* 121–23, *122, 123, 124,* 124, *125,* 126, 127; and gentrification, 128; prevalence in US, 128–29; in San Francisco, 129

homogeneity and community, 18, 209–10, 235n1

Huasicashca, Ecuador, 150, 158, 180, 182, 187

human agency: defined, 17; and inherent uncertainty about outcome of community participation, 221; Third World populations as prevented from exercising, 62–65

humanitarian design: and addressing issues of social justice through market, 61–63; and

humanitarian design (*continued*)
Architecture for Humanity's antihomeless
design, 126, 127; designers as local, 67–68;
failure of, to address structural factors, 63;
Foucauldian critique of, 61–62; imperialism
in, 25–26, 61, 65, 220–21; inherent inequalities in staffs of organizations, 66; "Is Humanitarian Design the New Imperialism?,"
5, 66–69; need for ethics in humanitarian
design practice, 65; Project H, 66–69; and
sustainability, 34. *See also* Architecture for
Humanity
humanitarian imperialism: in British Colonial
India, 220; comparative impact in social
design practice, 205; defined, 25–26
humanitarianism, 61–63
humanitarian starchitects, 10, 43, 208

iconicity: justification for, 11; as paradigm in
social design, 10; relevance of in present-day
social design practice, 206–7, 208. *See also*
Biblioteca España (barrio of Santo Domingo
in Medellín, Colombia)
imperialism: and being local, 24; colonialism
compared to, 23; defined, 22–23; designers'
solutions as, 61–62; focus of critique of,
70; and humanitarianism, 25–26, 65, 205,
220–21; of IFIs, 60; localism as solution to,
6, 70–71, 72; main argument of, 70; as main
challenge faced by social design practice,
69–70; modernism as, 47–48; morality as
rationale for, 50; in postcolonial theory, 23;
real versus stated goal of, 50; service learning studios to avoid, 64; of social design,
6; sustainability as tool of, 204; as theme
in critical literature on sustainability, 56;
"Torre de David" as, 95, 96; transition from,
to green imperialism, 50
indigenous people: adoption of traditional
designs of other peoples by, 169, 177–78;
in Brundtland Report, 48–50; definition
difficulties, 19–20; environment of, as prone
to exploitation, 49; and functionalism, 169,
178; identifying characteristics, 19; modern
culture as detrimental to traditions of, 168;
and paternalism, 161; resource efficiency
as implicit to, 49–50; as resource for global
sustainability, 49, 50–52; social class divisions within communities of, 211; traditional
material culture of, as political asset, 191–92.
See also ethnoengineering project in Ecuador; traditional people
Ingold, Tim, 28
Inhabitat, 121

Inter-American Development Bank (IDB), 28
Intermediate Technology Development Group
(ITDG), 136, 234n1
international financial institutions (IFIs): as
hegemonic institutions, 60; imperialism
of, 60; in postcolonial theory, 61. *See also
specific institutions by name*
International Living Future Institute (ILFI), 39
International Plant Medicine Corporation,
51–52
International Style, 21, 44
intervention and orientalism, 22
"Is Humanitarian Design the New Imperialism?" (Nussbaum), 5, 66–69

Jacanamijoy, Antonia, 51
Jacobs, Garrett, 127–28, 132, 210
Juan Bobo (project in Medellín, Colombia),
109

Kats, Robert van, 85–86
Kichwa traditional architecture, *46, 47, 139,
140, 149;* and cultural change, 146–51,
153–55, 159–62; issues with reimposition of,
162–75
Klumpner, Hubert, 34, 64, 89, 90. *See also*
"Torre de David" (Caracas, Venezuela);
Urban-Think Tank (U-TT)
knowledge as resource, 50–52, 61, 213
Koolhaas, Rem, 83

labor: of beneficiaries, 8, 29–30, 138, 181–85,
199–200, 212; cost of, 29, 79–80; as strategy
of community participation, 212–13
Laboratorio de Arquitectura y Urbanismo
(Architecture and Urbanism Laboratory), 98
Library of Spain. *See* Biblioteca España (barrio
of Santo Domingo in Medellín, Colombia)
LifeStraw, 63
"Lincoln Reimagine Project," 117, 234n11
Living Building Challenge (ILFI), 39
Lizarralde, Manuel, 49–50
local/foreign dichotomy, 24
localism: of Architecture for Humanity, 115–
16; defined in social design field, 24, 72–73;
of designers, 6, 9, 67–68, 73, 113, 205; limitations of, 9; of Medellín projects' designers,
113; premises of, 13, 14, 71, 135; and social
class, 73; as solution to imperialism, 6, 70–
71, 72; sustainability's focus on, 37
Lodaya, Arvind, 69
Lohmann, Larry, 49
Los Colorados, Ecuador, 150, 155, 157–58, 184,
184, 186

Said, Edward, 21, 22, 23, 25

Salazar, Alonso, 97–98

San Francisco Chronicle, 130–31

San Lorenzo, Ecuador, 52, 54

Saparoan traditional architecture, 141–43, *144;* adoption of, in Andes, 169–73, *170;* and cultural change, 149; redesign in Upper Amazon, 177–78, *178, 179*

Sarahuasi, Ecuador, 235n12

Schumacher, Ernst Friedrich "Fritz," 234n1

Sen, Amartya, 18

service learning model of social design, 31–32, 64

Shemede, Noah, 83, 84

Sieco_pai (Upper Ecuadorian Amazon indigenous group), 29, 224

Sinclair, Cameron: and Architecture for Humanity, 32–33; assessment of Burrows Street Pocket Park, 132; basic facts about, 233n8; benefit of using unused spaces, 128; fundraising strategy, 114–15; on Lincoln car brand and Burrows Street Pocket Park, 117, 132; as localism defender, 67–68, 114

Skene Catling, Charlotte, 95–96

Slum Dwellers International, 19

SLUM Lab, 91

slums/favelas: conditions in, 88; defined, 19; displacement of residents of, for social design projects, 104, 109; experimentation in, 89, 90–93, 98, 103; green gentrification resulting in rising costs of living, 111; high design and social improvement in, 97; lack of infrastructure in, 110–11; social design practice in, 64; and U-TT, 64, 88. *See also* Biblioteca España (barrio of Santo Domingo in Medellín, Colombia); Makoko Floating School (Lagos, Nigeria); "Torre de David" (Caracas, Venezuela)

social class: in bottom-up participatory process, 226–27, 229–32; within communities, 190–91, 198–99; defined, 16; environmentalism as marker of, 58; and localism, 73

social design: amateurism in, 137, 234n3; basic facts about, 1; as "cool," 2–3; culturally appropriate building as ruling principle, 45; defensive design, 119–25; with designers at bottom of hierarchy of process, 223–27; "design" synonymous with formal beauty, 11; ethics of humanitarian design practice, 65; and ethnoarchitectural approach, 229–32; example of paradigm of, 136–37; as experimental field, 8–9, 81, 87–89, 90–93, 98, 103; as field, 1–2; flexibility paradigm, 225–26; goal of, 6, 31, 197; governmentality

critique of, 62; high design as model for, 10, 205–6; iconicity as paradigm in, 10; imperialism as main challenge faced by, 69–70; as imperialistic, 61–62; imposition of First World–designed solutions in Third World localities, 62–63, 66–67; innovative products critique, 63; literature, 3–5; "local" in, 24, 72–73; nonprofit model, 64–65; personal brand in, 207–8; positive use of privilege in, 223, 224; poverty alleviation as disconnected from, 197; privilege as challenge for, 205, 222; proposed positionality shift, *231;* representation in, 25; role of iconicity in, 206–7, 208; service learning model critique, 64; in slums, 64; as stepping stone in architectural practice, 2, 10, 199, 206; sustainability as fundamental to, 31, 32, 42–43, 197, 204

Social Design Circle Honoree, 74

social equity and sustainability, 56, 57

social justice, 58, 62–63

social urbanism: awards and mentions, 99–100; basis of, 97; community participation as important in, 104; described, 97; and economic revitalization of neighborhood, 111; Green Belt, 111–13, *112;* main proponents, 97–98; pilot project in Medellín, 96. *See also* Biblioteca España (barrio of Santo Domingo in Medellín, Colombia); Northeastern Zone Project

Soe Ker Tie houses (Thailand), *2*

Spivak, Gayatri, 16, 220, 221

Stairs, David, 69

starchitects, 10, 58, 208

Stohr, Kate, 33. *See also* Architecture for Humanity

subalterns, 16–17. *See also* beneficiaries; Spivak, Gayatri

sustainability: adoption of, by banks and corporations, 41; as argument for imposing designers' ideas over beneficiaries', 12; and Biblioteca España, 100; and capitalism, 54–55; and climate change, 180–81; and consumption of green products, 54–55; as danger to progress, 57; definitions of, 15–16, 33–37, 39, 72; economic growth as essential to, 39, 40–42; elements of, 34, 36–37, 38; in emergency reconstruction, 35; and environmentalism, 204; in ethnoengineering project in Ecuador, 137–38, 196; fear component in, 54, 55; focus on localism, 37; as fundamental to social design, 31, 32, 42–43, 197, 204; and gentrification, 132; good/bad dichotomy in, 53–54; and green economy, 59; as hegemonic notion, 55–56; ignores issues

urban environments, sustainability and social justice in, 58. *See also* slums/favelas
Urban Land Institute, 99
Urban-Think Tank (U-TT), 34, 64, 88, 89. *See also* "Torre de David" (Caracas, Venezuela)
USAID and Medellín as living laboratory, 99
users. *See* beneficiaries

Velásquez, Carlos, 113
Venice Biennale, 74, 78, 84, 88, 89, 95, 99–100
Viollet-Le-Duc, Eugène, 20
visioning technique of community participation, 217

Whanyinna Nursery and Primary School (Lagos, Nigeria), 83, 87
Wilmes, Adam, 116, 127

World Bank: and defining indigenous people, 20; embrace of sustainability ethos by, 41; as hegemonic institution, 60; and Medellín as living laboratory, 99

yagé (*Banisteriopsis caapi*), 51–52
Yanaturo, Ecuador, *47,* 159–67, *160, 164, 165,* 182, 214

Zapata, Juan Fernando, 111
zinc (corrugated metal roofing), *47, 82, 83, 85, 109, 140, 141, 143, 147, 150, 179, 184;* combined with traditional elements, 140, 230; and community preferences, 7, 29, 146, 149, 173; and environment, 139; as iconic modern material, 21; safety issues, 186; used experimentally, 88